"READY . . . UP!"

Lutane pressed the pressure patch between her breasts, and jets soared as lox and hydrogen ignited, sending the squad up in a cloud of mist that wreathed the tower. Not the safest way to travel, Lutane thought dizzily, but effective, effective. . . .

Then she realized that Pachue was tilting. "Straighten out!" she called, but the private heeled over and headed for the ground. "Cut out!" Lutane screamed.

—— *Edited by* ——
David Drake *and* **Bill Fawcett**

THE
FLEET

BOOK 2

COUNTER ATTACK

ACE BOOKS, NEW YORK

This book is an Ace original edition, and
has never been previously published.

THE FLEET Book 2: COUNTERATTACK

An Ace Book/published by arrangement with
Bill Fawcett & Associates

PRINTING HISTORY
Ace edition/December 1988

ISBN: 0-441-24087-9

Ace Books are published by
The Berkley Publishing Group,
200 Madison Avenue, New York, New York 10016.
The name "ACE" and the "A" logo
are trademarks belonging to Charter Communications, Inc.

PRINTED IN THE UNITED STATES OF AMERICA

10 9 8 7 6 5 4 3 2 1

*Dedicated to
Two Who Led the Way:
Jack Williamson
and
Jack Vance*

CONTENTS
Book 2   Counterattack

CIVILIANS
by Christopher Stasheff

"THEY BROUGHT THEIR slaves with them, eh?"

"Yes, sir—from a dozen different species, at least."
Major Dromio laid a stack of reconnaissance pictures on
the desk in front of Admiral Vancouver. "Our Khalia have
been busy boys."

The admiral nodded, his mouth a grim line. "Pirates have
always taken prisoners for slaves. Well, we won't add
ourselves to their trophy case." He frowned down at the
reconnaissance pictures, each one showing a clothes-
wearing animal tagging along after a Khalia. "The scout
made it back in one piece?"

"Yes, sir. If they found out he was there, they didn't even
try to do anything about it. Not a single shot."

The admiral nodded. "Well, we can't be sure. That might
have alerted them, and they might be waiting to sucker us
in. When we hit, we'll hit fast, Dromio." He pointed at one
of the pictures. "This one here?"

"Yes, sir. The computer analyzed all the pictures and
found slaves of this race in ninety-three percent of them—
ninety-eight percent of all the ones that had sentient beings
in them. There are more of them than of all the other slave

species put together—22.7 times more, the computer says."

The admiral frowned at the picture of the alien, fore-shortened by altitude. It was squat and humanoid, but covered with a bright coat of many colors. "Why would the Khalia have brought so many of that one species?"

Dromio shrugged. "Must be damn good servants."

"Or victims." The admiral slid the pictures back into a pack and squared it on the desktop. "Tell the troops to avoid shooting civilians if they can, Major."

"Yes, sir." The Major's mouth tightened as though he'd tasted something unpleasant. "It won't be easy. They're all over the place."

The admiral shrugged. "There will always be a few civilians who get caught in the cross fire. Just keep their numbers down." He set the pictures aside and pulled over the meter-wide view of the provincial capital. A smile creased his face. "Well. How nice of them to make it easy for us. All the important buildings stand out like sunflowers in a cornfield."

Dromio winced at the homeliness of the simile. "Not quite all, sir. There's one of the timber and stucco structures that has a flock of antennas on top."

"Yes, and a transmitting tower next to it. Must be the communications center." The admiral pursed his lips as he studied the blowup. "I would have thought the Khalia would have tried to update their homes a bit more. After all, they've been stealing enough currency to buy all the construction equipment they want."

"Yes, sir. Intelligence's guess is that they devoted all their resources to expanding their navy. They only put up a new building when it was absolutely necessary."

"Yes, it's not as though they had invented the FTL drive themselves. That's still the best guess, isn't it?"

"*Guess,* yes—that they stole the FTL drive—or impounded it, from a spacer that had to make an emergency landing."

The admiral's shoulders shrugged with amusement. "Why not? Those thieves have stolen everything else they've ever come across."

"Yes, sir. The xenologists are pretty sure their culture hadn't moved past pre-industrial when they found it."

The admiral nodded. "No, of course their buildings would still be frame and stucco. So detail your best troops to take the state-of-the-art buildings."

"Yes, sir. The power plant's an old one, though."

"Odd." The admiral frowned. "I'd expect them to keep updating power stores. Maybe they have some respect for tradition . . . Well, send in the regiment from Cirwat. If those city tigers can't take it, no one can."

"Yes, sir. How about the comm center?"

The admiral shrugged. "No need for anything heavy; the Khalia seem to be naturally authoritarian. They won't know it's important." He touched the array of antennas with a forefinger. "I want that platoon from Galath detailed to take it. Half of them are electronics techs."

"Half of everybody is, on Galath—and the other half are still in school. What else can you make but circuit gear, when your only natural resource is sand?"

". . . and Fedor's platoon will take the comm center." Captain Rakoan looked up from the map and around at the faces of his lieutenants. "Any questions?"

They were quiet for a moment. Beyond them, the assault troops shifted restlessly, muttering to one another and chewing mild stimulants. A few were trying to keep card games going, but their hearts weren't in it.

The blond boondock woman straightened up, looking determined, and Rakoan braced himself. "Lieutenant Morna?"

Lutane Morna looked him square in the eyes. "You don't really think we should do this, do you, sir?"

The question took Rakoan by surprise—questioning orders was unheard of, especially when battle was minutes away. "Whether *I* think we should is beside the point, Lieutenant! Just take your Galathians down to Bay Four and get them ready to take that comm center!"

"Sir." Lutane pulled a brace and saluted, her face wooden.

Rage flared in Captain Rakoan at the covert defiance, especially aboard a destroyer on its way down to drop them in the assault zone. He almost reminded her that her beloved Galath had sold her and her squad down the river when it sent them to the Fleet, and she would blasted well do as she was told or be blasted, period—but he managed to catch his temper at the last second and remembered what a last-minute showdown could do to morale. The important thing was to get Lieutenant Morna and her platoon to do the job, not to make her blindly obey. He converted his blast of rage into a sigh of resignation. "No, Lieutenant, we don't have total information about Target. But we're pretty sure it's the Khalia's home world, even if we don't *know*. We do have reconnaissance pictures up to our gills, and that's almost as good as having a spy on the ground. Which we can't have, of course."

"No, sir." Lutane shifted uncomfortably. "We don't have anyone from any of the species that're down there, sir."

"No, we don't." Rakoan shrugged. "So what do we do, Lieutenant? Stand around doing nothing, while the Khalia gut ship after ship and leave them to drift into port with cargoes of corpses?"

"Well, of course not! But . . ."

Rakoan waited.

". . . we do what we can with the information we've got," Lutane finished lamely.

"And attack Target," Rakoan concluded. "But since we both know we don't know enough, Lieutenant, be on the watch for surprises, eh?"

Lutane straightened. "Yes, sir!"

"Particularly surprises from the squat humanoids with the feathery scales." Rakoan scanned the faces of all his lieutenants. "Intelligence says they're slaves—but if they are, the Khalia brought one hell of a lot of 'em!"

"Yes, sir." Lutane felt her insides loosen with relief; somebody else had noticed! "What else could they be?"

"Allies." Rakoan's face hardened. "And it *could* be that every one of those featherheaded fetchers is a veteran soldier, ready to jump your troops the second their backs are turned!"

"And ready to jump the Khalia if they see an opening?" Lutane's eyes glowed.

"Maybe," Rakoan said slowly. "Maybe we *can* divide and conquer—but we don't know that, yet. And our assault might just make them pull even more tightly together. So watch your back, Lieutenant!"

"Yes, sir!" But Lutane frowned. "So we really ought to try to learn more before we go in?"

Rakoan closed his eyes and counted to ten. Then he said, "Maybe we should. But the admiral says we're going in now, so we're going in now! Because for you, Lieutenant, the Fleet may be just an exciting place to visit—but for me, it's home! And my world and my universe, too—so whatever the admiral says, I'll do! And so will you, because I'll be right behind you and your fellow lieutenants when we hit the dirt! Understand?"

"Sir!"

"All right." Rakoan straightened into a brace. "Go tell your platoons what they're doing. Dis-*miss!*"

The lieutenants stiffened, saluted, and turned away to their troops. For her part, Lutane went with determination —Rakoan had voiced her own doubts, and answered them. In spite of her questions, she knew what it was like landing an assault force on the enemy's ground; she'd joined up when the Nietszean rebels had tried to take over Galath, and had been in on the end of it, chasing them back to their home province and going in to mop up their army and bring in the ringleaders. So she also knew what it was like to have every civilian turn out to be a soldier in retirement, or a soldier in training.

The floor lurched, and Lutane grabbed at a stanchion, waiting till the floor and her stomach settled. Her gaze darted to her troops, and she saw, with a glow of pride, that not one of them had landed on the floor. She let go of the stanchion and went on to them.

"Plasma bolt, sir?" Darby asked as she came up.

Lutane nodded. "They missed, though, sergeant."

One of the troopers brayed a laugh, quickly smothered. Lutane glared at him, then turned back as Darby said, grinning, "Reckon so. An they'd'a hit us, we'd'a heard it."

"Or felt it," a corporal muttered.

"We won't," Lutane snapped. "Our computer's got the records of a hundred battles like this one in it. But if we're close enough to feel the shock waves from their bolts, we're close to landing, too. Stand to!"

The men and women stood, grim-faced, shouldering their

packs and checking their weapons. Lutane walked down their line, glance flicking over each soldier from head to toe, checking to be sure all was in order. It was, and she felt that glow of pride again. She came back to the center of the line just as the boat lurched again and caught the stanchion just in time to save herself from the embarrassment of a tumble in front of her platoon. She recovered and said, just loudly enough to be heard above the noise of other platoons getting ready, "Okay. There's no point in my giving you a pep talk; you know why we're here. You've all heard how many ships the Khalia have taken, and what they've done to the people on them. Don't expect any mercy from them, and don't give any, either—they'll surrender, sure, but they'll stab you in the back if they get a chance. Just hit hard, and keep hitting."

Then she was quiet, glaring at the hatch in front of them. After a moment, her troops began muttering to one another. Somebody laughed, quietly, and Lutane felt an impulse to pray. In the nick of time, the transport hit dirt.

It hit gently, as such things go, but flexed knees and handholds were all that kept the soldiers from slamming to the deck. A crash behind them told them that one veteran wasn't as salted as he'd thought.

Then the hatch dropped away from them, and Lutane shouted, "Out!"

They shot out of the transport and hit the dirt in a semicircle as slugs peppered the hull behind them and troops slammed out of the transport all around its perimeter. It helped a little, knowing that three other transports were landing at the compass points around the city, so that the enemy couldn't devote its full attention to any one of them. It helped, but not much.

Then the transport's cannon began roaring, and Lutane shouted, "Now!" Her platoon surged to their feet and charged out under the transport's covering fire.

They hatched out of their egg like a thousand dragons, spawn of death spewing streams of bullets before them. The company spread out in a wave, firing at all and any near them in the city square. Khalia answered fire from the rooftops and doorways. Here and there a ricochet struck home, and a Khalian soldier toppled out with a death shriek almost too high to hear, but just right for abrading Terran nerves. The slaves were caught in the open and fell like stones—and they were all featherheads. Lutane felt her heart sink, but shot forward with her platoon. "Watch out!" she barked as they came up near a fallen featherhead. "It might be armed!"

Delacroix stitched the body with a stream of bullets. Lutane caught her breath; it hadn't been necessary. Or had it? But then they were beyond the corpse and charging in among the shadows of the houses, and she cried, "Halt!"

A rifle barked overhead, and one of her soldiers screamed, falling.

"Doorways!" Lutane shouted, and the platoon jammed into nooks and crannies. Something snapped, and the back of Lutane's nook crashed open, spilling soldiers onto a wooden floor. Lutane whipped about, rifle up and ready, covering her troops.

It was a sparsely furnished, almost bare room, but lighter areas on the walls showed where ornaments had been. All that was left now was a table and chairs, massively built and plain, but rubbed to a gloss. The featherheads around it were scrambling to their feet, backing away, two small ones, a medium-sized one, and a wide one, spreading his hands out, trying to cover the other three who retreated behind his bulk, cowering against a wall. Lutane couldn't read his facial expressions.

"Lieutenant," Gorman asked, "do they always shiver like that?"

"I don't know any more about them than you do, Gorman," she answered, "and I don't think any of our people do."

"I don't see any weapons," Olerein said.

"They got forks next to their plates, if that's what those slabs are," Delacroix pointed out.

Gorman made a noise of disgust. "Its paws are better weapons than that."

Something snored by overhead. Lutane went back and ducked her head out for a quick look. As she ducked back in, she studied the afterimage; Terran fighters wheeled across the sky, cannon blasting at Khalian patrol boats. But underneath them, Terran grav floaters moved. She risked another peek, and saw a floater drift over the rooftop across from her, where the sniper had fired from. His rifle stuttered, giving Lutane a hard smile; the weasel didn't lack guts. But his machine gun wasn't going to do much good against the floater's armor plate.

The pilot wasn't taking any chances, though; his own guns spoke. They stopped, and Lutane held her breath. Then an amplified voice boomed down, "Sniper cleared. Take the street."

"Up!" Lutane barked, and her troops scrambled to their feet and jogged out. Lutane looked back and gave the cowering featherheads a mock salute. "Sorry we couldn't stay." She pulled the door shut as she followed her troops.

The floater drifted ahead of them, firing as it went. "Don't think he's doing everything for you," Lutane called. "There're still windows."

Sobered, the platoon sprinted out, dodging from doorway to doorway in a staggered, always moving line. At its head, Ranton ducked into a niche and yelled in surprise as two rifles barked. Then a Khalian toppled into the street, and Ranton staggered out, hand pressed to his side, eyes bulging.

Lutane dashed up and caught him, lowering him back into the doorway and howling, "Medic!"

"They're following close, Lieutenant," Belguire called.

"They'll have you in a minute or two, Ranton." Lutane ripped his shirt open as she yanked the anesthetic bulb from his belt and shoved it into his hand. "Spray the wound with that. The bleeding's steady; you'll last till they're here. Good luck."

Her answer was a grimace of pain, and she dodged back out, frog-hopping from doorway to doorway, helplessness clawing at her gut. She wouldn't know whether or not he'd made it till an hour or two after it was all over. With a mental effort, she put it behind her and dodged for the next doorway, glancing up at the rooftops as she did. Ahead of her, the array of antennas loomed larger, closer.

Close up, the half-timbered building seemed to loom over them; Lutane had to remind herself that it was only three stories high. Three streets debouched onto the plaza surrounding the building; they were in the central one.

"Grelli, take your squad over to the left-hand street and set up a covering fire," Lutane ordered. "Jollin, take your people over to the right."

The two sergeants nodded and turned back to the alley-way, beckoning to their squads.

"What'll the rest of us do, Lieutenant?"

"What do you *think* we're going to do, Olerein?" Lutane snapped. "Have a tea party, of course!"

Olerein's face set into a regulation mask, and Lutane felt a moment's anger at herself for letting go like that—but it had been a dumb question.

Gunfire broke out from her right, Grelli's position. Thirty seconds later, Jollin's squad cut loose. Muzzle flashes showed at third-floor windows.

"All right, hotshot!" Lutane turned to Olerein. "Get those snipers!"

Olerein's eyes narrowed. He dropped to sitting position, rested his elbow on his knee, took deliberate aim, and squeezed off a shot. The window pane shattered, and the platoon whooped with glee. Then stucco dust geysered next to another window, and the pane broke on the third, as Grelli and Jollin got their own snipers working.

"Stay here and pin down that middle window, Olerein!" Lutane snapped.

"Wha . . . ! Lieutenant, I . . ."

"Do it! Everybody else—now!"

Lutane dashed out, sprinting in zigzags toward the big central door. The last two squads followed close. Occasional ricochets rang to either side of them, but the Khalian snipers didn't dare stick their heads out far enough to take proper aim.

Lutane jerked to a halt three feet in front of the door and started pouring automatic fire into the lock. Her squads slammed up right behind her and started stitching the hinge side.

"Hold!" Lutane cried. "Back!" She readied herself and slammed a kick into the lock. The door crashed down, and she sprayed the doorway with bullets. Answering fire from inside filled her ears with racketing, but her squad leaders ducked out to add their fire to hers. Pain blazed in her left arm and she knew she'd taken a hit, but braced her elbow against her belt and held the trigger down with her other hand.

Then the hammering stopped, and Lutane ejected the clip with a curse. She slammed in a new one just as the gunfire inside lessened, and her squad leaders leaped in. The move startled Lutane, so she was a step or two behind them, her squads streaming in after her.

Gunfire erupted from their right, and Lutane screamed, "Down!" as she threw herself prone. Soldiers screamed and fell behind her, and she cursed as she fired at the dim, elongated shadows lurking in a small, square room—they'd given her a sucker punch; they'd slacked off their firing to make her think she'd taken out all of them. Then, when her squads were in a point-blank range, they'd cut loose with everything they had.

It would be all they ever had, she decided grimly, as she thumbed down to semiautomatic and started picking targets. The Khalian in her sights jerked and fell; so did its mates, as her squad cut them down. The air was filled with their almost supersonic death cries, thin whines on the edge of hearing, tearing human heads apart . . .

Then the whines stopped. Automatic doors clashed closed, and Lutane leaped up firing at the heavy portal where the little room had been. A dozen automatics joined hers, and the door turned into a grating. "Cease fire!" She bellowed.

The entry hall went quiet.

"They got away," somebody snarled.

"Just make sure they don't come back. Sergeant Murghesh, set a guard on that door." Lutane looked around her, counting dead furry bodies. There were ten of them—and six of hers.

Enilho knelt over Kazruitin, setting a stitch-strip over a raw hole in her breast, then spraying it with plastic skin. Lutane felt a sympathetic ache and moved toward them. "You gave her anesthesia?"

Enilho nodded. "First thing, Lieutenant—the whole bulb." He finished spraying the plastic flesh, set the container back in her belt, and folded the slit uniform blouse back over her chest. "She'll last till the medics get her." He thumbed the beacon on her belt, and it started blinking.

Lutane nodded, feeling her heart sinking. "Any other casualties who aren't dead?"

Belardin shook his head. "She's the only one who didn't go right off, Lieutenant."

"Seven down." Lutane hefted her rifle. "Let's make it worth it to them. Clear the stairs."

Soldiers started dragging Khalian corpses off the steps.

"Hold still, Lieutenant." Murghesh ripped away Lutane's sleeve and pulled an anesthetic shot from her belt. She sprayed the wound, then peeled back the edges to inspect. Dimly, Lutane felt the pain, but it wasn't her arm it was happening to. "Clean wound," Murghesh said. "The bullet went through, and it just missed the artery." She slapped a patch on the underside and sprayed in the anesthetic. It smarted a little, but the bleeding stopped. Murghesh slapped a patch on the top. "Maybe we should call you a medic."

"All right, so I'm a medic." Lutane twitched her arm loose impatiently. "I'm good for a few more rounds, Sergeant—and I have some troops to avenge."

"Thought you already had." Murghesh glowered down at the Khalian corpses. "Stupid bastards! They got what they had coming."

"Not so stupid." Lutane frowned. "They gambled and lost, that's all. They suckered us in. When their mates on the stairs were dead, the ones in the lift stopped shooting. We figured they were all dead, and came in. When we were inside, the rest cut loose. But if they didn't get most of us in the first few seconds, they'd had it—and they knew it."

"But they made it up in the lift!"

"No—the *lift* made it up," Lutane corrected. "I very much doubt there was anything left alive in it—and if there was, it sure as hell can't do any fighting." She rubbed her temples. "Still, we can't know that. We just have to figure they reinforced the guard up top."

Guilt shadowed Murghesh's eyes. "We shoulda waited for your call, huh?"

"Yeah." But Lutane was glowering up the stairs. "But as you said, it was a stupid move. More than stupid—it was suicidal."

Murghesh shrugged. "They must have figured they didn't have a chance against us any other way."

"And they were right—there were just too many of us for them." Lutane scowled. "I'd have tried their trick, too, suicidal or not." She stared down at the corpses.

"Something wrong, Lieutenant?" Murghesh asked carefully.

Lutane pointed. "Only two of 'em are wearing bandoliers."

Murghesh followed her gaze. "That mean they were officers?"

"No, it means they were soldiers." Lutane pointed. "The other ones are only wearing armbands."

Murghesh shrugged. "I heard the Khalia weren't big on clothes, anyway."

"Yeah, but they need some kind of rank insignia—and that's all these ones had. They were reloading out of those boxes of clips, there." Lutane pointed. Murghesh looked and saw plastic cases stacked along the edge of the stairs. "Then what were the rest of 'em?"

"Communication technicians. They only had two guards stationed here, so the signal corps had to take defense stances as soon as the alarm went up."

"Comes to the same thing—all Khalia are soldiers." Murghesh shrugged.

"Yeah," Lutane muttered. "Kinda makes you wonder if there're any Khalian civilians anywhere." She had a brief, dizzying vision of newborn Khalia marching past with rifles on their shoulders.

Murghesh shrugged. "This is their home world. They've probably got more hidey-holes than a honeycomb. Nice to know we took 'em by surprise, though." Then Murghesh's eyes widened as she caught the implication. "That mean we got 'em all? That there're no more Khalia upstairs?"

"No." Lutane nodded at the corpses, her eyes hard. "Khalia do things by dozens, and only eight of those ten bodies belong to the building."

"Four more stationed upstairs?"

"Right." Lutane lifted her rifle with a wince. "Only four—but they're cornered, and they know they're dead. They're going to be trying to take as many of us with them as they can." She started up the stairs. "Let's get them."

She jumped back a split second before the stairs exploded with a hail of bullets.

"Lieutenant! How come you're still alive!?!" Murghesh was white as a sheet.

"Cause I was pretty sure they were up there. *I* would've been, if I were one of 'em." But Lutane was frowning up the stairwell, her brow creased in thought. Stairs . . . there was something subtly wrong about that, about the fact that the building had stairs. But what?

She shrugged the thought aside. There was a little matter of a battle, here.

"How the hell do we get through *that?*" Bonor grunted.

"We don't." Lutane stepped back, slinging her rifle.

"Lieutenant! How about the lift?"

Automatically, Lutane shook her head. "We'd open the door and find ourselves staring down a pair of rifle barrels —that is, *if* they didn't manage to turn off the power and strand us between floors." She turned to Murghesh. "Sergeant, hold this door with your squad. If anything comes down, blast it."

"Yes sir." Murghesh frowned, but she took up station, rifle levelled at the stairs—gaze levelled at Lutane. "But what's Nol's squad doing?"

"Going up the outside." Lutane turned to the door, nodding to Nol. "Let's go, Sergeant."

Nol herded his people outside, excitement flickering in his eyes. Lutane wished the rest of his squad looked the same. For that matter, she wished *she* did.

She stepped out to see Olerein's rifle levelled at her. When he saw who it was, he dropped his sights as though a marlin had taken his bait. "Lieutenant! What . . ." Then he remembered what might be behind her, and his rifle swept up again.

"At ease." Lutane stepped up to him. "Take off your booster pack and give it to Monsan."

Frowning, Olerein unbuckled his pack and swung it around. "Whatever you're gonna do, Lieutenant, you need me along. I'm . . ."

". . . the best shot in the platoon, and I need you here to make those weasels keep their heads down," Lutane finished. "Don't talk, Olerein." She turned away to the rest of his squad. "Doyle, Brill, Canche, Folar! Give your packs to Nol's squad!"

Reluctantly, the soldiers helped their mates into the booster packs. Nol already had one, of course—they were standard issue for officers and NCOs. But only half of the privates had them; HQ hadn't planned on whole squads having to lift.

"Shouldn't my squad go along, Lieutenant?" Olerein asked.

Lutane shook her head. "There're only five windows on that top floor, Olerein. Two soldiers to a window, that's all we need. You just make sure the bastards don't lean out to fire down at us."

Olerein grinned like a mountain wolf. "They'll stay down, Lieutenant."

"We won't." Lutane looked up at Nol and his squad. "Spread out all around the building. I'll take four troops up to the two windows on this side." Lutane pointed up. Nol followed her gaze, nodding. "You take six up on the far side," the lieutenant went on, "but don't fire until _after_ you hear our burst stop."

Nol frowned at her, puzzled.

"Just do it," Lutane grated.

"Yes, sir," Nol said stiffly, and strode away toward his sixty percent.

Lutane watched him go, simmering. Who cared if he was angry or not? As long as he followed orders.

Nol bawled at his squad, and Lutane waited, chewing at her gut instead of her lip. At least ulcers didn't show when you were out for R & R; that was some consolation.

"Ready," Olerein told her.

Lutane nodded. "Up!" She pressed the pressure patch between her breasts, and jets roared as lox and hydrogen ignited, sending the squad up in a cloud of mist that wreathed the tower. Not the safest way to travel, Lutane thought dizzily, but effective, effective . . ."

Then she realized that Pachue was tilting. "Straighten out!" she called, but the private heeled over and headed for the ground. "Cut out!" Lutane screamed.

Pachue couldn't have heard her, but must have understood the look on Lutane's face, because her jets died. Below her the squad scattered, pulling back into a circle as momentum turned Pachue upright again. When her head was at two o'clock, Lutane slapped her fist into her own chest, hoping Pachue would understand the impromptu sign. It must have gotten through, because the jets roared out again, breaking the kid's fall just in time. She hit hard, but she remembered to fold at the knees, and Lutane turned back to the comm center with a sigh of relief. Too bad they had to have replacements, but everyone had to be green once.

It left Lobrin without a partner, though. Lutane thumbed her altitude jet, swooping over to him, then straightening up again just as they reached the window. "Back!" Lutane called, and they both flattened themselves against the wall on either side of the window, throttling their jets down to maintain altitude, just as a fountain of bullets sprayed out of the window. Exactly what she herself would have done, Lutane thought grimly, and waited for a pause in the stream of bullets. It came, and she dodged into the embrasure, jamming the trigger down. Lobrin was a quarter-second behind her, but he matched her to the beat when she ducked back out again, loosing another geyser of bullets from inside the building. That was all it took, though; the defenders had had to turn back to Lutane's side, and Nol's troops at the opposite windows poured in hot lead as though the building was a crucible. Lutane waited, and waited; the hail of bullets seemed to go on, and on, and on . . .

Finally it stopped. The comm center was quiet.

Very quiet.

Somebody had to take the chance. Lutane ground her teeth. *What are lieutenants for, anyway?*

She spun through the window, rifle blazing—and let the burst die.

Four Khalia lay on the floor—all around. What was left of their bodies was hamburger, with a few jigsaw puzzle pieces thrown in.

Her stomach heaved, and she just barely managed to choke it back down, lifting her glare to the comm gear. There was a lot of smoke rising, but a few consoles seemed intact.

"Come on in," she called. "Don't look down."

Nol ducked in, then Lobrin at Lutane's back, then the rest of them. Some looked at the floor, and looked away again quickly, turning a delicate shade of chartreuse. Maybe, Lutane thought, that was why they called new troops "green."

The veterans could have taken it, but they had sense enough not to look. Porthal and Elab went straight to the two intact consoles, frowning down at the dials and sliders.

"Can you figure it out?" Lutane demanded.

Porthal nodded slowly. "Take a little experimenting, Lieutenant—but this grille is either a mike or a vent, and that meter's either amps or volts."

Elab didn't speak; he was already kicking aside the tilt-board and pulling a chair over.

Lutane stared. A chair? What was a chair doing here? The Khalia's tilt-board backrests, sure—but why would there be chairs in the comm center, too?

Later. Speculate after the job's done. Lutane pressed the patch on her bracelet and talked into the mesh. "Everybody in. Squad one, hold the door and the stairwell. Squads two and three, search the building by the square foot. If there's anything bigger than a gnat, I want it dead."

"Yes, sir," her bracelet answered in duplicate.

"And watch out for booby traps!" Lutane snapped. She lowered her arm and turned about slowly, surveying the big, open room. There—the lift. It was over against the side wall, doors open—and filled with dead, bloody bodies. Lutane nodded with grim satisfaction—she'd been right. The last Khalian alive downstairs had pushed the up button, and died as the lift rose.

She turned back to Nol's squad. "Anybody with a strong stomach, help me throw this mess into a tarp and find the mops and buckets. Everybody else, get busy repairing equipment."

She shouldn't have left it open like that. It came down to Nol and herself on the cleanup crew.

The floor was so clean that it glared. The equipment had stopped smoking, and the soldiers had started to repair it.

"All set?" Lutane asked.

Porthal nodded. "It works, Lieutenant. Long-wave and medium-wave audio. Video, too, but there's nothing to feed into it yet."

"We'll find the pick-ups soon enough," Lutane assured him. "Okay, power up." She raised her voice. "Who speaks Weasel?"

"Here."

"I do, Lieutenant."

"Me, too."

"Okay. You three, over to the pick-ups."

The three troopers came over and sat down next to the signal operators.

"Send this out broadcast," Lutane said. "This city has been conquered by the Terran Fleet . . ."

"Uh, Lieutenant?"

"I know, I know, we don't know for sure that we've conquered anything more than this center! But we're after propaganda, not news. Just broadcast it, private."

"Yes, sir . . ."

"All civilians are to remain indoors until further notice. Do not obey orders from any Khalian. Instead, report their locations to the nearest Terran soldier." Lutane frowned in thought for a moment. She had to make it sound like a good deal for the slaves. "Citizens, rejoice! The conqueror is vanquished; your freedom is won!"

"Yes, sir." The translators turned back to their pick-ups and eyed the operators, who scowled at their panels for a moment, then nodded. The translators began to talk in falsetto, trilling syllables. Lutane watched them for a few minutes with grim satisfaction, then lifted her big commset and keyed in Captain Rakoan's code. She waited impatiently until the little plate lit up with his face, frowning. "Lieutenant Morna?"

"Yes, sir. Objective accomplished—we've taken the comm center."

"Yes, I heard your broadcast. You might want to add to it that the other platoons have taken their objectives, too."

"Yes, sir." Lutane felt her belly weaken with relief and realized that, at the back of her mind, she'd been haunted by the possibility of being a Terran island in the middle of a Khalian sea.

"How many enemy have you taken?"

"None, sir. They all died fighting."

Rakoan nodded as though he had expected it. "That seems to be the rule. Your fellow officers only took two alive, and they're so badly mangled that we may not get anything out of them. Any noncombatants?"

"No, sir." Lutane frowned, realizing for the first time that there hadn't been any slaves in the building.

Rakoan nodded again. "That's the pattern. Featherheads in the houses, slaves of all species in the streets—but none in the objective buildings."

"Slaves wouldn't have anything to do with running the place, anyway," Lutane said cautiously.

"No, but I would have expected a few of them to be in the government buildings, just as servants." Rakoan frowned, brooding on the question for a moment. Then he shrugged it away. "Well. There'll be time enough to find out why when we've mopped up. Well done, Lieutenant. Listen in on the comm and pick out the details to broadcast."

"Yes, sir. Out."

Rakoan's picture vanished. Lutane racked her commset on her belt, and turned to frown out over her new domain. Something niggling at the back of her mind had become clear—the fact that the comm equipment wasn't placed to full efficiency in the room. The consoles were set around in a horseshoe, which made sense for a single officer in charge—but the horseshoe sat in the center of a rectangle, with all kinds of room between it and the walls. Even allowing for technicians needing access for repair, there was still way too much space left over. That, plus Rakoan's comment about the lack of slaves, ignited an insight—she was looking at a conversion. Sure, the original building predated interstellar technology—but presumably, it would have had the same kind of function in the early industrial civilization that preceded it.

No, it hadn't. Why else would there be so much room left over?

Lutane nodded slowly. She was looking at the inside of what had been a public meeting hall of some kind, adapted for use as a comm center.

"Here, Lieutenant. We found an extra."

"Huh?" Lutane looked up just as a private shoved a chair toward her knees. "Oh. Thanks, Londol." She folded into the chair, then had to fight to keep herself from folding, period. "You were a journalist back home, weren't you, Londol?"

"Yes, sir. I worked on the *Galathian* with Bullam over there."

"Well, the two of you get busy being reporters again. Listen in on the comm, then call in and get the details on how each unit won. Then assemble them for broadcast."

Londol smiled. "We know the process, sir."

Lutane just nodded wearily, and settled back to watch as the room quieted. There were comments back and forth between technicians, broken by occasional warbling announcements in Khalian—but aside from that, the comm center was mostly quiet. Londol and Bullam settled themselves at desks and began making calls. Lutane listened idly, feeling a glow of accomplishment—and the regret of having killed sentients, no matter how vicious they'd been.

After a while, she frowned, realizing that a pattern was building up. The units reporting in had taken terrible losses, between thirty and fifty percent, but the Khalia had been virtually annihilated, since they fought ferociously and refused to surrender. The only prisoners were the ones who were wounded too badly to fight back—and most of those would probably die in a few hours.

But that wasn't the case with their "allies," as Captain Rakoan had called them. The featherheads were running at the first sign of a fight, which wasn't surprising, since none of them seemed to be armed. They didn't even carry belt knives. But they did have an appalling tendency to get caught in the cross fire, and there were more dead featherheads than dead Khalia.

"Lieutenant!"

Lutane looked up to see Olerein coming up to her. Then her eyes widened, and she came to her feet, because in front of Olerein marched two featherheads, hands pressed to their chests, trembling—and in front of them was a much smaller one, doing a good imitation of an earthquake. Lutane stared at the little one, remembering the two other little ones she'd seen in the featherhead house, and a lot of things began to make sense. She lifted her head and called, "Anybody speak featherhead?"

The room was quiet. Then Londol said, "No, Lieutenant."

Lutane cursed and yanked out her commset. "Lieutenant Lutane calling Captain Rakoan."

The plate glowed. Then Rakoan's face appeared. "Yes, Lieutenant?"

"We have some featherhead prisoners, sir."

"Those we have plenty of, all sizes. Anything interesting about them?"

Lutane eyed the aliens. "Guess not, sir. I was, uh, hoping you could, uh, spare a translator."

"'Fraid not, Lieutenant. The ones we have are all busier than a beekeeper without a mask. Let me know if you find out anything interesting, all right?"

"Uh . . . yes, sir." Lutane killed her commset and racked it as she looked up at Olerein. "I hate to give up my chair, but it's the only thing to tie them to. Make 'em sit down, Olerein. Londol!"

"Yes, sir?"

"Bring some rope."

She studied the featherheads as Olerein and Londol bound them. There wasn't enough chair for the two big ones, but at least they had some support for sitting. She picked up the little one—it squalled frantically and struggled like an eel—and put it on the laps of the big ones just as Londol looped a rope around it. "Bring another chair as soon as you can find one, Olerein. Where'd you find 'em?"

"Ground level, Lieutenant. There's a lift-tube at the back of the building . . ."

"A lift-tube?" Lutane looked up, startled.

"Yeah." Olerein grinned. "We could have come up the back way and caught the weasels in a cross fire. But, the door that opens into the entry fits the wall so tightly we passed it by. Besides that, there's just the room at the back, where I found these two. They were cowering in a corner, hugging each other."

Lutane's eyes narrowed. "What else was in the room?"

Olerein shrugged. "Just knives, ladles, pots, ovens . . ."

"Food preparation." Lutane scowled at the featherheads,

who shrank in on themselves at the sight of her glare. "What have we got here, the cook, the butler, and the pot-boy?"

Londol nodded. "That would make sense, sir. From the way they're cowering, I'd sure say they aren't soldiers."

"Yeah." Lutane frowned and pulled out her commset. "Lieutenant Lutane to Captain Rakoan. Over."

The plate glowed to life, with Rakoan glowering out at her. "This had better be good, Lieutenant."

Lutane swallowed hard. "I hope so, sir. Remember your hypothesis, that the featherheads might be allies instead of slaves?"

Rakoan frowned. "Of course."

"Well, mine are quaking in their boots, sir. I don't see any way they could have been *any* kind of soldiers."

Rakoan's frown softened to brooding. "Yeah. You're not the only one who's said that. In fact, everyone who's taken featherhead prisoners says they're scared gutless."

But Lutane heard a report coming in to Londol. "Wait, sir! The assault on the admin center?"

"Successful, Lieutenant, though they took more than fifty percent casualties. They had to fight their way up those ramps, inch by inch. Why?"

"Because of the stairs!"

"Stairs? *What* stairs, Lieutenant?"

"The ones in this building, sir! The admin center was one of the new ones, wasn't it?" She rushed on, not waiting for an answer. "And our comm center is one of the old buildings! It has stairs!"

Rakoan was turning thunderous. "Explain the import of this contrast, please, Lieutenant. What difference does it make if they've updated their architecture?"

"Because they would have had no reason to change from stairs to ramps, sir! None of the Khalia ships we've captured have ever had stairs—and their bases haven't had them, either! Khalia have very short legs; ramps are much more convenient for them! They probably never even invented stairs!"

Rakoan straightened, understanding coming into his eyes. "Assuming you're right, Lieutenant . . ."

"If I'm right, the building I'm in wasn't built for Khalia! They captured it and converted it, but the stairwells didn't

give 'em room for ramps, so they had to suffer with the steps
or put in a lift."

Rakoan nodded slowly. "That makes sense, yes. But I still
don't see its import."

"Then think about this one with it—why aren't there any
Khalian juveniles here? Or teachers? Or nursemaids?"

Rakoan began to look thoughtful. He reached off-plate to
key a pick-up. "All stations that have wrapped up hostili-
ties, report. Have you found a juvenile Khalian? Out."

Lutane waited on tenterhooks as the other platoons
reported in, one by one. Finally, Rakoan looked up at her,
his expression dark. "Not a single juvenile, Lieutenant—
and of course, no Khalian responsible for taking care of
one. Would you like to . . ."

"But there are featherhead juveniles, sir! I've got one!
How many have the other platoons found?"

Rakoan frowned and keyed the unseen pick-up again.
"All stations report. Have you found small-sized featherheads?"

Lutane held her breath as the seconds ticked by and tinny
voices buzzed through the plate.

"Out." Rakoan looked up, nodding heavily. "None of the
troops in any of the public buildings have found any small
featherheads, but the ones who are conducting the house-to-
house search have found a lot."

"Have they found any Khalia?" Lutane burst out.

Rakoan frowned and admitted, "Only a few. And in those
houses, the featherheads have been huddled in fear."

Lutane frowned. "They aren't cowering in the houses
where there aren't any Khalia?"

"Not really. When our troops break in, they run for
cover—*then* they cower." He sighed. "I see your point,
Lieutenant—the featherheads aren't Khalian allies. Command was right—they're slaves." He frowned. "But I still
say there're way too many of them. Why would the Khalia
have imported so *many* slaves of this one race?"

"Yes, sir. There are so many, many more of them, than of
any other species—and *vastly* more than there are Khalia."

Rakoan sighed and shrugged. "I suppose it's not all that
unlikely for slaves to outnumber the masters, Lieutenant."

"Yes, sir, but not at interstellar freight rates. FTL ships

have to be the single most expensive way of importing labor ever developed."

"Where else do you think the Khalia would get their servants?"

"From every ship they've conquered," Lutane answered, "as excess baggage—but *not* as the primary cargo. If they were, there wouldn't be any more of the featherheads than of any other race. And I don't think the Khalia are so swollen with booty as to be able to bring in *that* many more of any one species—with their children, too."

"So maybe the children were born here. After all, what're . . ." Rakoan broke off, his eyes widening.

"Yes, sir." Lutane nodded. "The Khalia got bored with stealing ships and moved on to bigger and better things. This time, they hijacked a whole blasted *planet!"*

Rakoan nodded, his gaze never leaving her face. "And if they did, then the featherheads aren't allies *or* imported slaves."

"No, sir." Lutane shook her head. "They're the natives."

INTERLUDE

The papers said the name was Neuton Bedfort Smythe. To Isaac Meier he represented a greater threat than the Khalia. Smythe was the special investigator appointed by the Alliance Council to investigate the "Target Fiasco." He was currently at the Admiral's desk, the heels of his shoes scraping gouges in a redwood desktop (that had been imported from Earth at Admiral Meier's personal expense) randomly accessing the files and reading them.

"Just trying to get the feel of it," the special investigator had explained. The grapevine (admirals listen to it as well; that's why they are admirals) was saying that he was looking for atrocities. The Admiral had a private theory that waste was first on the special investigator's list. Senators like waste; finding it makes the taxpayers happy. Happier yet as they were still smarting under the recent increase required to finance the expansion of the Fleet to a wartime establishment.

Even though all this interfered with his preparations for the final attack on the real Khalian home world, Admiral Meier had to admit the Council's dissatisfaction was justified, if ironic.

Politicians always look for the quick fix, for the easy, and

more importantly, cheap solution. Some of those fools on
the Strategy Board had been only too willing to tell the
Council what they wanted to hear.

The attack on Target had been billed as the final solution
to the entire Khalian problem. Instead it had unquestionably demonstrated that problem to be ten times as serious as
was previously thought. Now the Strategy Board looks like
fools and he has to deal with Smythe.

With a resigned sigh the aged Admiral settled back and
slaved his console to the one Smythe was using. Now he
could be aware of what the investigator was viewing. Meier
was relieved when the next file accessed was labeled Medical Corps. No chance of trouble there, not even a combat
unit.

LAB RATS
by Jody Lynn Nye

THE CENTRAL LIFE-MONITOR screen lit up, pinpointing the positions of soldiers down on Target wearing Fleet medical monitors in their gear. Even as the dots glowed into life, some of them began blinking distress, and just as quickly, others went blue. By watching, one could map out where action was taking place, and where the Fleet was losing ground. As positions stabilized, the medical ships moved in to pick up the survivors who were not able to get to their personnel carriers on foot. And the bodies of those that didn't survive. It was the Fleet tradition to bring back every combatant, alive or dead, for reasons of honor, if not because of what the Khalians did to those left behind.

Hospital ships were supposed to be inviolate in battle. *Elizabeth Blackwell,* though unarmed herself, had an escort of three heavily armed battle cruisers to make that so. The *Elizabeth,* as the main hospital ship, had a complement of over six hundred doctors, researchers, diagnosticians, and technicians on board and standing by.

Sixty scooters—medical shuttles—were already flashing their way between the ship and the battle, carrying away the Fleet's wounded and dead. Each worked its own territory which overlapped slightly with that of its nearest neighbors, so that no wounded man would go untended.

The streamlined scooters, at just under twenty-five feet in length, were among the smallest ships employed by the Fleet. They consisted mostly of engine, fuel, and powerful boosters designed for easy, rapid landing and takeoff. They were sprinters, not intended for long trips. The small cabin contained a compact primary care unit where a doctor could sustain life in up to sixteen beings while they were evacuated to a full-service hospital.

Inducer units were as much standard issue on a scooter as in the hospital ships. They were used during surgery to put a subject under without chemical anesthesia by broadcasting relaxing alpha waves to the lower centers of the brain, and did not interfere with normal dreaming or REM sleep. Violent or distressed patients often lay under its influence to halt manic spirals of energy. And it was common practice for doctors to use the device on themselves when running long, irregular shifts. It relaxed them enough to get in a little shut-eye. In fact, for anyone used to its effects, it would work almost instantly.

The computer woke Dr. Mack Dalle up from under the inducer in his research laboratory. He had crawled under for a much needed nap when he realized he wasn't going to be able to sleep because of the excitement and anxiety surrounding the coming battle. Which, obviously, must be going on right now. He pushed the square metal hood up and lurched over to his intercom. "Dalle," he grunted into the audio pick-up, almost falling against the switch in the effort to turn the com unit on. Six hours of sleep, the holographic analog clock face informed him. Almost his normal allotment, though induced sleep tended to be more restful. He felt as though he had been under for over eight.

"Can you wake up, Mack?" a female voice requested from the unit. The color monitor screen resolved into the image of a human woman with large brown eyes and dark blue hair streaked with white.

"Yes, ma'am," Mack said, stifling a yawn and giving her his whole attention. Commander Iris Tolbert, herself a neurochemist, and a good friend of Mack's, had been assigned as dispatcher of the Medical Shuttles for the assault against Target. "Just inducer sleep. I'm fine."

"Good. I need a pilot," she told him, looking as if she was under great strain. "Scooter FMS–47 is not responding to signal, and I haven't been able to raise the scooter-jockey, Leodli Schawn. The computer reports no life forms on board except a couple of critical patients who were reported by Leo herself. Fleet controller refuses to lend me a pilot to retrieve a medical shuttle, so I'm forced to deprive myself of the services of a doctor." Commander Tolbert let one corner of her mouth go up in a sour half-grin. "You."

"Whatever you say," Dalle said matter-of-factly, moving out of the viewscreen's range. He assembled clean medical coveralls from a storage cabinet and made for the small bathroom attached to the lab suite. He caught sight of himself in the mirrors over the line of scrub sinks and groaned. He looked like a terminal patient himself. Bags under his eyes, lines around his mouth, hair ruffled into a shock. He swiped at the hair with one hand.

"I say we have to get those soldiers aboard," Tolbert's voice said, fiercely. "You won't have time even for a shower," she commanded, guessing his thoughts. "You'll go down with Dray Kavid in FMS–38. I've called the flight deck. He's expecting you, so you'd better get a move on. Tolbert out." The screen went blank just as Dalle moved in front of it. With a sigh, he stepped out of his sweat-smelling off-duty jumpsuit and reluctantly pulled the white flight coverall up over his tall, thin frame. The suit was stencilled on both chest and back with the stylized red caduceus of the Medical Corps. On his way out of the lab suite, he called Stores for an extra diagnosti-kit to be waiting for him at the launch bay.

The scooter shot away from the *Elizabeth* like a waterbug on a pond, frictionless. In the distant blackness around Target, Dalle could see the tiny rectangles of other scooters moving to and fro, silver in the planet's reflected corona.

"The battle is gone from our sectors," Kavid told him. He was a somber black-haired pilot with some paramedical training, and a lot of experience in bussing live freight. "Half the scooters are still hovering. God, the place is full of those stupid feather-faces. If they're not staring at you in droves, they're getting in the way. They live here, you know? It's been all over the waves. They're the native life-form. And they're greedy little buggers. I caught one of the short ones trying to make off with my medikit. They'll steal anything."

"So you've been down once?" Mack asked, swallowing a quick cup of caffeine.

Kavid waved a negative, still staring at the forward viewscreen, and presented four fingers. "Four times. Once because they steered me in while the fighting was still going on. I felt like a damned pogo stick: *Boing,* down, up. It's a good thing I was strapped in. Damned near lost my teeth. The other three times I brought wounded back. The prep rooms are full. I'm going to get good and drunk when I go off duty." He punched a control button, and the view changed briefly to their aft. The gigantic ring-shaped form of *Elizabeth Blackwell* was quickly receding.

"I believe it," Dalle said, and sipped his coffee in silence. He read down the list of shuttles and their pilots on a side screen, noting the indicator which showed whether the scooter was in the docking bay, in transit, or dirtside. "FMS–27, Jericho, bay; FMS–28, Otlind, transit; FMS–29, Cooper, Target . . ." and all the way to one which was flashing: "FMS–47, Schawn, Target."

He pictured Leo as she was the last time he had seen her, laughing over a game or a drink in the rec room, surrounded by their friends. The pilots did fraternize with the doctors, at least on *Elizabeth,* during the years he had been assigned aboard her. There were so many who overlapped into both functions, like Mack himself, both shaman and bus driver. Leo was a birdlike female—with a long, swanlike neck, and vestigial feathers along her forearms and the nape of her neck—from some interesting genetic cross between an avian race and some humanoid stock. She put up with the usual bird jokes with grace, retorting with wit directed at monkeys and pigs.

Target zoomed in on them from the corrected view. Kavid cut in the jets, and the shuttle tilted and set down on its side in a dirt area that was obviously normally used for livestock. Empty feed troughs stood at the perimeter of the field. "Your shuttle's that way," Dray pointed to planetary west between two of the wooden troughs. "Sorry I can't get you closer, but I've got to get moving."

Mack shouldered his diagnosti-kit and picked his way out of the farmyard, avoiding the newest deposits of excrement. He passed through a wooden gate into a beautifully laid out garden of exotic flowers and pretty stones. Three of Kavid's "feather-faces" peered out at him timidly from a glassless casement, their multicolored faces almost as exotic as their garden. Dalle and they stared at each other for a moment, and then he went on westward.

His monitor tracer gave him no clear idea where to look for the scooter. Undoubtedly, there were more wounded around than Leo had managed to pick up before she disappeared, so there wasn't a concentration of red lights by which he could judge. He was afraid that she must be dead. He couldn't believe that in an organization so rife with communications backups as the Fleet she could be conscious anywhere and still remain out of touch.

A handful of Alliance marines, their tan uniforms coated with dust, saluted him as they passed. He returned the salute sharply. "Have you seen a grounded med scooter?" he asked them. They pointed back over their shoulders, and he plodded on.

Scooter FMS–47 lay in the rubble of a blasted cottage, smooth blue-grey surrounded by splintered brown. There were five feather-face bodies lying outward near where the door had been, surrounded by pots and rolls of textiles: residents fleeing with their little household goods. A clutch of dead Khalia sprawled nearby, fur mottled with laser burns and bullet holes. No Fleet or Alliance dead. This must have been one of the more successful skirmishes. Dalle had to step right over one of them to get to the starboard hatch. He rolled the Khalian over with one foot. Its face had been punched inward and charred black with a laser blast. Dalle gave it another push so it landed facedown again.

He put his palm on the doorlock and waited. A beep deep sounded within, and the door slid back. Dalle took a step to the side. A low, wide ramp extruded itself at his feet, and he walked into the ship, bowing a little to pass under the arch.

The two patients were there, and one of them stirred as the door opened. "Doc?"

"Yes?" Dalle came over to the woman and took her wrist. The stocky woman's pulse was strong, and the monitor showed her vitals to be good. At first he thought the bandages over her eyes hid the only wound, but when she sat up, he saw that there was a leg missing. Her hair was scorched, leaving a bald place over her left eye that stretched to the crown of her head.

"You're not the same doc," the marine accused, gently touching his chest with one hand.

"I'm Mack," he said, in a soothing, professional voice. "Hasn't Leo been back? Is anyone else here?"

"Nope. Just the guy breathing over there." Mack glanced over at the other marine, who was in deep sleep. His wounds were more extensive than the woman's, though not as severe.

"Do you need anything, corporal?"

"Nope," the woman said. "Doc told me they'd try to do something about my eyes later. I'm okay for now."

Stoic, Mack thought. Or shock. "Fine. I'm going to look for Leo and the rest of the wounded out there, and then we'll be heading back to the hospital."

"That's okay, Doc. Thanks." The woman settled back onto her bunk, patting her bandage to keep it in place.

There were no other sounds within except the chuckling sounds of the ship's systems maintaining themselves, but he heard shuffling feet running outside. "Leo?" he called.

Mack was just in time to see a white-backed shape vanishing around the corner of a mostly intact house to his left. "Hello?" He stabbed at the communicator button on his sleeve, on general immediate-range broadcast. "Hello? I am Dr. Dalle. Please identify yourself." No reply. It couldn't have been Leo, or any other Fleet personnel. He hadn't received even an echo from a nearby transmitter. A Khalian? A live Khalian in this area? His hand twisted forward to his sleeve.

Mack took another quick look around for the missing pilot, his hand curled under to the arming switch that operated the weapon hidden under the medical insignia on his sleeve. It was a laser, with a self-contained battery good for three short-range but powerful shots. He admitted at last that Leo was nowhere around, and went back to the scooter to begin his rounds.

"Doc?" the marine called out.

"Just me," Mack said, and started gathering equipment. The motorized travois, a rolling two-tiered gurney for four, was moored just forward of the inside hatch. He unfastened the straps holding it in place, and manipulated the control lead, a long, curving neck of metal that terminated in a tiny ten-button keypad, until the trolley followed him at heel out of the ship like an obedient three-wheeled dog. His medical paraphernalia rode on the near end of the cart, ostentatiously marked with the same red caduceus he wore. He had no armaments in plain view, but the laser was ready. He was also running through everything he knew about unarmed combat with opponents that bite, a required course ordered by Commander Tolbert.

He passed hundreds of featherhead natives, who all stared at him without comprehension. "I bet they don't even understand they've been invaded twice," Mack said to himself, sarcastically, stopping to run the portable monitor over the body of a very large Alliance marine. There were no wounds visible, not even bruises, but the man was deeply unconscious. Mack couldn't even guess what had happened to him. The echo of the heartbeat and brain functions was weak, but the frequency monitor remained clearly on red, not blue. The cleanup shift would come in for the dead, later on after the battle had ended or moved on, led by the blue frequency band.

After dispensing a "shock absorber" to the marine, Dalle pushed, pulled, and shoved him into the shelter of the low eaves of a hut. To pick him up on the outward journey made it more awkward to haul the motorized travois Dalle pulled behind him. It made more sense to haul it out empty, and pick up the wounded on his way back to the ship. He had three other life monitors on his scope along this vector. In his condition, the man would last until Dalle came back.

A sharp *crack!* startled him, and Dalle stopped cold, listening. Someone was stalking him. The image of the white figure haunted him. He wished that he had been able to get a clear look at it. *Pok,* the sound of a footstep, came

right behind him. He spun and dropped just as a laser blast
seared overhead and gouged a five-inch strip of plaster out
of a wall. The plaster exploded with a loud *bang!* Mack
gulped. On his belly, he wriggled over to the travois, hid in
its shelter. A second blast ricocheted silently off the shiny
metal of the travois's surface, heating up the place just in
front of his head, and peeling more stucco from a building
facade with a *crack* that echoed down the street. He peered
around the gurney's front end, readying his laser, but there
was nothing to shoot at. His assailant was well hidden.
Mack didn't want to expose himself, but he could have a
long wait before being rescued, and there were the wounded
to consider. He craned his neck around the metal frame,
and swept an eye over the square. There wasn't much left of
the buildings on that side, but the ragged lean-tos formed by
fallen timbers and panels made terrific places for snipers to
hide.

A bullet zinged past him from the other direction. Mack
buried himself in the broken quartz paving and tried to
scramble backward out of the way. That shot came from a
walkway between two of the brown and white wooden
houses. Dalle lay flat and spat out gravel. The laser shrieked
again, sounding near to overheating. At the same time more
bullets flew from the other side of the square.

"Stay down, dammit!" barked a male voice. Another
scream, animal this time, tore the air, and the laser bolts
stopped coming. There was a rush and rumbling, and more
of the masonry fell in. Dalle, with a cautious eye on the
heaped rubble, rose and dusted himself off.

"You're a doc?" a voice gritted from the walkway. Dalle
activated a powerful tight-beam torch and shone it into the
alley. He let out an involuntary hiss. There was an Alliance
marine sergeant lying braced against a wall with a broad
hand pressed to his side. His helmet was gone, and his
eyebrows were drawn down with the pain. "Help me." The
left side of the man's face was torn open, and his other arm,
thickly muscled, rested bonelessly on his lap. Blood dripped
purposefully from his wounds, showing the heart muscle
was still working hard, and nothing had clotted yet. This
must have happened just before Dalle moved into the
middle of the firefight. Dalle swallowed, looking around for

Khalia. Dead ones lay at grotesque angles all over the street, some spilling out of a crashed floater. No living ones were in sight. He knelt by the marine, prying the man's strong fingers away from the wound. He squeezed anesthetic and antibiotic over it, and probed gently with his fingers. There were shards of bone mixed in with the shredded muscle. "Slug-thrower," the marine told him through gritted teeth. "Big one."

"I hope you got him," Dalle said, without looking up. He pulled bone splinters away from the great blood vessel and held the vein shut with his fingers until he could clamp it with a temporary. He unfolded a heavy soft dressing and fitted it over the tear. It would hold together until they got back to the hospital ship. He didn't want to plant new skin on it until he had a chance for adequate debridement, and this was no place to do it.

"I do, too," the marine assured him. "Can you get me out of here?"

Dalle rose to his feet, wiping his hands down the sides of his jumpsuit, leaving red streaks in the dust. "Wait here for me. I won't be more than five minutes. I've got two others on scope. They're just a little way from here."

"No!" The wounded man tried to struggle to his feet. "You've got your trolley. Take me back!"

"I can't yet." Dalle tried to explain about the travois's limited capabilities, but the marine drew his sidearm and levelled it on him.

"Let's go, doctor," he said in a low voice trembling with pain and stress. "Now. I'll die if you don't get me to a hospital right away."

Dalle stood his ground. This was not his first battle, or his first threat. War affected strong men in odd ways. "I can't, soldier, but more than that, I *won't*. Those could be men from your command out there. Even if you won't, I must give them every chance of survival. You'll last." And he turned purposely away, looking into his monitor and not at the wounded sergeant. The man had behaved in a perfectly understandable and predictable manner, and so, after much practice and many battles, was Mack's response. He kept his muscles taut as he walked. If the man was going to shoot at him, it would be . . . *Now!* His head jerked up nervously in anticipation, but the shot didn't come. He relaxed with a sigh. The sergeant would wait. The logic, however inhumane it seemed at first, had gotten through to him. It did, in eight times out of ten—and only one of those other two had had decent aim.

The other two marines were easy to find. They were the only dull-colored humps in the midst of a particolored "rug" of Khalia and feather-faces dead in a town square. The square was surrounded by the typical low-eaved buildings, and one tall structure with antennas on top stood off to one side. The Alliance men's khaki uniforms were stained with dirt and much blood, but they still managed to respond when Dalle sought to rouse them. One, who had lost a foot and had a deep bite under his collar bone, crawled onto the gurney under his own power, and helped Dalle to drag his buddy on board. When they turned him over, the doctor could see the second marine had been lasered across the back. In a way, he had been lucky: the strip of dark pink flesh showed that he'd been broadside to the gunner. On the other hand, it would take time to see if there had been nerve damage in the spine. The man could end up being paralyzed from the ribcage down. Dalle sprayed him with antiseptic, not wanting to numb the endangered nerves with anesthesia. He put a patch on the other's wrist to feed antitoxin into the bloodstream, to counteract any infection that he might get from the weasel bite; he closed up the bite itself and the end of the leg. Mentally, he was already doing surgical prep on these men.

The marine sergeant was waiting patiently where Dalle had left him. He straightened up when he heard the travois trundling toward him. "Hi, Doc," the sergeant said, in unaccustomed embarrassment. "It's bad luck to shoot at a doctor. Hope you didn't take offense before. You know . . ."

Dalle nodded. "I know. I'll get you home, sergeant."

"Shillitoe is my name. Alvin Shillitoe, but my mates call me Tarzan."

Dalle grinned. "At least it's not as bad as Hound Baskerville."

"Yeah. I knew him," Tarzan acknowledged. "Unngh!" he grunted, using his good hand to lever himself aboard. "Another good old nickname." He struggled to flatten out as the gurney bumped into motion. The other men gave him faint grins of greeting.

"Yo, sarge," one of them said, noticing Shillitoe's insignia.

"And they call me Sunday Driver," Dalle smiled, watching the man try to disguise his discomfort as they moved over the ridged dirt streets. "No, really. I'm Mack, but you can call me Doctor."

"Thanks, Mack," the sergeant said, relaxing.

Dalle stopped only once more, to pick up the comatose patient. There was still no response or signs of awakening, but his heart beat was a tiny bit stronger. Not enough, Dalle thought, with a wrench.

"He won't last," Shillitoe observed.

Privately, Dalle agreed with him, but aloud he said, "Everyone gets his chance."

He got them all stowed in the bunks aboard FMS–47, patched, and started plasma on the three with deep wounds; he slapped a fibrillator alarm onto the chest of the fourth in case his heart should go into arrest in the doctor's absence. The woman had fallen asleep, and Dalle was glad to see an improvement in her blood pressure. They should be stable enough until he got back. With a thoughtful nod, he rolled out and down the ramp for a second load.

The streets were so cramped along his second vector that Dalle was forced to leave the travois and step carefully among the massed bodies to search for his quarries. There were three on his screen, and he was still hoping one of them would be Leo Schawn.

The rough walls caught at his sleeve with protruding wooden splinters or dribbled stinking gray plaster dust all over him. Floaters and jet-packers had been through here. Dalle could tell by the odd streaks where lasers had hit and gouged, yards above the reach of anyone at street level.

Dead bodies, Alliance, featherheads, and Khalia, were crowded together against a crumbling wall as if they had been bulldozed aside. The Fleet personnel, most of them technicians and doctors, had all been tied up and then killed. Most of them showed bullet or laser wounds, but

others had suffered more gruesome deaths. He recognized
Leo's shocked, open-eyed face among the dead, realized
with a hollow feeling inside that only her head was there.
Her body, dressed in its white jumpsuit, hands bound with
a thong, was ten feet away, with another heap of bodies on
the stones. The neck, which was narrow enough to be
encircled by one of Dalle's long hands, had been violently
severed. He gagged out of sheer reaction, then swallowed
and went over to place the head with the body. With a gentle
hand, he closed her eyes and drew her jaw shut.

"Dalle, FMS–47, on Target," he said into his wrist
communicator, and waited for acknowledgment. A hissing
crackle came, which was the dispatcher hooking in. "Confirm that Pilot Schawn, late of FMS–47, has been found.
She's dead. Khalian-style killing. Her neck was chewed
through. It's nasty."

A sigh came out of the grille. "I thought so, Mack," Iris
Tolbert said. "If you've got room, bring her back up.
Otherwise, leave her for the cleanup squad."

"I'll bring her back," Mack said, grimly. "Out."

The sight of her open eyes stayed in his mind all along the
rest of his vector, while he loaded up two surviving marines
and turned back along a detour. The third man's life
monitor had turned to blue as he watched, unable to halt
death, and under the circumstances, unwilling to try. This
marine had caught the edge—only the edge—of a plasma
blast, which had cauterized the places where his right
ribcage, arm, neck, and jaw used to be. He looked as though
someone had taken a giant bite out of him, like a ginger-
bread man. A husky male voice sputtered out of the
helmet-communicator, demanding attention. "Marlowe?
Do you read me?"

Dalle lifted it off the dead man's head and thumbed the
switch which would normally be pressured open by the neck
muscles. "This is Dr. Dalle. Who is speaking?"

"I am Sergeant Villanova," the voice snapped in surprise.
"Where is my marine?"

"He died a minute ago, Sergeant. I'm sorry."

There was a quiet, sad growl out of the speaker. "He was
talking to me. I was keeping him awake 'til we could get

back there. He was hurt bad?" It was a question.

"Very bad," Dalle confirmed. "I don't think I could have saved him. Are you in need of assistance?"

"Nope," Villanova said, curtly. "Thank you, Doctor. Out."

As Dalle stood up to drag away his travois, he saw a flash of white. The tension took over his reactions, and he turned and fired his sleeve laser in the direction the shot came from. Then he screamed. His left sleeve had been punctured, and a laser had etched a hot pink line in his forearm up to the back of his hand. To his amazement, he heard an answering scream from his assassin.

Cautiously, he edged over and peered around the corner. On the ground a Khalian lay. The fur of its arms and upper body was bleached white, some mark of vanity, or perhaps a sign of rank. One could never tell with the Khalia.

With an eye on the claws, he checked under the pointed muzzle for a pulse. His shot had only grazed its head, but it was nearly dead from a half-dozen other wounds. There was an entry and exit wound from one of Alvin's bullets, Dalle was sure. Its weapon holsters on crossed leather straps were empty.

"Spot check, FMS–47!" Dalle's communicator crackled. It was Iris Tolbert. "How're ya doing, Mack? I'm not going to lose touch with another pilot."

"I'm okay, Commander," Mack replied. "How do you think the lab boys would like to play with a weasel?" While he talked he was squirting anesthetic on his arm. He unwound strips of plasti-skin and pressed them over the pink line. In a moment, the pain died down. There was no need for antibiotics: lasers made clean wounds, but the sonovabitch hurt like hell.

"We've got all the dissection subjects we need, Mack."

"I've got a live down here. He's beat-up, unconscious, but I think he'll make it. He'd better. I think it might be one of the ones that killed Leo."

Tolbert was silent a moment, considering. "Good idea. We don't get many live ones. Bring it aboard. I'll tell Security to expect you."

"Thanks, Commander. Out."

The limp weasel body was astonishingly light. Dalle felt

almost no strain as he carried the alien over to the cart and strapped it down. Its breathing was very shallow. There was little of life left in it, but perhaps the lab techs would have enough time to study its responses before it died. Most Khalian prisoners suicided after capture, but this one wouldn't be given the chance. He gave it a general antibiotic booster, hoping the drug wouldn't kill it. Leo's light skull rolled from side to side in its gurney bed just across from the pinioned Khalian. Her narrow jaw had flopped open, and she looked like she might be screaming. Betrayal. Dalle felt a stab of guilt for possibly saving the life of the very Khalian who had taken hers. On the other hand, making it so her killer lived the short, proscribed life of a laboratory rat was perhaps apt revenge.

He saw a few of the feather-faces robbing supply packs from the dead. He made no move to stop them. Those that the Fleet reclaimed would get tossed into the disposer anyway. Someone may as well get use out of them. Except for their scratching and quiet conversation, there was no sound at all for miles under Target's sun.

Dalle bandaged the Khalian's injuries and left it strapped down on a bunk, ignoring the questions of his other patients. "Prisoner of war," was all he would tell them. Tarzan squinted a question at him, but Dalle looked away. The last vector he needed to cover showed only two pinpoints of red. Out of curiosity, he turned the monitor dial to blue for the same tangent, and cringed at the vast number of indicator lights that appeared. Some sectors were just overlapping blurs of blue. Quickly, he snapped the control back to its original position, unable to deal emotionally with the scope of violent death. He chided his subconscious. It wasn't as if he hadn't seen war before, but he never got used to it. He didn't *want* to get used to it.

One of the two soldiers was kicking and twitching his arms feebly by the time Dalle brought him back to the scooter. His eyes were open, but he was not seeing Dalle. He was reliving the battle, fighting off the assailants who left the pattern of deep scratches on his skin and shredded his uniform. He must have been beset by a whole gang of weasels. The knife Dalle had found near his hand was bloody, but his slugthrower was never pulled out of the holster. He was a good candidate for inducer-rest. Perhaps the man would need psychotherapy anyway, but his anxiety level could be significantly reduced in the meanwhile.

He hit the hatch control and guided the travois up the ramp. At the top, he nearly let go of the metal leash in shock. The room was an abattoir. His patients lay in their own blood, dead, unable to have defended themselves. Some had died without ever having regained consciousness from their first encounters. And the bunk where the Khalian had been was empty, the straps chewed through. "By the hand of the goddess, what have I done?" Dalle whispered. He dashed around to each bed, searching for signs of life. It was a vain pursuit, except for two bodies, the female marine, knocked unconscious with a heavy plasma cannister that lay nearby; and another, stretched out on its side on the floor.

"Doc," Alvin croaked, his jaw and neck covered in blood from his face wound. One eye was glued shut and bruised. "Your pet weasel—"

"Where is it?" Mack looked around, but all he saw were dead men.

"Don't know. It attacked me and I grappled it. Damned things don't weigh much, and I coulda taken it down in spite of my busted arm, but see what it did to my eye? Kicked me in the gut, too."

"Yeah," Mack said, retrieving a flat, blue leechpak from the refrigerator unit. It didn't draw out blood, as its name suggested, but did assist in promoting circulation in hematomae. Alvin put it over the side of his face.

"Little bastard. Why'd ya bring it in anyway?"

Dalle took a moment, teeth in his lower lip, to confirm that all of his other patients were dead. Where was the Khalian now? "Did it get out of the ship, Alvin?" he asked, ignoring the marine's question.

Shillitoe cringed at the sound of his given name. He glanced around. "No. It's in here somewhere behind the panels. It couldn't figure out how to work the controls."

Warily, Dalle moved to the console, turned on the ship's security system. He didn't have any taste for playing

hide-and-seek with a bloodthirsty monster, in spite of the
fact he must have a good two feet in height on it. There, on
the schematic, was a life-form moving toward the other five
life-forms, his and the living patients. Dalle twisted, stared.
The Khalian, dripping blood, was racing toward the open
hatch.

Quickly, Dalle pounced on a control, slammed the heel of
his hand down on it. The door whooshed shut almost on the
alien's claws. It let out a panicked squeal. Whirling, it
dodged toward the tiny bridge, and even as Dalle lunged for
it, discovered there was no door to shut on its pursuer, and
backpedalled toward the bank of storage cabinets.

Mack ran after it, trying to guess what its next move
would be. Having been in the thick of hand-to-hand skirmishes with Khalia before, he probably knew as much or
more about their fighting style than any other doctor in the
Fleet. They were smaller, weaker, lighter than human
beings, but they were faster than hell, and they had a lot of
energy.

He got a sudden inspiration: he could throw it under the
inducer. Kayo it with waves, and it would be no more
trouble. He cursed, looking at the bodies of the dead and
wishing he had thought of that solution earlier. Keeping his
eye on the Khalian, he sidled over to the device, a more
portable version of the one in his lab, and switched it on.
The inducer's gentle hum filled the air.

The Khalian's shiny black eyes followed Dalle suspiciously. It had no idea what the soft-skin's machine did, but it
had no intention of getting anywhere near it to find out. The
device smelled dangerous. Teeth and claws were no use
against the walls of this ship, and its position of mere
soldier had never allowed it to learn such intricacies as
technology. It would have to make him open the door
before it tore his throat out.

Dalle moved purposefully toward the weasel, seeking to
maneuver it toward the inducer. It cringed, flattening its
back against the wall and spreading out its front claws.
Dalle feinted toward the left, driving it out of its niche to
the right. It flashed across the room, pounding on the
control console to make it open the door, then turned at
bay. Mack moved inexorably toward it, cornering it, until it

found that it had its back to the deadly machine.

The weasel sprang at Dalle, teeth bared. It was still very weak from blood loss and its wounds, but it was determined to go out fighting. Dalle looked at the long, sharp incisors, and regretted not pinning it down with metal straps when he had gone out. Ironically, it was his own fault that the weasel had enough strength to fight. The shock absorber and local anesthesia had done their work; the weasel didn't feel its wounds. He had set it free to kill. It made him sick to see the mangled dead strewn about his control room.

The Khalian leaped at him. One claw whistled through the air. Dalle nearly loosed off another of his laser shots, but remembered in time how much damage it would do to the inside of the ship. He stiff-armed the weasel in the face, bending backwards to grab the heavy plasma cannister off the floor. The weasel raised a back claw and raked down his leg, came up again, and grazed the cloth over Dalle's abdomen. It ducked its head around his arm to bite at the exposed side of the doctor's neck. To its owner's surprise, the claw caught in the fabric, halting the Khalian's strategy momentarily. Dalle let go of the weasel's face, linked his arm under the leg, and flipped it up and over.

The weasel went flying, but it regained its feet in a blur and fixed its teeth into Dalle's shoulder. Mack screamed, and a tingling raced down his left arm to his fingers, followed by a shock of numbness. The can fell from his hand with a *boom!* as it hit the deck. Instantly, the weasel tried to break to the right. In automatic response, Dalle's arm tightened around it and squeezed.

The weasel gasped involuntarily through the corners of its mouth. Its front claws let go, but its teeth didn't.

Ignoring the deadening of his left hand, the doctor locked his right hand on his left wrist, and lifted the small Khalian off its feet, waltzed it struggling toward the inducer. As a creature so close to base animal, Dalle was confident that the effect the waves had on the lowbrain in so many Allied species would put the beast quickly under.

He body-slammed it against the side of the table, trying to bend it backwards, but its spine was designed to bend only forward and to the side. He was afraid he would snap its backbone, and twisted instead to the side, pinioning the

Khalian's paws over its head. It brought them both within inches of the edge of the inducer's beam. The weasel doubled over between its own forepaws, jaws reaching for Dalle's throat. The doctor recoiled, remembering what had happened to Leo. His head moved just under the focused beam of the inducer.

Dalle saw the writhing white figure of the Khalian change, until the face was Leo's, screaming at him as his hands closed around her throat. It was a waking dream, and he was fighting the urge to fall asleep as much as his furry opponent. He kept convincing himself that it wasn't Leodli he was fighting, but a Khalian, and the face changed over and over again. He was determined not to lose his prize. He wanted to bring the alien home still breathing. It became Leo again, this time pleading with him not to kill her. "No more," she begged.

The Khalian took advantage of his uncertain grip to scratch at him again. Dalle felt the gouge across his belly and thigh from very far away. It was as if it was hurting someone else, not him. The soft, cottony wadding of unreality around his mind was starting to work on the rest of his body. He realized that his brilliant strategem was more dangerous to him than to a weasel. If he moved fully under the inducer's beam, he would be instantly asleep. There was no telling how long it would take the Khalian's unaccustomed brain to be affected. In the back of his consciousness, he could hear the intercom screaming at him, Commander Tolbert wanting a progress report. He heard the murmur of voices in the background near him, but none of them made any sense.

He batted away a claw he couldn't quite see. It kept metamorphosing as it moved closer to his face. He was losing the fight. If he moved one more inch under the hood, he would be helpless, and his opponent could quite easily kill him. He was becoming groggy. It was overwhelming him now, pushing him, forcing him . . .

His attention was dragged back to the surface just then by a magnificent, full-throated yell. His limbs twitched and jerked, all control lost from the startlement.

But that was nothing compared to the reaction of the

Khalian. It jumped high in the air, whiskers out, fizzing and spitting, and spun at bay to face the attacker who loomed behind it, gigantic in the glaring white light.

Without the alien's pressure to keep him on the table, Dalle slid out of the inducer's influence to the floor, where he banged his head on the tiles. He rolled over, gained his hands and knees by inches. The war cry sounded forth again, forcing the weasel into an attitude of defense. Alvin stood before him, waving the plasma cannister and uttering the huge sound that had the weasel frozen in its place. Without hesitation, Dalle wrenched himself upright, enveloped the small figure of the alien in a hammerlock, and threw it bodily under the inducer beam. In a few moments, it was still. Mack let go and leaned back against the wall, panting, then grinned up at Shillitoe, who was supporting himself against the travois. The other two patients were cheering.

"Now I know how you got your nickname," Dalle joked weakly.

Colonel Bar Kochba of the security occupation force, from the planet that orbited Magen Perdido, was on hand with five of his men to assist with the transfer of Mack's prisoner. They put restraints on the helpless Khalian before dragging it out of the inducer unit. Until they were gone, Mack was more than half convinced he would be led away in irons too, to face court martial for letting an enemy murder helpless patients. Instead Bar Kochba threw him a casual salute and grinned through his beard at him. Mack returned the salute, and bent to care for the survivors. Gently, orderlies from the Morgue lifted Leo Schawn's body from the stretcher bed. Mack watched them roll away with her and the other dead before turning to care for the remaining living passengers of FMS–47.

He went to visit Alvin in the ward after the big sergeant had been through surgery and recovery. The torn place on the sergeant's face was patched up, with a ring of white wadding around the eye to keep seepage out of the new skin graft. Mack's other three patients were all doing well, and seemed to bear Dalle no ill feelings for accidentally turning a Khalian loose among them.

"Fortunes of war, doc. If the brass let you off, I can forgive you," the female marine told him philosophically. If anything, they respected him for capturing one alive single-handed. Shillitoe promptly offered to take him on as medic for his unit, the Apes.

"No, thanks," Mack said, laughing. "I'm happy at what I'm doing: Research and Diagnosis. If I can ever get back to my lab and do some."

"You're missing a great opportunity, Mack," Alvin chided him, shaking his head. "Ooooh." He touched a hand to the eye patch.

While he and Alvin were chatting, a mate came up and touched Mack on the shoulder. "Excuse me, Captain, Admiral Duane requests your presence on the *Caffrey*. We've got a wounded Khalian. It's unconscious, I think."

"Why me?" Dalle demanded.

The aide shrugged. "The Admiral's decided you're the closest thing we have to an expert."

Dalle ignored the grin on Shillitoe's face as he followed the aide out.

PRISONER OF WAR
by Judith R. Conly

The acrid tang of the fallen foe
still seared my tongue and stung my nose
when the unseen skulking smooth-skin,
whose greatness of size and strength
outweighed a heritage of skill,
shackled me to defeat and life.

From forbidden captivity I cast my complaint,
not to the kin who mourn my death unknowing
but to the void we travelled, wizard-guided,
in whose depths my words at least find rest.
Dishonor binds and weights my chest
where once my weapons shone with pride.
(Yet my brave sons may rest secure,
for no witness to my disgrace survives
to erase all traces of my tainted line.)

My claws ache to rend furless flesh,
to drown with alien blood my shame
and the voice of my fettered soul that asks:
what more will my cloth-clad captor,
vindictive in victory, require that I endure,
that I might earn the right to die?

INTERLUDE

Admiral Meier leaned back in his chair. If that's what the medics were doing on Target, he wondered what the combat files read like. And he wondered what Smythe thought of it. The thought took the edge off the excitement he had felt reading about the doctor's adventure. Deciding there was only one way to find out, the admiral switched on the intercom.

"Mr. Smythe?" he said, trying to sound as if he weren't annoyed at calling his own office. Why hadn't that pompous Pat Jamesen turned his own office over to Smythe instead? Jamesen had rarely bothered to report here for duty anyhow since his brother was elected to the Council Appropriations Committee.

"Yes, Admiral?" the investigator answered almost instantly.

"Could you come into my, ummm, the next office to your left?"

"Be happy to," Smythe actually sounded cheerful. Well some people enjoyed dirtying others. Meier braced himself.

When the investigator had settled into a chair, Meier decided to dispense with pleasantries and loose his broadside.

"That was a damn fine action on Target, a lot of good men died." He tried not to sound defensive. "Even if it didn't end the Khalian threat, it moved 'em further from the border."

"They still occupy Bethesda, Triton, and Dibden Purlieu," Smythe retorted, but in a level voice.

"Exactly," Meier agreed, having maneuvered the conversation to where he wanted it. "And your being here is doing nothing but complicate our efforts to do something about that."

He plowed on before the investigator could respond. "You must be aware that we are planning a major action to recover Bethesda. When we reoccupy that planet, the Khalian position on the others becomes untenable."

Meier's voice was becoming louder. His agitation with being investigated was complicated by his growing concern over the Bethesda operation.

They simply weren't ready yet. It takes months to recall and reassign a thousand ships and not disrupt everything they have to maintain inside the Alliance. Duane had nearly caused disaster on McCauley by withdrawing too much force.

The memory that his grandson had done such an outstanding job calmed Meier. As if waiting for the Admiral to be ready to listen, Smythe choose that moment to answer in his perpetually level voice.

"I am here to help, not hinder."

Meier suppressed a snort.

"No really," the investigator added quickly. "Perhaps it is time I explain. You have to keep this in the strictest confidence. Even from the rest of the Strategy Board."

Admiral of the White Isaac Meier wasn't sure whether he should feel insulted or not.

"Go on," he said in a voice that echoed reserved judgment.

"There is something wrong with the Khalia," Smythe began gesturing with his shoulders. "It just doesn't feel right."

"We're at war with the hull-pocked weasels," the Fleet officer interjected more vehemently than he intended.

"At war yes, but are the Khalia like any enemy the

Alliance has ever faced? Do they act like any navy, any culture we have ever dealt with?"

"It's a big galaxy, Mr. Smythe. Lots of strange things in it. That's part of why The Fleet is needed." Meier couldn't resist interjecting the commercial. This Smythe certainly thought he knew it all.

"Not so big that a race capable of causing this much trouble shouldn't even be listed on the old Imperial records." The investigator launched his own broadside. "A preindustrial, semibarbaric culture doesn't become capable of what the Khalia are doing in less than a thousand years." Smythe leaned forward, warming to his topic.

"Look, how would you characterize the individual tactics of the Khalians?"

"Deadly," Meier answered instantly. Was this man casting doubts on the fighting ability of The Fleet?

"Will you permit me to show you another file? You may find it more interesting than the med corps one." The investigator not too subtly put the admiral on notice he was aware his actions were being monitored. "After that I'm going to need several weeks alone to plough through a gigabyte of memory. I'll count on you to throw up a barrier around me that will keep everyone else out."

Meier didn't respond. Something didn't fit about Smythe either. He was much too competent to fit the mold of Alliance Council flunky.

"You'll just have to take my word that I am not here on a witch hunt . . . We already know where your espers are quartered," Smythe finished with an obvious attempt at levity.

"A file?" the admiral inquired, reserving judgment.

The investigator's smile remained, though more strained. He reached over and keyed in a command he must have had preset. Meier realized he was being maneuvered, but couldn't figure out why. With the clout of the entire Alliance Council behind him, Smythe certainly didn't need to be concerned about the opinions of one admiral.

THE ANTAGONIST

by Janny Wurts

JENSEN STEPPED BRISKLY from the orange-lit access corridor, and a thrill touched him as the confined echo of his footfalls fell away, lost amid the din of Point Station's docking hangar. Through the bustle of mechanics stripped to their thinsul suits, and the cross-bracing of gantry arms and loading winches, he found the object of his passion instantly. A smile of predatory satisfaction lit his face. She was exactly as they had described her, in tones that varied from frustration, to thwarted fury, to outright, obsessive longing: ugly, patch-painted, and scuffed, a typically hard-run small-time merchanter. Yet the awkwardly configured spacecraft under Jensen's eager scrutiny was nothing of the sort. His trained mind could admire the artistry with which her weaponry and shielding had been installed without marring her image of innocuous decrepitude. Jensen squared his shoulders, missing the stiff scrape of his ensign's collar. Like the deadly, efficient bit of machinery he viewed, he would use camouflage to disarm his prey. For the *Marity* was the love and the pride of MacKenzie James, a skip-runner wanted on eighty-six Alliance planets for illegal trafficking in weapons, treason, theft, and sale of classified Fleet documents. Piracy was not a trade for the cautious; the

Fleet's autonomous diligence ensured that most skip-runner captains paid for their wealth with imprisonment or early death. But "MacKenzie, James," as the criminal files formally listed a man whose true name was only a matter of conjecture, was no ordinary skip-runner.

Mostly he was too good. The captains, officials, and highly placed admirals he had evaded, avoided, and unabashedly fooled in the course of his career made him dangerous, a topic of wild speculation in the barracks and the bars but one most scrupulously avoided in the company of superiors. To Michael Christopher Jensen, Jr., anyone who could engineer the skip-runner's long overdue arrest would gain promotion, accolades, and a reputation of undeniably proven merit. For a young man who had yet to earn "his paint" in battle against the Khalia, MacKenzie James was a piece to be manipulated.

Jensen adjusted the unfamiliar ties of the Freer over-robe he had acquired with some difficulty for the occasion. He looked the part, he knew, with his rangy frame and dark hair and eyes; meticulous to the point of fussiness, he had made certain no detail was out of character. Like many a fringe worlder, Freerlanders liked independence a bit too well to submit to Fleet sanctions; skip-runner captains knew them as a dependable market for illicit weaponry. They were ornery enough, or maybe just proudly stubborn enough, that only the reckless interfered with them in public. Still, as the young officer strode into the chaos of the loading lanes, his palms sweated. His plan might be soundly designed, but he was not quite brash enough to be unafraid. *Marity*'s master had ruined many a promising career before an unscheduled repair stop had delayed him; and though inconvenienced, MacKenzie James would never be caught unprepared.

Especially here; Point Station was a crossroads for the remote boundary of Carsey Sector, a center for commerce and intrigue only sporadically patrolled. Betweentimes, those goods and outbound colonists who were of questionable legal status arrived and departed with all the speed that over-used, outdated equipment could command. The ratchet of the winches was loud enough to drown thought, and the reek of heated machinery a metallic taint in the musty,

recirculated air. Jensen made his way cautiously. Ducking a
trailing power cable, and wary of stepping into the path of
the squat, radio-controlled light-loaders, he noticed the
stares prompted by his black-fringed Freer robe. He adjusted his hood, careful to carry himself with the right
degree of arrogance. His mimicry seemed effective. A dock
worker stumbled clear of his way, and behind the periphery
of the hood, someone else muttered, "Pardon,
Freerlander."

Jensen buried his hands in red-banded cuffs and kept his
steps light, as if he had grown up walking icy, wind-carved
sands; nothing less than perfection would deceive MacKenzie James. As *Marity*'s spidery bulk loomed closer, the time
for second thoughts narrowed. Now, Jensen no longer
regretted that necessity had forced him to include Ensign
Shields in his plan. That she drifted just beyond Point's grav
field perimeters in the dispatch courier Fleet Command had
assigned to the pair of them now offered great reassurance.
Though technically his senior, and compelled to collusion
by a veiled threat of blackmail, she would not let him down.
The moment her courier had altered course for Point
Station, the Ensign was committed.

Jensen managed not to trip on any cables as he crossed
the apron which separated *Marity* from the adjacent berth.
Eyes narrowed beneath the fringe of his hood, he promised
that overcoming Shields's reluctance would be the last time
he traded upon his father's influence for his own gain. The
man who arranged MacKenzie James's arrest could write
any ticket he wished and with this in mind, Jensen studied
the slots that recessed the studs of *Marity*'s entry lock. The
young Fleet officer repressed a whistle of admiration at the
evident strength of her seals. No Freer ever uttered anything
that resembled music outside of ritual. Such attention to
detail was not misplaced, for a moment later he found
himself noted by the ferret-quick gaze of the individual who
served *Marity* as skip-runner's mate.

The man was typical of the type signed on by MacKenzie
James. Young, athletic, and guaranteed to have no ties, he
turned from wheeling a cargo capsule that had overlapping
layers of customs stamps to mark a conspicuously legal
course across Alliance space. The Freer robe drew his

attention. An instant later, Jensen found his path blocked, and his hooded features under scrutiny by a pair of worldly eyes.

"You're here to see Mac James," said the mate.

He placed slight emphasis on James, the Mac more a prefix than first name. Jensen considered this idiosyncrasy while returning a nod of appropriate Freer restraint.

The man smiled, suddenly older than his years. His thinsul suit hung loosely over his frame, no doubt concealing weapons. "Godfrey, wherever we alight, and no matter how unexpectedly, you people seem to find us." But his easy manner was belied by the tension in his stance.

Yet skip-runners could be expected to treat strangers with caution. Careful to pronounce the name precisely as *Marity*'s mate had, Jensen said, "Then Mac James is available?"

"Mac's topside." His appraisal abruptly complete, the mate jerked his head for the young officer to follow, then gestured toward the open jaws of the lock.

Jensen took a slow breath, readjusted his Freer hood, and ducked under *Marity*'s forward strut. He set foot on the loading ramp, and quashed a panicky urge to retreat. The burning ambition which held him sleepless each night drove him forward as the mate disappeared into shadow.

Jensen passed the lock. *Marity*'s interior seemed dim after the arc lamps that illuminated Station's docks. His spacer's soles clung lightly to metal grating, the sort that adjusted on tracks to vary storage according to the demands of different cargos. But as Jensen blinked to adjust his vision, he heard the clang of an innerlock; a cool draft infused the outer hold and by that he guessed that on the far side of that barrier *Marity*'s resemblance to a merchant carrier must end. Only a craft that carried state of the art shielding and navigational equipment would trouble to control its atmosphere while in port.

The mate paused at the head of the corridor and called. "Mac?"

A grunt answered from the ship's upper level, distorted into echoes by the empty hold.

"Company's here asking for you." The mate waved for Jensen to pass him and continue alone down the access corridor. "Ladder to the bridge is there to the left."

Startled to be left on his own, Jensen crossed the threshold of the innerlock with his best imitation of Freer poise. He set cold hands to the ladder beyond. Faintly over the mate's receding footsteps, he heard the muted grind of light-loaders laboring outside on *Marity*'s hull. Then the innerlock hissed shut. Irrevocably sealed off from Station, and isolated amid the hum of the air-circulating system, Jensen recognized the sizzle of a laser pencil cutting through cowling.

"Come to talk, or to tap-dance?" *Marity*'s master called gruffly from above.

Jensen climbed. Sweating under his Freer cowl, he emerged in the windowless chamber of the bridge. Dead screens fronted the worn couches of two crew stations. The controls beneath were sophisticated and new, and somehow threatening without the array of labels and caution signs indigenous to Fleet military vessels. Jensen repressed a slight prickle of uneasiness. The man who flew *Marity* knew her like a wife; his mates without exception were pilots who could punch in and out of FTL or execute difficult dockings in their sleep.

"You're no Freer," the captain's gravelly voice observed from behind.

Jensen whirled, fringes sighing across the top rungs of the ladder. Bent over the far console was the skip-runner half of Fleet command would trade their commissions to jail. Through the dazzle of the laser-pen, Jensen made out a dirty coverall with the clips half unfastened, knuckles disfigured with scars, and a profile equally blunt, currently set in a frown of concentration. Shadowed from the laser's glare by a flip-shield, eyes light as sheet metal never left the exposed guts of *Marity*'s instrument panel, even as Jensen shifted a hand beneath his robe and gripped the stock of the gun hidden beneath.

"Care to tell why you're here?" The laser-pen moved, delicately, and the shift in light threw MacKenzie James's scarred fingers into high relief. With a small start, Jensen recognized old coil burns, from working on a ship's drive while the condensors were activated. The story was true, then, that Mac James had changed a slagged module barehanded to make his getaway the time he had sabotaged the security off Port.

Mesmerized by the movement of fingers that should by rights have been crippled, Jensen opened, "You run guns," and stopped. The man's directness had rattled him and he had neglected his guise of Freer restraint; but then, Mac James had already observed he was no Freer. Why, then, let him in at all? Taken aback, Jensen was unable to think, except to notice how remarkably deft the scarred hands were with the electronics.

"You're not here to negotiate business." MacKenzie James joggled a contact, applied his pen, then thumbed the switch off. The laser snapped out, and *Marity*'s master swung around, a hulking bear of a man with a spare brace of contact clips dangling from the head strap of his eye shield. He snapped up the plate, revealing a face of boyish frankness entirely at odds with his reputation.

Jensen opened his mouth to speak, and was cut off.

"You're Fleet, boy, don't bore me with lies." Mac James whisked clips and shield from his forehead and threw them with a rattle into the disjointed segment of cowling. "That makes you trouble, unwanted being the least damning complaint I have against you." He leaned heavily on the back of the nearest crew chair, his manner distinctly exasperated. "Don't bother with the gun, I know it's there."

"Then you'll surrender your person without a fuss," said Jensen, his confidence buoyed by the realization that the man he covered was sweating. "*Marity* has skip-run her last cargo."

MacKenzie James raked scarred fingers through a snarl of uncombed hair. "Boy, you've put me in a very bad position, and I'm not known as a nice man."

"That doesn't concern me." Jensen eased the pellet gun from his robe, pleased that his hand was so steady. "Your papers, Captain. Tell me where they are."

MacKenzie James slung himself into the gimballed couch. Light from the overhead fixture flashed on the worn tag he wore on the chain at his neck. The lettering stamped in its surface was ingrained with dirt, legible even in dim light: "MacKenzie, James, First Lieutenant." That rumor also was true, Jensen reflected; or maybe part of it, that a

two-credit whore from the Cassidas had gotten herself
knocked up, then smuggled herself and her byblow into the
quarters of her officer lover. An emergency call to action
came through, and when the Captain in command had
discovered a civilian on board, he had dumped her through
the airlock into deepspace as an example. Her lover had
subsequently died in action. The kid, who may or may not
have been related, had been signed over to some Alliance
charity orphanage. Though given a legal name, he never
called himself by anything but the inscription on the dogtag,
surname first; and harboring no love for the military, he
grew up into the most wanted man in Fleet record.

MacKenzie James raised tired eyes. "Boy, if you continue
with this, all the wrong people are going to suffer."

Jensen gestured with the barrel of the pellet gun. "Who?
Not all your clients are like the Freeborn, who think to beat
the Khalia single-handed. The guns you skip-run are as
likely to be used by criminals as in defense."

"Godfrey," said MacKenzie James with exactly the same
inflection his mate had used earlier. "Nobody informed *me*
I was such an idealist."

Marity shuddered slightly, as if jostled by on-loading
cargo. MacKenzie James sighed with apparent resignation
and said, "My flight papers are in the starboard vault.
Here's the key."

His coil-scarred fingers moved, very fast, and switched on
the laser-pen.

Jensen ducked the beam in time to save his eyes. He even
managed to keep his pellet gun trained on the patch of
sweaty chest exposed by MacKenzie's gaping coverall; but
the young officer didn't fire, which proved a mistake.

Hands that by rights should have been ruined flicked a
switch, and *Marity* came to life with a scream of drive
engines. She tore her gantry ties, stabbed upward with her
gravity accelerators wide open and smashed through the
closed hangar doors. Jensen was thrown to the deck. He
heard the wail of sheared metal as landing struts wrenched
off. *Marity* jerked, half-spun, and yanked free, burning
outward into deepspace and trailing a tumbling wake of
debris. Horrified, Jensen imagined Point Station thrown
into wobbling chaos: alarm sirens smothered by the inrush

of vacuum, and the light-loaders magnetic treads plodding mechanically over the dying thrash of the workers *Marity* had sacrificed to rip free.

MacKenzie James sat immobile in his threadbare deck chair. "This craft is fitted with several sets of back-up engines," he admonished. "Point Station personnel and Carsey sector authorities know better than to meddle with us."

"Bastard," Jensen said thickly. He moved gently against the pressure of acceleration, his pellet gun trained steadily on his antagonist. "Your mate was equally expendable?"

"Evans?" MacKenzie James did not change expression as the glare of the laser pencil snapped out. "No Freer ever approached us without elaborate clandestine overtures and a meeting in private. Evans should have remembered."

But Jensen's equilibrium had recovered. The vibration just prior to takeoff, surely that had been the lock cycling closed? Evans in all probability was on board. The control panels on the bridge seemed utterly dead; but with back-up systems, even now the mate might be piloting from a remote station elsewhere on *Marity*. If Evans was at the helm, Ensign Shields was going to have to fly her shapely ass off to keep up. Fortunately her ability was equal to her boasts.

Right now the primary directive was to take control before *Marity* gained enough charge to sequence her FTL drive. Icily composed in the half-light cast by the bridge control panels, Jensen shifted the target of his gun and squeezed the trigger.

The light-pen in MacKenzie's hand shattered. Fragments of casing raked his wrist and drew blood while the expended pellet screamed past his groin and imbedded in the stuffing of the adjacent crew chair.

Mac James moved, but this time Jensen was ready. Before the captain reached cover behind the bridge cowling, the Fleet officer had him cornered. Breathing hard, and sweating beneath his Freer robes, he trained his weapon squarely on the skip-runner's heart. "Roll over. Cross your wrists behind your back. One wrong move, and you're dead."

MacKenzie James grunted, eased his weight off his right

forearm, and carefully extended it behind his waist. "You're Marksman Elite?"

"Unfortunately for you," said Jensen, concentrating more on the left hand of his captive than acknowledging the accolade he had striven for, and won with such pride at an exceptionally early age. Gun at the ready, the young officer loosened his robe and retrieved a pair of loop nooses, the thin, cutting type Fleet marines used to restrain everything from murderers to brawlers. He hooked the first over James's upraised wrists and jerked tight.

"Now raise your ankles, captain." James did so, and the second noose shortly trussed his legs.

Smiling raggedly from triumph and excitement, Jensen locked the ends and began to search the captain's person. The man was tautly muscled, which was unusual enough to inspire caution. Most skip-runners were slender to the point of fragility, the result of long hours lurking in null gravity, their ship's systems shut down to a whisper to avoid notice. MacKenzie James also carried no side arms, only a small knife in a sheath sewn into his boot. Jensen confiscated this, then shoved his prisoner awkwardly onto his back.

MacKenzie returned a cool, appraising stare that, even behind a pellet gun, Jensen found disturbing. "You will tell me where Evans is piloting, clearly and quickly."

The captive smiled with brazen effrontery. "By now I expect what remains of my mate is being bundled up in a body bag."

"Back at Station?" Jensen resisted an urge to step close; even bound, the captain was bulky enough to roll and knock him down. "I'm not a fool, James. If Evans died on Station with the rest of the dock personnel, who guides this ship?"

MacKenzie's grin turned thoughtful. "Well now, I could say with reasonable certainty that *Marity* flies on a hard-wired connection between her accelerator banks and her coil regulator. Assuming I don't lie, any fool knows she'll blow when the condensers overheat."

Jensen considered this, unpleasantly confronted by the mulish courage that had confounded so many officers of the law before him. The captain *might* be lying; but his reputation said otherwise, which placed Jensen squarely on the prongs of dilemma.

MacKenzie James stopped smiling. "Don't think too long, boy. Since you so proudly blasted my laser-pen, I'll have to rummage around for my cutter tool to break the bridged circuit."

"Shut up." Jensen needed a second to clear his mind. Somewhere on *Marity* would be a kill switch to cut the drives in the event of emergency; the other fail-safes and override systems would be nonexistent, for skip-runner captains as a rule pushed their machinery over margin. The complication that this ship held to no specs, that she was a jumble of ingenuity and modifications hung together by the cleverest criminal in the Alliance meant Jensen was in too deep. If MacKenzie James were freed to right his bit of sabotage, chances were he would create additional havoc in the wiring, perhaps even contrive to regain advantage.

"I'll take my chances," Jensen decided. But his confidence was forced. If Evans had made it on board, he was now in serious trouble.

With the nooses secured without slack to a deck fitting, MacKenzie James could not roll onto his stomach. Nothing important lay within range of his feet. Certain as he could be that his captive was secure, Jensen sealed the bridge behind him and descended into *Marity*'s service level. Away from Point Station's fields, the descent shaft had no gravity. Already the chill of deepspace seemed to have penetrated its shadowy depths. Jensen drifted in a faint fog of condensation left by his breath, the ladder rungs icy beneath his sweating hands. His feet tingled with the knowledge that at any second a plasma weapon might sear upward and fry him like a fly on a web. The Freer robe swirled and caught at his ankles and knees. Jensen longed to shed the fabric, but dared not. Sewn into the sash was the transmitter that enabled Ensign Shields to track him, and *Marity*, through the deeps of space.

Jensen reached the base of the shaft without incident. Gun at the ready, he barely waited for his soles to grab on the decking before he started forward. His danger now redoubled, for the access corridor extended in both directions; MacKenzie's mate might easily slip into the bridge behind him and set his captain free. The fact that the mate had no key to release the nooses, and that the material of which they were made was extremely difficult to cut offered only slight reassurance. Under Mac James's spoken guidance, Evans might take control of *Marity* from the bridge.

Jensen glanced nervously over his shoulder, then rounded the crook in the corridor near the access door which had first admitted him. Beyond lay the hold, dark except for the blink of the indicator that showed the life-support system which served that portion of the ship was currently switched off. Jensen agonized for a moment in indecision. If the outer lock was sealed, then Evans was surely on board. No sense in crippling his judgment with worry if the man had died back on Station; crisply Jensen punched the stud he found near the hold's double safetied access latch.

Arc lights flashed on, lancing uncomfortably into pupils grown adjusted to the dark. Jensen squinted through glare off the port's bubble window. Beyond the crosshatch of struts and decking, the lock was securely closed. Nearby, garishly colored in the severe illumination, lay the cargo capsule Jensen remembered from the apron back on Station. Fear raised gooseflesh at the nape of his neck. Whether or not MacKenzie James had triggered a remote control in the opened pilot's panel, that capsule had not wheeled on board by itself. Skip-runner's mate Evans had assuredly made lift-off, which made light of any sort a liability. Jensen set his hand on the stud to kill the arcs, and stopped, caught short by something bulky that drifted above the grating which floored the hold.

The thing twisted gently in null-grav. Jensen made out the limp form of aman, and realized he'd been lucky. The automatic cutoff functions of lift had trapped Evans within the hold. Jensen glanced swiftly at the gauges in the panel by the lock controls. *Marity*'s hold maintained atmosphere, but no recirculation for oxygen. As a safeguard against stowaways and other breaches of security, cargo areas as a rule did not allow manual access to the habitable portions of the ship. Dependant upon rescue from within, *Marity*'s mate was probably hypothermic, for the cold of deepspace would swiftly permeate the uninsulated hold.

Jensen considered, then cold-bloodedly stabbed the light stud off. By now a steady whine pervaded the corridor; *Marity*'s engines climbed steadily toward overload. Evans probably knew the location of the emergency cutoffs, but it would likely take too long to force the information out of him. Jensen quashed his last pang of conscience.

The gloom seemed deeper on *Marity*'s lower deck, and the cold more cutting. Though the breath came ragged in his throat, the young officer clung righteously to his purpose. The mate was a skip-runner's accomplice, a criminal no invested Fleet officer could condone.

Jensen ducked through a companionway. His eyes reflexively traced the layout of cables on the far side. Guided by their convergence, he pressed forward and ascended a small ramp, half-stumbling over the shallowly raised treads. The transmitter sewn into his sash dug into his waist, reminding that he *had* to succeed, or leave Ensign Shields to answer to Fleet admiralty for diverting a courier from dispatch duty.

The whine of stressed engines rose relentlessly, throwing off unpleasant harmonics. Jensen covered his ears with his hands and hurried blindly forward. The cables threaded through a conduit above a small hatch, and, by the shielded panels, Jensen figured the drive units lay immediately beyond. If he were forced to tear the coils out barehanded to prevent an explosion, he wondered whether the burns would prevent him from manipulating his gun.

But that concern became secondary when Jensen discovered the shielded doorway was secured with a retina lock, inoperable except to Mac James, and maybe his mate. With no alternative left but to fetch Evans, he returned down the access corridor toward the hold.

But when he banged the switch once again, the arcs glared off a vista of empty grating. The cargo capsule lay open in the harsh light, and Evans was nowhere to be seen. With a crawling chill that had nothing to do with sweat, Jensen spun and raced for the bridge ladder. He'd made an idiot's misjudgment. *Marity* was a skip-runner's craft; he should never have assumed her specs would conform to those of a common merchanter.

The rungs themselves hampered, spaced as they were to a design that differed from Fleet regulation. Clumsily shortening his reach, Jensen made more noise than he intended. Above, the gruff voice of MacKenzie James called warning.

"Company, mate. Initiate without cross-check and take

cover. I trust your coordinates from memory."

Evans returned a protest, just as Jensen reached the upper level. The shift from weightlessness to induced gravity blunted his speed, yet still he managed to fling himself into cover behind an electronics housing. Aware of him, Evans still did not turn, but lingered to fine-tune something in the control panel. Noosed helplessly to the crew chair, Mac-Kenzie James cursed viciously.

Driven by threat of failure, Jensen raised his gun and fired. His pellet hammered Evans in the back of the head. Instantly dead, the mate pitched forward into the control banks. His body quivered once, and slipped to the deck, leaving vivid smears on the cowling.

Jensen shivered with relief. In the icy clarity of adrenaline rush, he noticed that MacKenzie James said nothing at all; but his steely eyes bored with steady and unsettling intensity into the Fleet officer who had gunned down his mate. He seemed almost to be listening for something.

Jensen discovered why a moment later. *Marity*'s engines died to a whisper. There followed a peculiar hesitation in time, that blurring transition which signalled the drop into FTL.

Jensen knew a chill of apprehension. He had not killed swiftly enough. Now she hurtled through deepspace toward a destination only MacKenzie James and his dead first mate would know. Still, though the ship was untraceable to the courier, Jensen did not lose control. The prize, the skip-runner captain whose capture would gain him advancement, was still at his mercy.

Jensen dug in the pouch sewn into the Freer robe for another round of ammo. His fingers snagged in the fabric; he swore and wrestled them free, while from the deck, MacKenzie James broke his silence.

"Most Freer carry their weapons on a belt across their chests. The pouch is for pills to kill parasites, and the clip on the seam hangs their water skins."

Jensen clamped his jaw tight, methodically busy with reloading. If Mac James chose to make conversation, he would have a purpose other than boredom.

"Godfrey, who's left to shoot but me?" The skip-runner

never glanced at the corpse, oozing blood an arm's length from him.

Jensen snapped a fresh round into the magazine of the gun and tried to figure why Mac James might wish to distract him with chatter. Quite dangerously, the stakes had altered. He might hold the upper hand, but the captain was not entirely at his mercy. With *Marity*'s major controls stripped of function and her FTL hurtling her toward an unknown destination, Jensen shoved back the first, creeping stir of doubt. He could defeat the retina lock over the drive access hatch by dragging his captive down below and manhandling him up to the sensors. But disabling *Marity*'s FTL condensers would do no good if he had no inkling of her position. Jensen stepped over the mate's sprawled feet. Most of the screens were opaque, empty of data as the rest of the controls. As he surveyed the opened cowling and tightly racked maze of exposed boards, it occurred to him that Mac James might have prepared his own diabolical sort of defense: *Marity* was probably inoperable by any hand but her captain's. Jensen clenched his hands, rage at his predicament momentarily making him dizzy. He *would* come out of this on top, with the promotion he was long since due. Freshly determined, he searched out the stop-marker coordinates that glimmered on the navigational board.

The fix was still within Carsey Sector, and surprisingly familiar. That James would wish *Marity* to emerge only hours away from the wreckage he had left on Point Station bespoke unsettling confidence. Jensen hid his hands in his robe, too careful to give way to elation as he identified the fix as Castleton's World, a lifeless planet until recently, when Fleet Command had cut ground there for a large-scale outpost. Two squadrons patrolled there, with a dreadnaught in synchronous orbit to maintain security for the duration of the construction.

Jensen turned slowly from the controls, startled to find that MacKenzie James seemed to be sleeping. Ripped with an irrational desire to destroy the man's nerveless peace, the Fleet officer said, "Castleton's isn't the refuge you hoped for, not anymore."

MacKenzie James replied without opening his eyes.

"You're not much in the confidence of your superiors, are you, boy? Or maybe the news is too recent, or the planned assault on Bethesda makes Fleet brass too busy to keep current."

The assault on Bethesda was supposed to be top secret. Horrified that a common skip-runner should be party to Fleet secrets, Jensen stiffened. He leveled the barrel of his pellet gun just as the gray eyes of his captive flicked open. They reflected a cold and bloodless amusement that made him ache to pull the trigger.

"Khalia," said MacKenzie James with uninflected plainness. "The new base on Castleton's was overrun, utterly, and stripped of all survivors."

Disbelief made Jensen tremble. Even the hand which held his weapon was not exempt. The captain had to be lying, his words a ploy to provoke a careless reaction. Only Jensen made it a point never to be careless.

Mac James shrugged. "If you aren't going to kill me out of pique, you might want to clear the remains of my mate from the bridge. Because unless you wish to become a slave of the Khalia, I'll need to reconnect some circuitry without tripping over dead meat."

The sheer effrontery of the suggestion undid Jensen's poise. "You think I'm a fool?"

Mac James stirred against the confines of his bonds. "Yes, but how much of one I'm waiting to find out."

Jensen's jaw jerked tight. He pointed his gun to the deck, viciously flipped on the safety, then turned his back on his prisoner. All sensor displays were lifeless; when *Marity* broke out of FTL, no method remained to determine whether the ships which would greet her were Fleet, or enemy; and hell only knew if the defensive shields had power. Jensen felt a detestable sense of helplessness. Mac James had him boxed; not being a hardware man, he lacked the knowledge to hack the electronics back into working order.

Mac James drawled lazily at his captor's back. "The sensors and analog screens are operational, boy, but you'll need to engage the power switch."

Jensen hesitated out of principle. The control panel might possibly be booby-trapped. Yet logic dictated that Mac

James would hardly plot murder while still under restraint, not unless he planned to die slowly of dehydration. Alert for surprises, Jensen hunted among the controls and flipped the appropriate switch. The analog panel hummed to life, and snow hazed the monitor, while the sensors gathered data. Presently, the haze subsided to black, which was normal; no image would resolve until *Marity* re-entered normal space.

Jensen tried the power switches for weaponry, without success. The guidance computer also proved to be dead, and only the watching presence of MacKenzie James prevented Jensen from hammering the panels in frustration. The chronometer by *Marity*'s autopilot alone showed any indicators, the most maddening of which informed that re-entry into sub-light at Castleton's was barely thirty minutes off.

Jensen paced. Careful to stay within the perimeters of *Marity*'s artificial gravity, he avoided the congealing runnels of Evans's blood, and also that portion of deck included in MacKenzie's field of view. He dared not give the skip-runner captain his liberty. Yet to risk re-entry near a base under Khalian control without fire power or maneuverability begged the most terrible fate. Not least, a concern the young officer would never have admitted out loud, was the fact he had never seen action against the enemy. Jensen had never doubted his courage. But the possibility of closing with the enemy in a small, converted merchanter like *Marity* frayed his confidence to tatters.

The chronometer on the autopilot clicked over; seven minutes to re-entry. Mac James once again appeared asleep. His behavior seemed inhuman, until Jensen recalled that *Marity* had docked at Point Station forty-eight hours before under emergency priorities. By the grimy, unkempt appearance of the captain's person, he probably had not slept while he effected repairs on his ship. Jensen himself had not rested for nearly as long, but excitement and stress had put him on a jag that precluded relaxation.

At a minute and a half to re-entry, MacKenzie James opened his eyes. The corpse of his mate lay undisturbed on the deck. Jensen stood at the analog screen, his gun clenched in anxious fingers. Beneath the Freer robe, his left hand gripped the keys to the nooses which secured Mac-

Kenzie James with white-knuckled indecision.

One minute to re-entry; Mac James quietly recommended pressing the toggle to unshutter the shield generators. Though to do so felt like capitulation, Jensen did not cling to foolish pride. A suspicion crossed the young officer's mind, that more of *Marity*'s systems might be operational than the control monitors indicated. But no time remained to run cross-checks. The buzzer signalled phase-out of *Marity*'s autopilot, and the eerie instant of suspension which heralded transition from FTL to normal space followed after. Jensen watched the analog screens with taut anticipation.

Castleton's appeared as a dun ball, mottled gray at the terminator; the larger of two moons showed as a sliver to dayside, but Jensen spared the scenery barely a glance. The sensors finished processing data, and the screen became peppered with silvery specks; scouts by their formation. Larger shapes nestled among them, unquestionably cruisers, with a third one tucked away behind the mass of Castleton's.

"Godfrey," Mac James observed, his neck craned awkwardly to allow a view of the screens. "They didn't waste time expanding their strike force, now did they?"

"They might not be Khalia!" Jensen snapped.

A buzzer clipped his outburst short. Lights flashed warning on the analog panels, and one of the flecks gained a faint halo of red.

"Well, Fleet or enemy, boy, one of them is about to fire on us." Mac James shrugged irritably at his bonds. "If you like slavery, or maybe even vivisection, just keep sitting there doing nothing."

Jensen raged, uncertain; *Marity*'s sirens wailed with sudden violence, her shields crackling under the impact of a hit.

"Warning rocket," Mac said tersely. "Probably they're provoking to see whether we want a fight. Power up the transmitter, boy."

Jensen hesitated.

"Do it now!" barked MacKenzie James, adamant as a Fleet rear admiral.

Another red halo bloomed on the analog screen. Jensen

slapped the transmitter switch. The gabble of alien speech that issued from the speaker caused the last bit of color to drain from his face.

"Now listen carefully, boy," said the hell-begotten captain from the floor. "Do exactly as I tell you, or we'll both get our guts ripped out."

"You planned this!" Jensen accused, horror sharpening the immediacy of their peril.

"Yes, now shut the hell up and listen!" MacKenzie said.

The patter of Khalian changed inflection, and a singsong voice in poorly prounounced wording began a demand for the surrender of *Marity* and all human personnel on board.

Still clutching pellet gun and keys, Jensen rubbed his hands over his blanched face.

"You will surrender my ship to the Khalia," MacKenzie James instructed tersely. "But add that you will submit only to a great captain, one who has proven his merit. That one, you will say, is the Khalia cruiser currently in orbit over the night side of Castleton's."

Jensen lowered his hands, incredulity spread across his features.

Before he could draw breath to speak, Mac James cut in, *"Just do it!"*

Instead Jensen spun and stabbed each of the firing studs in frenzied succession. Nothing happened. *Marity*'s weapons remained utterly unresponsive. Furious that his career should be finished without a single rocket fired in protest, and whipped by recognition that no option at all remained to him, Jensen crumbled at last into panic. "Why disable the weaponry, man? Why, if you planned this cruise into an effing Khalian fleet?"

"I probably wanted to commit suicide." MacKenzie's vicious sarcasm jarred like a slap. "Maybe, though, I'll get slavery or vivisection instead."

A shudder shook Jensen's frame as the voice on the transmitter changed from a demand for surrender to threats. Rather than be blasted to vapor, Jensen pressed the toggle to send. He surrendered *Marity* and all on board to the Khalia in a voice he barely recognized as his own. Only as an afterthought did he include MacKenzie James's stipulation: that prize rights and conquest be awarded to one of proven merit, the great captain who cruised the dark side of Castleton's.

The effect upon the Khalia was profound. By their belligerent and bloodthirsty reputation, Jensen expected the enemy would converge upon their prize without delay. Instead, the scout ships clustered tightly to their respective cruisers; as if locked in deadly partnership, the closer pair of warships wheeled and advanced upon the one which even now accelerated from the shadowed side of Castleton's.

"They'll challenge," MacKenzie broke in, answering Jensen's puzzled frown. "Khalian war leaders can't bear to defer without a fight. That lends you a very narrow margin to get this bucket operational. Which means my release, boy, because this is the only break you're going to get."

Jensen rounded upon the captain. "You never intended to surrender!"

Mac James returned a withering stare. Mollified by a knowledge of the enemy not even Fleet intelligence could equal, Jensen thumbed the safety toggle off his pellet gun. Then he took the release key in his other hand, stooped, and unclipped the nooses from MacKenzie James's feet. The man shifted forward to better expose his hands; the noose was soaked with blood. Nerves, or tension, or sheer frustration had caused the skip-runner captain to wrench at his bonds until his wrists tore open. Jensen keyed the catches, a sick clench in his gut causing his guard to slip. In that instant, MacKenzie's elbow hammered upward into his face. A spin and a kick relieved Jensen of his weapon. The young officer crumpled to his knees. Feeling as if every knuckle in his hand were broken, he fumbled to pull the knife he had confiscated earlier.

Mac James reached it first, and tossed it rattling into a corner. Disregarding Jensen completely, he retrieved the fallen gun, discharged the single round into the stuffed seat of a crew couch, then hurled the weapon without ceremony down the companionway ladder. With no break in movement he bent over the opened cowling of the control panel and furiously began to work.

Lights flashed to life under the captain's ministrations,

casting baleful light over his frowning features. To Jensen, who moaned through clenched teeth at his back, he said, "Clear Evans out of here, boy. If I trip over him at the wrong moment, some Khalia butcher'll hack off your balls."

Jensen obeyed to buy time, lull the captain into the belief he was cowed. Evans's corpse was already cool to the touch, his bulk limp and awkward to lift. Hampered by his injured hand, Jensen was forced to drag him. Blood from the dead man's shattered jaw smeared the white deck. Dizzied with pain from his hand, Jensen choked back a wave of nausea. He reeled into the nearest crew chair, just as *Marity* roared to life. MacKenzie James crowed over the controls like an elated child. Scarred fingers kicked in the accelerators.

On the analog screen, the first pair of cruisers closed to do battle, scout ships circling to one side like swarms of angry bees. Now and again the bolt of a plasma discharge flicked through the flashes of heavy rockets.

"They're pounding themselves to a pulp," Jensen observed in amazement.

"Better hope they do." MacKenzie twisted a lead, then punched up *Marity*'s screens. "The one who's not joining the cockfight will be on our butt quick, before the survivor calls challenge on him."

"How do you know?" Jensen hated himself for the admiration which colored his tone. "Where did you learn so much about the enemy?"

MacKenzie never glanced up from the controls. "Evans could have told you. Right now, I'm too busy." He flung himself into the adjoining pilot's chair, took the helm, and almost immediately *Marity* veered.

Still nauseous, Jensen sought stability in watching the analog monitor. As the attitude thrusters opened wide, the pared disc of Castleton's fell away, replaced briefly by space sprinkled with fixed stars, and the moving points of enemy warcraft. These were eclipsed in turn by the disc of Castleton's sun; MacKenzie flicked the stabilizers and banged the heel of his hand down, shoving the gravity drive into full acceleration.

Jensen made a sound in protest as several g's of force ground his body against the crew chair. "Out of the frying pan," he managed, before discomfort forced him silent.

MacKenzie James said nothing. His profile seemed motionless as laser-cut quartz in the lights off the monitors as *Marity* picked up speed. Fuelled by the gravitational field of Castleton's sun, she gained velocity at a rate that was frightening. Jensen battled for equilibrium. He was not the pilot that Shields was, but he could recognize when safe limits were transgressed. As if his worn old craft did not hurtle full tilt for annihilation in the fires of a star, Mac James sat back and flexed his scarred fingers in a manner that suggested habit. Then, as *Marity*'s course held stable, he shoved forward against the force of acceleration and busied himself again with the circuitry.

"Haven't you done enough?" Jensen demanded, mostly to distract himself from fear. With the Khalia behind, and the inferno of Castleton's star raging forward, what composure he had left was faked.

Mac James pulled a wire from the cowling and unceremoniously stripped it with his teeth. He twisted the bared end into a hook which he clamped to some unseen contact below. Another panel on *Marity*'s control boards flickered to light; satisfaction made her captain expansive. "You're better endowed with luck than brains, boy. You're not going to burn. Just maybe you'll be spared the hell of being bait for Khalia as well."

He added no explanation. But as the third Khalian warship swung to intercept, the captain responded with hair-raising innovation. He spun *Marity* into what seemed a suicidal trajectory toward Castleton's sun. Like some terrible vulture, the Khalian cruiser swung into position, shadowing their descent into the inferno. If Mac James even once tried his drive brake, *Marity*'s occupants would be weasel meat.

Jensen masked fright with bravado. "You're sending yourself to hell, by way of the inferno."

MacKenzie James said nothing. The staccato buzz of an alarm sounded, and the control board transformed to a field of warning lights. Caught in horrified absorption by the star swelling on the analog screen, Jensen almost forgot the Khalian warship until it fired.

The rocket lanced across the screens, violet against the glare of Castleton's star.

"My god," Jensen said angrily. "Do they believe in miracles, or what? They may as well vaporize us, for all that we can stop."

"They think we're what we seem," MacKenzie James said softly. "A merchanter caught without escort." He paused, as if that explained everything. A second Khalian rocket seared across the screens. In the fitful, flickering light of its passage, the captain seemed to recall that the man in the crumpled Freer robe who sweated in his crew chair was not his knowledgeable mate.

"The Khalia believe that we have chosen suicide rather than be captured. They fire to salute our courage, for by their honor code, our action is admirable."

Which fit with the accuracy of truth, Jensen reasoned. With a crushing sense of frustration, he cursed the fact that he could not return the information to his superiors. Surely such knowledge would have earned him a commendation and promotion—but the closing proximity of Castleton's sun foreclosed any chance of survival.

MacKenzie James seemed peculiarly indifferent to the end his own subterfuge had created. Hunched like a bear over his controls, he grinned. "Watch now." But the corpse of the mate which oozed by the companionway showed as much enthusiasm as Jensen. "In a moment, the Khalian ship will brake and pull off, just enough so she'll bounce off the gravity well at a tangent."

"So what," Jensen shot back. The captain was crazy; they'd melt just as handily by hydrogen fusion, but the man acted as if he was ignorant of the fundamental rules of physics.

"Now," murmured Mac James. The Khalian cruiser shifted. His scarred hands moved at the controls, and *Marity* responded with a roar like a Chinese dragon. Jensen was tossed backward as her entire aft quarter opened up into a fireball.

Jensen saved himself from a bruising fall with the hand Mac James had injured. Pain exploded like white heat. His head spun and his vision momentarily went black.

"We're not a merchanter," admonished MacKenzie James from the dark. By the time the officer's eyesight cleared, *Marity* had burned into a new trajectory, a searing arc that would carry her into a parabolic orbit just within survivable limits. This, with an antique mess of a drive unit that ran on explosive propellants—no sane captain would have such a relic on a space-going vessel.

"But the quick acceleration is damned handy in a pinch," the skip-runner captain said brightly. "It's saved my butt more than once."

Mac James stretched in his chair, flexing his fingers in a hellish glare of warning lights and attitude meters. Jensen held his opinion. *Marity* might be safe at present, but only by the grace of surprise. Khalian raiders would be waiting once they rounded Castleton's sun, and even Mac James's famous cunning was not equal to combat against a cruiser.

The skip-runner captain met Jensen's skepticism with a stinging honesty. "Boy, your officer's handbook doesn't list every known fact in the universe. The systems they have are infrared, which happens to be our salvation, because the emissions from that star out there will blind them."

And it dawned on Jensen then, that both of them were going to survive. The Khalia believed they had burned. Once eclipsed by Castleton's star, *Marity* could hammer her way into escape trajectory with her anachronistic fusion rockets, then power down. With her gravity drives turned off, no infrared scope could distinguish her from an asteroid. Hopelessness and lethargy vanished in a breath. The pellet gun which Mac James had carelessly tossed down the companionway became of paramount importance.

Jensen measured the distance to the opened hatch with his eyes. The expanse was wider than he liked, particularly since the Freer robe would encumber him. Still, with Castleton's world and the threat of the Khalia keeping MacKenzie James preoccupied, there might never be a better opportunity. Jensen gathered his courage and jumped.

He completed no more than a step when a weight crashed into his shoulders from behind. He fell heavily to the deck. At once the muscled bulk of MacKenzie James bore him down. Jensen countered with a wrestler's move that should have freed him in short order. Instead the captain anticipated him, caught his wrist, and twisted. Jensen cursed, forced to fall limp or scream with the pain of dislocated joints.

Just shy of injury, Mac James let up. "You're trouble," he said bluntly. And as though he handled a vicious animal, he rolled and jerked Jensen upright. The strength in his hands was astonishing. Very quickly, the Fleet officer found himself noosed and helpless in the coils of his own restraints.

"Also, you talk too much," MacKenzie added. He ripped away the sash of the Freer robe, pausing as his fingers encountered the bulk of the transmitter. A wicked flash of amusement touched his features as he went on and twisted the material into a gag, which he tied expertly in place. Jensen struggled but gained nothing except cuts on the ribbon-thin metal of the noose. Shoved into the nearest crew chair, he glared back as the captain studied him in passionless silence. The directness of the man's gaze unnerved Jensen as nothing had before.

"What chance did you give Evans?" Mac James's voice held a roughness that might have been grief, except his expression showed no feeling at all. The captain flexed his ruined fingers, one after another. Tortured with the certainty his fate was being weighed, Jensen recognized more than habit in the movement; such exercise had once restored mobility to hands crippled with coil burns. The driving persistence of the captain's character abruptly became frightening to contemplate.

Jensen closed his eyes, opened them to find the captain watching him still. The ambition that had driven the attempt at his capture withered away to diffidence. The gag tasted of sweat and desert spice and stale saliva, and the sick fear in Jensen's gut coiled tighter by the minute.

Aware his captive's composure was crumbling, MacKenzie James jerked him to his feet and spun him around. "Evans never did like to kill," he said in contempt. "For that, you'll leave *Marity* alive."

But reprieve was not what MacKenzie James had in mind as he hefted his captive through the companionway. Towed through null gravity like baggage, Jensen had to writhe ignominiously to keep his face from banging the bulkheads. The hiss of the lock to the cargo hold spilled icy air over his skin. Left to drift, the young officer could not see his captor, but an echoing flurry of footfalls and the clang of something metallic did little but amplify his apprehension. Then hard hands caught his legs. His view of the hold spun horizontally, and through dizziness he glimpsed customs seals and the opened hatch of the cargo capsule. Then MacKenzie James brutally started cramming his body inside. Jensen exploded in panic.

He struggled, and got a bang on the head for his effort. Mac James shoved his shoulders down. Scarred fingers reached for the latch.

Jensen twisted frantically and managed to tear the gag loose. "Wait!" he said breathlessly. Desperate now, his ambition reduced to a fool's dream, he begged. "I could take Evan's place for you!" Except for the piloting, he was qualified; and he wouldn't defect, not really. Once he gained MacKenzie's confidence he could alert Fleet authorities.

But his proposal met with silence. Shoved protesting into the cargo capsule, and panicked by the prospect of confinement, Jensen abandoned his pride. "Damn you, I'm the son of an Alliance Councilman! That should be worth enough to hold me for ransom."

No spark of greed warmed the eyes of MacKenzie James. Single-mindedly efficient, he banged the hatch closed over his captive's head. Jensen kicked out in disbelief and managed to skin both his knees. The slipped gag constricted his wind. Over his ragged, frantic breaths came the unmistakable click of latches, the inexorable deadening of sound as the seals of the container clamped closed. He banged again, uselessly. He might suffocate, or die of hypothermia in *Marity*'s unheated cargo hold; surely Mac James would see reason, contact his father and arrange an exchange of money.

Jensen felt the capsule bump and rise; through its shell he heard the unmistakable hiss of a lock. He screamed in uninhibited terror, then; but nothing prevented the sickening, tumbling fall into weightlessness and cold which followed. He curled up, shivering in the bitter end of hope. MacKenzie James had jettisoned him, living, into deepspace.

The cargo capsule's seals preserved atmosphere. For

awhile its honeycomb panels would conserve body heat, but with no air supply it was an even draw whether Jensen would die of asphyxiation, or tumble back to fry in the fury of Castleton's star. At best, he might be salvaged alive by a Khalian scout ship. Worst and most galling was the fact that MacKenzie James went free.

Jensen shouted in frustration. Unable to forget those coil-scarred fingers flexing and curling, tirelessly beating the odds, he longed for one chance to shoot his antagonist, even as he had Evans: from behind, with no chance for recriminations, just death—fast and messy and final. But anger only caused the nooses to rip painfully into his wrists. In time, all passion, all hatred, unravelled into despair. Jensen's tears soaked the hood of the Freer robe and curled the dark hair at his temples. After Mac James, he reviled his disciplinarian father, for stifling his career with the stipulation that under no circumstances was undue favor to be granted him. Competence became a sham. Such was the influence of fame and politics, no board of officers dared to grant promotion without performance of outstanding merit. One by one, Jensen had seen his peers advance ahead of him. Balked pride and rebellion had landed him here, trussed and sealed like flotsam in a cargo capsule. Too late, and in bitterness, he questioned why the promise of money had failed to motivate MacKenzie James.

The air in the capsule quickly became stale. Jensen's thoughts spiralled downward into a tide of black dizziness. His limbs cramped, then grew numb; the transmitter in the Freer sash dug relentlessly into his neck, but he was powerless to ease even this smallest discomfort. Presently, none of that mattered. Resigned, Jensen directed his last awareness to cursing MacKenzie James; as consciousness began to dim, sometimes the name of his father slipped in . . .

Something banged the cargo capsule. Jostled against the side panels, Jensen heard the whine of grappling hooks. Fear roused him from lethargy as they clamped and secured his prison. Suffocation seemed a kindness next to threat of Khalian cruelty; but the young officer lacked strength to do more than shut his eyes as whatever being had salvaged him popped the capsule's release catches. Clean air rushed in around the seals, and light fell blindingly across Jensen's face.

"I'm surprised he left you alive," said an acerbic voice he recognized.

Jensen started, drew a shuddering breath, and ducked sharply to hide cheeks still wet from crying. "My god, how did you know where to find me?"

Perfectly groomed, and correct to the last insignia on her uniform, Ensign Shields regarded him with that whetted edge of antagonism she had affected since the morning he had compelled her collaboration in his scheme to capture MacKenzie James. "*Marity*'s instruments weren't shielded," she said at last. "You're living lucky for that."

Jensen tried to scrub his damp cheeks against his shoulder, and awkwardly found he couldn't, not with his hands still bound. His embarrassment changed poisonously to resentment. He faulted himself bitterly for lacking the presence of mind to note the implications of *Marity*'s opened instrument panels. Evans had programmed the autopilot for the FTL jump with the keyboard circuitry wide open to surveillance; if the scout ship assigned to Shields was not one of the fancy, new brain models, she still carried a full complement of electronics. "You read our destination coordinates from our tempest signal," Jensen murmured, shamed by memory of Mac James's amusement as he allowed the transmitter to remain twisted into the Freer sash. The captain had known then that his victim would be rescued. He must have considered Jensen a fool, harmless or incompetent enough to be no risk if he were set free.

"Maybe not so lucky after all." Shields shoved the cargo capsule over, interrupting Jensen's thoughts and spilling him ignominiously onto the courier ship's lock platform. "You'll wish you'd died in deepspace when our dispatches come in late. Serve you right if the old man himself calls you onto the carpet."

Stung by more than humility, Jensen twisted until he gained a view of his shipmate's eyes. "Play things right, and we'll get a commendation."

Shields stepped back. Rare anger pinched her face;

Jensen had never thought her pretty, but she had slenderness, and a certain grace of movement that had half the guys back at base off their feed. "You're obsessed, Jensen. *Commendation for what?* You've been an overambitious jackass and now, finally, the brass in Fleet Command will know it too."

Jensen made a vicious effort to sit up; but the nooses cut into his wrists, and he gave up with a curse at the pain. "You'll go down with me," he threatened. "'As my senior officer, piloting a Fleet dispatch courier off course calls for court martial, not a dressing down."

He heard Shields's sharp intake of breath, and could not look at her. Once he might have veiled his threats in gentler language; but now, the cruelly injured dignity inspired by MacKenzie James impelled him to roughness. "Don't be a stupid bitch." But he couldn't quite bring himself to finish; by the whitely locked knuckles of Shields's hands he saw he did not have to mention her brother, who was ill and under treatment in an Alliance medical facility, a benefit of her enrollment in the Fleet. Should she be discharged now, he would lose his benefits. But pity came second to necessity. Ambition and his driving desire to command a vessel that carried weapons instead of dispatches cut with a need like agony. Coldly Jensen outlined his alternative.

The dome at Port was packed to capacity on the day the citations were read. Banners overhung the stage where the Fleet high command were seated. At attention alongside Ensign Shields, Jensen surreptitiously checked his uniform for creases. Finding none, he stood very still, savoring the moment as the speaker at the podium recited his list of achievements.

". . . commendation for bravery; for innovative escape tactics, when asked at gunpoint to surrender to three Khalian warships, which imagination and daring in the face of danger has resulted in the furtherance of Fleet knowledge of enemy behavior; for performance above and beyond the call of duty, these two young officers will be promoted in rank, and be decorated with the Galactic Cross . . ."

Shields went very white when the Admiral laid the ribbon with the medal over her shoulders. She shook his hand stiffly, and looked away from the cameras when the press popped flashes to record the event.

Jensen also stood stiffly, but for very different reasons. Warmed by his father's proud smile, he reflected that the story they had presented to Fleet command had held as many half-truths as lies; the tactics which had brought word of the takeover at Castleton's had been real enough, though only Shields and he knew they had originated with the wiliest skip-runner in Alliance space. The weight of the Galactic Cross which hung from his neck carried no implications of guilt; at last granted the command of a scout ship with armament, Jensen swore he would redeem his honor. One day MacKenzie James was going to regret the humiliation he had inflicted upon a young officer of the Fleet. Jensen intended to rise fast and far. In time he would retaliate, find means to bring down the antagonist who had bested him. The honors he took credit for now were only a part of that plan.

INTERLUDE

Neuton Bedfort Smythe looked terrible. His eyes were red and his color sallow. He looked very much like what he was, a man working alone against time on a vital project. Even his obvious exhaustion couldn't mask the enthusiasm with which he burst into Meier's new office.

"I have found something important. A first clue in the mystery," he announced. "If you will." With a flourish he inserted a memory chit into the comconsole on the admiral's desk. The astonished officer just had a glimpse of the title. It appeared to be the occupation report from one of the levies garrisoning the planet.

Meier had to admit the investigator had been true to his promise to stay out of the way. Except for the inconvenience of having to shift offices, approving his access to an astonishing number of files, and a personal concern about his redwood desktop being badly abused, Meier had hardly even been aware of the Alliance Council's investigator's presence in Port.

Before he could reply the screen was filled with images.

TRAITORS' SAGA

by Robert Sheckley

ON EMBARKATION DAY there were a thousand of us who marched down Maccabee Boulevard behind Colonel Bar Kochba to the reviewing stand, where Solomon Gottshaft, the Planetary President of Eretz Perdido, gave us the salute, and told us to go out and show the universe, or whatever part of it happened to be watching, what sort of stuff Perdido's Ten Lost Tribes were made of. We proceeded past the enormous stone doors of the New Temple, cheered by the multitudes, and then we were loaded into trucks and taken to Theodor Herzl Spacefield on the edge of our capital city of New Jerusalem. There we were loaded aboard the Fleet destroyer *Swiftsure* for the short trip to the dreadnought *Valley Forge,* which waited in geosynchronous orbit above our planet.

The *Valley Forge* was twelve hundred feet long, displaced well over one hundred thousand tons, and carried a crew of two thousand and eighty. Our hundred men were assigned quarters and canteen privileges, and were given self-locating maps so we could find our way between sleeping quarters, mess hall, exercise area, PX, and recreation hall. Our own officers relayed ship's instructions: we were to deploy immediately to our assigned sleeping places, which also served as acceleration couches, and strap down for takeoff.

It was a fine moment when the siren sounded and we felt the tingling vibration as the ship's sub-light convertors came on. There was no sense of motion, but strapdown is traditional, besides sometimes there can be vertigo when first getting underway. We watched our progress on overhead screens, and the readouts made clear to us what was happening.

There was very little physical sense of acceleration, but we knew that *Valley Forge* was getting up to standard one-quarter speed of light very quickly, powered by the gravity potential of our nearby star, Perdido Primary. Theoretically, this ship could continue accelerating in sublight drive until it approached C, the speed of light, or until the magnetic engines came apart. In practice, the big ships rarely go beyond ½C, and use that mainly for maneuvering around planetary systems. The really long-distance travelling is done in an entirely different mode, by means of the FTL drive. Using FTL, the largest ships can cross the thousand light-year diameter of the great spherical volume of space which contains the more than three hundred Alliance planets in about three standard Terran weeks.

Our trip would take twenty-five days, because we were going to the periphery of Alliance space, the Galactic northwestern frontier, to the planet Target, which The Fleet intelligence services had determined was the home planet of the Khalian raiders. The establishment of a Fleet base recently on the planet Klaxon had paved the way for this final assault on the enemy's key position at Target, the planet from which the Khalian raiders attacked our shipping and raided the home planets of Alliance members.

For this purpose, the Fleet had gathered together elements from all its far-flung frontiers and guard posts, stripping the interior defences of the home worlds, timing everything so that one gigantic blow could be struck against the enemy. It was the largest concentration of ships in the Fleet's thousand-year history, and it seemed impossible that any force could stand up to it; though pessimists pointed out that the fortunes of battle were uncertain, and that if the attack should fail, or be destroyed before it began

by the sudden appearance of a rogue black hole or an
unseasonal time-storm, we would be delivering the future of
humanity into the hands of our enemy, the alien Khalia.

The Combat Troops of the Fleet are made up of levies from
the various planet members. The troops served under their
own officers who were under the orders of the Fleet high
command. At the time we embarked it was still a toss-up
which group was going to be picked to lead the commando
ground assault onto Target. Among the hundred or more
who had volunteered, several of the planetary levies were
suitable and trained for the job. The Zyandots of the planet
Zyandot II came well recommended, as did the Mahdists of
the planet Khartoum IV. The Sons of the Albigensian
Heresy, from the planet Janus, were especially eager to lead
the assault, because their planet had only been a member of
the Alliance of Planets for seven years and they hoped to
achieve recognition and status by the doing of an heroic
deed. There was intense lobbying in the Chamber of
Delegates at Alliance Headquarters on Earth for the privi-
lege: planetary honor was at stake. Less than an hour after
we boarded *Valley Forge,* it was announced that our
thousand-man battle group from Perdido had won.

   This should not be ascribed to our popularity. We were
the compromise candidate. The major planets lost less face
if we got the assignment rather than one of their rivals.

   I know, I protest too much. It is a universal Jewish
tendency. We Jews from Perdido have more than the
normal amount of Jewish paranoia. This is due to the
uncertainty of our status. Our co-religionists on Earth won't
admit that we are Jews, will not even consider our claim
that we are descendents of the ten lost tribes who were
kidnapped by aliens and taken from Earth to Perdido.

   We pointed out that it was the aliens' fault that no torahs
had been brought on the flight across space, no Talmuds,
none of the commentaries of the learned Rabbis, not even
Martin Buber's stories of the Baal Shem Tov. We were
aware of the existence of these things due to our racial
memories, but we had no knowledge of the things themselves. The Jews of Earth said that since we had no holy
books, no prayers, no knowledge of Hebrew, a very feeble

grasp of Yiddish, and several more points that I forget, we couldn't be Jews. We pointed out that although we didn't have those things—through no fault of our own—we did have the shrug, the habit of answering a question with another question, the habit of addressing hypothetical bystanders, the custom of smiting ourselves on the forehead with the flat of the hand when perplexed, the almost racial trigger that forced us to say "Oy, vey!" from time to time, and to reproduce out of alien foodstuffs, and in a climate hardly suited for it, the tastes of dill pickles, stuffed cabbage, varnishkas, pastrami, chopped liver, and stuffed derma with plenty of brown gravy, the latter a triumph of the will when you consider that our entire planet is a steaming rainforest and we had to create a food like salt herring without ever having tasted one. Interesting, the Jews of Earth said, freaky, even, but hardly proving anything. My God! we cried, smiting ourselves on the forehead with the flat of our hands, if that doesn't prove anything, what does prove anything?

The matter is still under discussion.

Meanwhile, not even in Israel are we considered Jews. Only on our own planet Perdido, and in some parts of New York City.

That sort of treatment would be enough, you must admit, to make any group a little paranoid and eager to win a measure of glory for itself as a way of taking the pressure off the eternal Jewish question of identification which the Jews of Earth don't even admit that we, just like them, suffer from.

My name is Judah ben Judah. I am stocky, I have a round head with tight dark curls, as if that mattered. I am thirty-three years of age, and, before my enlistment in the Perdido Expeditionary Force, I was an assistant professor of Jewish Cultural Apologetics at the University of Stetelhaven on Perdido. The reason I was not a full professor has no bearing on this tale, but rests, let me assure you, on the incompetence of the examiners.

I enlisted in our planetary levy and was given the rank of captain and put in command of a ten-man assault squad. We took basic training together at Camp Sabra. After a few weeks we had worked out our basic disagreements and my squad had voted to take my orders unconditionally, at least for the present. Some peoples of the Alliance have found it strange that we Perdidans—to use a neutral term for us—ask each other things rather than give each other orders, and that so entrenched is this custom among us that we stick to it even in our armed forces. Why do we do it that way? I can only say that through trial and error we have discovered it's a lot easier to talk matters over with us than to try to tell us what to do. Asking may take a little longer, but it ensures that the job gets done cheerfully and well. And if you're told no, you just shrug your shoulders, perhaps mutter oy vey, and go ask someone else. That's the way we handle these matters. It seems so logical. Not everyone sees it that way, obviously.

II.

Colonel Bar Kochba called me and the other squad leaders to his quarters soon after the ship was in FTL drive and we were able to move around again. Kochba was a short, bull-necked man with a neatly trimmed white-flecked black beard and the upright bearing of the professional soldier. He was one of the few trained soldiers of field rank on Perdido, having graduated with honors from the Fleet College at Academia on Hellas II. We try to keep a few trained officers ready at all times, even though our planet has never had a real war in the sense of large professional armies and navies fighting it out with their counterparts. Perdido is too isolated and too poor to tempt anyone except the Khalian raiders. We had had more than enough of those, however, and were looking forward to this opportunity of striking back with what we expected would be a crushing blow.

Bar Kochba proceeded in logical fashion. There was going to be a great space battle centered on the planet Target. This battle would be preceded by a commando-style raid on the planet itself. Bar Kochba explained that we would be taken to the surface of the planet in destroyers specially equipped for the mission. By taking out their main armament, the destroyers could mount multiple screens and probably avoid detection long enough to put us on the ground. He outlined the order of battle, issued maps of our region which were little more than blank spaces with coordinates, since we had not been able to map Target yet. Our attack was to be made in just sixteen hours: now that the assault had been announced, it was imperative to get it moving before the Khalia had time to learn about it through their various allies.

After dismissing us, Bar Kochba asked me to stay behind.

Lighting his large and malodorous pipe, he told me that after reviewing the qualifications of his ten officers, he had decided to ask me to take on the job of Intelligence Officer.

I was a little puzzled. "I wasn't aware that I had any particular qualifications."

Bar Kochba smiled in his affable way. "I have chosen you," he said, "because the records show that you are an inquisitive fellow, always poking your nose into matters that do not concern you. That is exactly the sort of fellow we need to do our intelligence work."

"Just what did you have in mind, Colonel?" I asked. "You're not expecting me to spy on my fellow soldiers, are you?"

The Colonel was surprised. "What gave you that idea? That's Counterintelligence and it's not at all what I'm interested in. I need an intelligence officer to help me find out what to expect on this planet we're going to, this place called Target."

I shrugged. "You've seen the briefing reports, same as I have. What more is there to say?"

"Nothing, yet. But in sixteen hours—closer to fifteen, now—our battle group spearheads the assault on Target itself. Once on the ground, I suspect we're going to be staying a while. There will be important things to be learned, things that can affect the whole course of the war. I need a man to collect and coordinate all the discoveries made by our battle group."

I thought it over. It sounded like an important job. "I'll do it," I told him.

"That's fine," Bar Kochba said. "But let's get one thing straight. I don't mean that you, personally, should do it. I'm not sending you out on a spying mission. I'm asking you to collect and coordinate information, and that's all. Is that understood?"

"Of course, sir," I said. I saluted and left, and went back to prepare my squad for action. I thought about my new job. And I realized that I had not, in fact, promised not to do any spying myself. I had merely agreed that I understood that Bar Kochba had asked me not to. I mention that because there was some talk of a court-martial after what actually happened later, after Wyk-Wyk Kingfisher came to our camp.

III.

The Land Combat Forces of the Fleet, drawn as they are from hundreds of planets with differing levels of military technology, to say nothing of local preference and personal taste, always equip themselves, carrying with them a small ordnance department to keep the weapons working and to handle ammunition and repairs. Our group was no different. We had adopted the standard Gushi Plasma Piece, the GPP, as our standard artillery arm. These weapons look like lengths of pipe four feet long by six inches wide. They can fire three five-pound cartridges without reloading, but are limited to line of sight operation. They produce a fireball upon impact with their target, and the energy release is on the order of half a ton of TNT. My squad had four such weapons, more than is usual for ten men, but we were the spearhead.

Aside from that we carried our own weapons as developed on Eretz Perdido. We had several varieties of dart gun, a simple laser pistol, and various types of grenade. And it is with these we were armed when the time came to board the Fleet Destroyer *Reliant* and go down to the surface of Target below us.

Our descent to the surface of Target was swift, and yet it seemed long indeed, because we didn't know what awaited us below. It seemed entirely possible that this attack had been betrayed, for it was known that there were spies even among the professionals of the Fleet, men with a taste for money, whose easy consciences allowed them to sell out their own people in the comfortable expectation that the Alliance would win anyhow, so what difference would it make? The Khalia could set a trap for this destroyer as it dropped noiselessly through Target's atmosphere. Their best strategy would be to let it land without opposition; then destroy it and everyone aboard it in a single overwhelming assault, mounted and carried out before any support could be brought in. Indeed, we couldn't even ask for help; for the entire operation was to be performed in radio silence.

Treachery, indeed, is the theme of this story of mine, but this is not where it occurred. Our destroyer put down without incident, kissing the dark ground of Target without a sound as we officers urged our men out of the hatches, fast, fast. The black night sky was pocked with distant silent explosions of light and color as the Fleet, high above us in battle formation, opened up a bombardment on the advance scout ships of the Khalia coordinating this action to mask our landing.

The last of our battle group tumbled out, and the destroyer went into lift mode even before the hatches were dogged shut, pushing away from the planet like a gale-driven schooner clawing off a lee shore, hoping to find maneuvering room in space before it was detected and brought down by the Khalian defence batteries.

As for us, once on land, I and the other Captains took command of our squads and by prearrangement led them in different directions. Our first necessity was to disperse, get under cover, make an assessment of the situation, find out what troops were opposing us and in what numbers, and then hit the enemy and hit him hard.

We were hampered at the beginning by a lack of decent maps, because very little mapping of Target had been completed before the assault. We had bought plenty of maps of course—seamen from the merchant fleets often came into contact with aliens who were themselves in contact with the Khalians. They sold their maps to the Fleet, and the Fleet paid them and hoped for the best. As I had feared, what I had in my hand didn't correspond to what lay around me. So different was the reality from the fanciful documents which the Fleet had given us that I told my men to put the useless things away, since they would only serve to confuse us, and sketch out new maps as they went along.

We had come down to the south of a small city or camp, artificially lit, with streets running for many miles along a bay that opened into the ocean. We had named it Enemy City and assumed it was of some importance. Above us the skies were turning lurid and bright with plasma explosions as more and more ships joined the space battle. It was time we did something for the war effort. I checked out my men, then led them toward Enemy City, hoping that the other commanders shared my view that it was the obvious target.

We set up the four plasma cannons on two ridges commanding the city, sited to pour down enfilading fire. The remaining men were dug in facing the rear, to defend the gunners if our position should be attacked. I took time to make sure that the gunners had the necessary windage corrections. Dawn was just glimmering when I stood up, lifted a white handkerchief, easily visible in the lightening gloom, and brought it down sharply.

Golden tracks arced across the sky in a flat trajectory. By the erupting fireballs which rose upon contact we saw that we were hitting the target. For a moment we could see a dust-colored earth-hugging city of one-and two-storied adobe buildings, with a scattering of larger structures. I was reminded of photographs I had seen of Timbuktu and Omdurman on Earth. Was Enemy City a place like those? I wish I had had time to photograph it, but we blew a lot of it to bits before it fully registered on our consciousness, and then I assembled the men and marched them away at the double. I hated to give up the high ground, but I had to assume that someone would begin firing back.

We stumbled down the hillside, charging toward Enemy City. We ran through narrow ravines that snaked toward the city gates. A hundred yards from the low mud wall that surrounded the city we encountered our first resistance: a small rectangular guardhouse with slit windows, like some old Crusader fortress. We blew it apart with two hits from the laser cannon, and the first Khalia we saw were dead, slender chestnut-furred creatures with gunbelts around their waists, from which depended a variety of pistols and swords.

We had barely regrouped when a mob of Khalia came running toward us from the burning city. Backlit by the flames, unable to see us crouching in the ravine, they ran toward us and died, and we killed them with the plasma cannons until we ran out of cartridges, and then we killed them with stingers and cluster pistols, and at last with our bent-bladed knives, until there were no more around to kill. Not long after that we took possession of Enemy City.

IV.

Full daylight found me and my squad occupying a small tower in the center of the city. We had chosen a building made of heavy granite blocks, miraculously not destroyed by our bombardment. This structure, which we later learned was called Guildhall, sat by itself in the middle of a plaza, giving us an open field of fire on all sides. This was important, because we expected a counterattack to be mounted against us at any moment. So far, we had had it all our way, but we knew that couldn't last forever. After all, we were sitting somewhere on the Khalian home planet. I just hoped that Colonel Bar Kochba had arranged for a second wave to be sent in. I expected all hell to break loose any minute.

The light on our field radio started flashing soon after noon, signalling the end of radio silence. It was Colonel Bar Kochba, and he asked me to report my squad's situation.

"We've taken over a city," I told him, "Not much resistance. No casualties. But I don't know what happens next. We're sitting right in the middle of this place and expecting to get attacked any time."

"You can relax a little," Bar Kochba said. "We have visual and radar surveillance over your entire sector. There are no Khalian troop concentrations in sight."

"What about the other squads?" I asked him.

"They've all reached their objectives. We had some losses when Teams 4 and 7 hit the spaceport. Only four men. So far we're coming out of this miraculously well."

"What about the spaceport?"

"We destroyed it."

"And the battle in space?"

"A very big victory for the Fleet. The Khalia seemed to have no general battle plan. Just a mass of ships attacking on an individual basis. The Fleet knocked down a lot of them. The rest went into FTL drive and got away."

I needed a moment to digest all this. "Then we've won!" I cried.

"Yes, obviously," Bar Kochba said. He didn't sound too excited about it. "I guess we could call it winning."

"I don't understand your reservations over this," I told him. "We've mauled their fleet and captured their home planet. Doesn't that mean that the war is over?"

"My dear ben Judah," Bar Kochba said, "I guess I must bring you up to date on the latest findings. Preliminary reports show that the planet Target is or was an important staging area for the Khalian raider ships. We have won an important victory. But this planet Target seems *not* to be the Khalian home planet."

One of the members of my squad had come into the room I was using for radio transmission. He was making gestures and pointing outside. I made a gesture at him which was meant to mean, wait a minute, can't you see I'm talking on the radio?

"If this isn't the Khalian home planet," I said, "then who does it belong to?"

"How the hell should *I* know?" Bar Kochba said. "You're the Intelligence Officer. Find out."

"All right," I said, "What about the Khalia?"

"You'll have to be on your guard at all times. Preliminary reports indicate there are at least a few thousand of them left on the planet."

"Right, sir. We'll be careful. How much longer will we be down here?"

"Quite a while," Bar Kochba said, with what might have been a dry chuckle. "Our Battle Group has done so well that the Fleet Command has assigned us to garrison duty here."

Bar Kochba signed off. At last I was able to give my attention to my gesticulating squadman.

"What is it, Gideon?"

"Some people outside are demanding to see you at once."

"People? Do you mean human people, or Khalian people?"

"Neither, Judah. These are what I guess are the indigenous people who live on this planet."

"Good," I said. "About time we found out who this planet belongs to. I'll see them at once."

Gideon nodded. Our armed forces are very casual. "I'll show them in." He had a curious expression on his face. Almost like he was laughing about something. I couldn't figure it out until a few minutes later, when he led the delegation in to the room.

I suppose that "people" can refer to anything that can carry on an intelligent conversation. We sometimes call the Khalian "people," and they resemble four-foot weasels. So perhaps I shouldn't have been surprised when Gideon ushered in four bipeds of approximately six feet in height, dressed in long robes which concealed the greater part of their bodies. What I could see of their bodies, however, were scaled and feathered. Their feet were clawlike, and their small heads, at the end of skinny scrawny necks, were the small heads of birds.

V.

Thus I met my first Nedge, as they called themselves, the nomadic bird-people of Target. And while other humans turned to the major question of the day, the question of where the Khalian home planet was, since it wasn't here, I turned to rounding up the remaining Khalia on Target, gathering intelligence, and arbitrating the differences that come up between our troops and the Nedge.

My first meeting did not have too auspicious a beginning. I welcomed the four Nedge, had chairs brought for them, offered them refreshments. I was trying to begin on the right note, because I knew we would need their cooperation to help us find, capture, or kill the remaining Khalia.

But my words, intended to put them at ease, seemed to give them problems. They conferred hastily among themselves, gabbling and clucking and shaking their wattles.

Finally they reached some sort of decision, and the eldest among them, whom I later came to know as Kingfisher, since his Nedgean name was unpronounceable, stepped forward, flapped his rudimentary wings twice, cleared his throat, and spoke in quite passable English, though marked, inevitably, with a broad avian accent.

"You do us much honor," Kingfisher said, "but that's your problem. If you wish us to sit, we'll sit. Just remember, we didn't propose anything of the sort ourselves."

I had Gideon fetch some of the folding canvas chairs that had been sent down with our supplies from the Fleet. The Nedge tried to imitate the way I sat, but it soon became obvious that their bones weren't jointed like ours. Still, they managed finally, at cost of putting their feathers into considerable disarray, and Kingfisher said, "Am I correct in assuming that this is a form of abasement or does the posture have some other meaning?"

"It has nothing to do with abasement," I told him. "I am honoring you as my friends and guests."

"This is how you treat a friend?" Kingfisher said, "I'd hate to see what you make an enemy do."

"Where I come from," I told him, "sitting signifies a meeting of equals. But suit yourself, stand up if you want."

"No, no," Kingfisher said. "We are honored that you consider us your equals. Sitting is grotesque and uncomfortable, but what does that matter when you consider the honor it conveys?" He translated this for the others, who gobbled their appreciation.

"Gentlemen," I said, "let me start off by telling you how happy I was to be able to rid you and your people of the oppressive rule of the Khalia."

"Is that what you call them?" Kingfisher said. "Panya. That's what we call them. We also call them 'the dwarf people with too many teeth.' There are other names. Yes, we meant to thank you for that. Of course, the Khalia aren't really gone, you know."

"We'll soon take care of that," I told him. "We will expect your cooperation, of course."

"I cannot speak for the rest of my Guild," Kingfisher said. "For myself, I can assure you, you will get the full honors suitable to your rank."

Kingfisher was a high official of the Tinker's Guild. The others represented, variously, the Nest-Builder's Guild, the Seaweed Purveyor's Guild, and the Interior Decorator's Guild.

These were by no means all of the guilds of the Nedge. This intelligent avian race had divided itself into more than three hundred functions or duties, each of them the prerogative of a guild. Even murder was represented in the form of the Assassin's Guild, known poetically as the Guild Without a Nest.

Their planet, poor in minerals and deficient in croplands, had been little disturbed by the various waves of traders and raiders that had become manifest over the last thousand years or so. The Khalia had come across the Nedge only about fifty years ago, had found their planet a good staging ground for their space fleets, and had taken over the political power from the guilds. Before the arrival of the Khalia, the Nedge had been ruled by a council made up of the leading members of all the Guilds. This council decided matters requiring arbitration between the guilds. The Khalia had left this structure intact, but had placed themselves at the head of it. Until our arrival, all the larger questions had been decided by a Khalian overlord, and the Nedge had greatly resented this.

Now I told them, as tactfully as I was able, that we, the representatives of the Fleet, were the ones who had to be obeyed. They didn't like this, of course, but it had to be said.

Kingfisher and the others held a hurried conference. They gobbled and chittered with each other, in that bad-tempered, exasperated way some birds have. At last they seemed to agree about something, and Kingfisher turned to me.

"We agree that you Fleetmen have the power. We Nedge will not act against you."

It was a weak sort of statement, and not entirely satisfactory. But I had to be content with it. I radioed Bar Kochba later in the day, reporting on the conversation.

"The other commanders have reported much the same thing," Bar Kochba said. "I don't think we'll have any trouble from the Nedge. I'm getting reinforcements sent down. It should take us no more than a week or two to kill or capture the remaining Khalia."

Ben Kochba was a little hasty in saying that, and I do his reputation for sagacity no good by quoting him. A month later we were still mopping up the Khalia. A month after that—so unexpected are the fortunes of war—we found ourselves on the defensive.

VI.

People get the wrong idea when they refer to the Khalia as weasels. Yes, the resemblance is there, the long, supple body, lustrous fur, pointed snout. But there is something ludicrous about the idea of a weasel four or five feet tall. And the Khalia were not ludicrous. In their style of attack, they were more reminiscent of wolverines, pound for pound perhaps the fiercest fighter in the animal kingdom.

The Khalia had great powers of concealment and a sure instinct for camouflage. On the attack, they had a talent for instant acceleration. Individually, they loved to do the unexpected. A Khalian brave might come at you in great bounds, or he might slither toward you like an impossibly agile snake. Tactically, it was impossible to predict what they would do next.

They soon gave up any attempt at fighting in formation. It was a style that didn't suit them. They were individualists, as I was to learn, with a taste for fighting that reminded me of stories of the ancient Norse berserkers. Their skill with handguns and edged weapons was uncanny. It took a trained swordman among humans to be a match for a Khalian brave with his wavy-edged swords and his foot-knives. They would come boiling up almost at our feet while we were on patrol, or dart at us from alleyways in the cities of the Nedge. Their aim was to inflict casualties. They gave us much more trouble than we bargained for. They gave us so much trouble that the occupation of Target became a matter of concern to the officers of the Fleet, who dreaded having to send the casualty lists back to the home planets of the deceased. Almost a dozen levies were involved in the occupation of Target. Unless matters could be turned around rather dramatically, there was a real problem of a collapse on the part of the Alliance ground troops.

We were hampered in dealing with the enemy by our concern for the indigenous population. They were not our enemies. But they were not our friends, either, and somehow the Khalia were able to move among them, were often concealed by them. The Nedge didn't like the Khalia, but they didn't turn them in, either. I learned the reason for this later.

It was a merciless war, in the cities and villages, in the countryside. The strain on our forces was so great that there was a danger Fleet Command would withdraw us, because our casualties have grown alarming, if not to us, then certainly to the constituencies on our home planets. And it is the peoples of our home planets, after all, who vote the funds that keep the Fleet in operation. If the constituency thinks an operation is being bungled, politicians distance themselves from it. They may disregard strategic interests and give up too soon, hoping to achieve easy, bloodless victories in a different sector.

Unfortunately, wars are not necessarily won by those who lose the least men. Some of the greatest victories of past wars have been won by the army that stayed in the field longest, that kept on going, stayed cohesive longer than the other, in spite of perhaps equal casualties. And wars have been lost by the timid—their prototype being those Carthaginian merchants who hesitated too long to supply Hannibal in Italy, who wanted easy "strategic" victories.

It's a difficult problem, because simple pugnacity and stubbornness isn't enough. You have to be the judge of when to move back, when to stick it out at all costs. It calls for a nice genius, knowing when to dodge and run, like Fabius Cunctator, and when to pound home the attack at all costs, like his successor, Scipio Africanus, at the walls of Carthage. These two great generals, both of whom saved Rome, did so one by retreating without a blush when that was the thing to do, the other pressing relentlessly for final victory when that was the thing to do.

We on the front line that was everywhere on the planet and nowhere felt that there was something important to be won here. You could tell it in the desperation with which the Khalia fought us. There was nothing specific we could point

to, nothing for the computers to quantify, but despite that
you can't discount the gut feeling that something important
is going on, something which may take a little while to
clarify, but will prove more than worth the effort. And we
also felt that it was a test of wills, and that the final victory
would be determined by who put forth the greater effort in
imposing his will.

It has never been revealed just how badly the tide ran
against us. We managed to hang on, concealing our losses
from Earth, lying about our victories. It was as though we
could see acted out, here in this single planet, issues which
affected the rise and fall of whole species, factors of
determination and will which determined which race would
live and which would die.

In the end, the decisions of the bird-people's guilds were
crucial. They were frankly in doubt as to whether to
exchange rule by the Khalia for rule by us. Because that's
what it came down to. We tried with a straight face to
promise them freedom, but finally we couldn't do it. We had
to tell them the truth because we couldn't help giving
ourselves away when we tried to lie. We of the Alliance were
going to take over Target, at least for the immediate future.
The planet was important to us. Because the Khalia had
been here for many years, there was a lot we could learn
about them here. And, also, this planet was the last known
assembly place for the Khalian raiders. It was from here
that we expected to pick up the clues that would lead us to
their real home, the planet where the power came from, the
head of the snake, so to speak, so that we could finally cut it
off. But to do that we had to solve the riddle of the Khalia on
Target. And it was a bird-man, at last, who provided the key.

VII.

It was two months after our landing on Target that I met the
young Nedge named Tsk Otaî, and whom I nicknamed
Woodpecker. He was taller than most of his people, with a
red crest on his head that stood up when he became excited.
He was a Master in the Tinker's Guild. I knew that this was
a considerable accomplishment for one so young, and I

congratulated him on his rank.

"There was considerable opposition within the guild to granting me Master status," he said, "But I demonstrated my mastery of the Seven Manipulations, and the Three Ways of Joining Material, and this in front of the full assembly of masters. So they had no choice. But they made me pay dearly for the honor."

"How so?" I wanted to know.

Otaï told me that his home was about two hundred miles from here, in an area of steep little hills and boulder-filled ravines, close to the Karnaian Wilderness. It was a favorite hiding place for the Khalian guerillas, who could not be run down in these sun-beaten stone labyrinths. The Khalian irregulars visited the Nedge from time to time, demanding food in the manner of guerillas throughout the universe. One day, however, one of the Khalian fighting bands came to the Nedge with a different request: they wanted a Master Tinker to accompany them to their camp and assist them in repairs.

"And you were chosen?" I guessed.

"Against my will."

"But I thought guild members are free to accept or refuse any job that comes along?"

"That's generally true. But in this case, the Khalia invoked the code of sinik-duty, and the Elders of the Guild had to comply. But they should have chosen by lot among the Masters, rather than merely ordering me to go because I was the youngest."

"What is sinik-duty?" I asked.

"It is a period of labor which an overlord can demand from a guild. It is considered a sacred obligation."

"But the Khalia aren't your overlords," I pointed out. "Not any longer."

"True. But they were armed and desperate, and you Alliance people were far away, and all in all, we decided not to argue the point."

"So they took you away with them?"

"They did indeed. To their hidden encampment. There I did the sort of simple tinkering of which the Khalia themselves seem incapable, fixing simple mechanical contrivances such as hinged doors, and all the time bearing with stoicism their rude and boisterous behavior and living for the day when I would be released."

"That day seems to have arrived," I said, "since here you are now in our camp."

Woodpecker shook his head gloomily. "They granted me a week's leave so that I could go home and put my affairs into order. But I must return to them, hateful though the prospect is to me."

"Why return?" I asked him. "There's nothing they can do to you here."

"You don't understand. The Guild stands surety for me. If I don't return as I promised, they will have to send someone else. In that case, they would expel me from the Guild."

"Why not take up some other line of work?" I asked him.

He shook his head. "Even if I desired to do that—which I don't—it is impossible. We Nedge are born into our Guilds. One without a Guild affiliation is considered dead. He would have to scratch out a living alone, staying well away from the habitations of the people. No female would ever look upon me again. My children, if I had any, would curse my name."

"Is there no way out?" I asked.

"Only one. The Khalia must themselves terminate my contract. But the contract is void if the Khalian chief who claimed my sinik-duty were to die."

I pondered. "You couldn't kill him yourself, could you?"

Woodpecker gave a short whooping laugh. "Me kill Tostig Manslayer, leader of the war band to whom I am indentured? I wouldn't be capable of it. Only members of the The Guild Without a Nest are permitted to kill, and they have turned me down."

"So you come to me with your request."

"It is your business to kill the Khalia. You have told us so often enough."

I thought about it, and my thoughts were not pleasant ones. I had no confidence in these bird-people, who helped us only grudgingly, and seemed fonder of their murderous masters than they were of us. The possibility of treachery here could not be discounted. It was a long journey into the

Karnaian Wilderness, through difficult country that afforded a determined enemy many chances to set up a devastating ambush. I really was not justified in leading my men so far afield, and on such a dubious enterprise.

I was about to turn Woodpecker down. But then he said one more thing, and this made me decide differently.

"I will also be able to show you," he said, "the place where the Khalia fix their spaceships."

That got my full attention. The location of the Khalian factories, their supply warehouses, and refitting yards was a mystery we had been trying to solve since landing on the planet. We had destroyed their spaceport, but still their ships appeared from time to time, to hit and run, dodging away before we could scramble a pursuit, going to ground somewhere in the wilderness that made up the greater part of Target.

"You have actually seen this place?" I asked him.

He cluck-rattled in the affirmative. "I have seen it. And it is vast, vast."

"Tell me where," I said, "We will call up the Fleet."

"I could not tell you even if I wanted to," Woodpecker said. "It is somewhere in the Karnaian Wilderness, and I can find it, but maps are beyond my capabilities. And besides, I must personally see Tostig Manslayer dead in order to claim termination of the contract."

I thought about it. If true, it would be a matter of the utmost importance. And the opportunity of wiping out a Khalian war band was nothing to be taken lightly, either. It could mean the beginning of the end of the difficult war on Target. And if I could locate their factories, find the places where they rearmed, that would be worth almost any risk.

It was nothing I would care to expose my men to. And anyhow, this called for a scouting mission, for stealth and secrecy, because the idea would be to find the location and then get back and direct the attack upon it. It was a job for one man, and a guide.

And it was in my mind, too, that if I could kill this Khalian leader, this Tostig, that would be a great blow as well.

"Wait for me here," I told Woodpecker. "I'll be back in an

hour. Tell me, Otaî, do you believe in a supreme being?"

"Of course," he told me, "The god of my guild is called Thalatak."

"Not even Thalatak will save you if you have lied to me," I said, in suitably impressive tones, I hoped.

VIII.

Four days later, Woodpecker and I were camped in a narrow dried-out riverbed just a few miles within the Karnaian Wilderness. We had taken a lightweight Scout skimmer as far as I dared to go, flying mostly at night at only a few feet above the ground in order to escape surveillance.

We had hidden the vehicle away on the edge of the Karnaian and proceeded on foot. We picked our way through a rocky wilderness, a high desert of tumbled stone and shale. The wind screamed and tore at us without letup, and I was thankful I had brought goggles when the quick deadly dust storms came boiling up out of the south. I had left Gideon in charge of the squad, and had sworn him to secrecy as to my destination. When I told him about it, he was eager to come along, and put up several good arguments as to why he should be taken. When I turned him down he had accused me of trying to hog all the glory. But it wasn't that at all. I had the fear that I was on a fool's errand, and I wouldn't risk the lives of any of my men on it.

We had been discussing the Khalia, Woodpecker and I. Although he purported to despise them, there was always an odd air of grudging reverence in his voice when he discussed them. Whereas when he talked about us humans, his tone was somewhere between bantering and scornful. I had noticed this in other of the Nedge, and had put it down to sheer cussedness. But now I was growing exasperated, and decided I'd really heard all I wanted to about the Khalia and their lordly qualities.

"Otaî," I said, "it seems to me that you and all your people have a problem. On the one hand, you keep on talking about how you despise the Khalia. On the other hand, you talk about them as though they were something special. Okay, let's get it out into the open. What, in your estimation, is so special about the race you refer to as 'Dwarf Men with Too Many Teeth'?"

"Why, obviously," Otaî said, "the Panya are despicable and hateful. But it is equally obvious that they have *feii*."

"And what," I demanded, "is *feii*?"

"Feii," he told me, "is the quality that makes one person or being of higher or lower social rank than another. It emanates from a variety of factors."

"I've never heard the expression before," I told Otaî. "Is it much in use among your people?"

"It's something we think about quite a lot, or rather, take into consideration. Probably nobody mentioned it to you humans because we didn't want to hurt your feelings."

"What do you mean?"

"It's just that you humans have very little *feii*."

I became immediately and irrationally angry. How dare this six-foot chicken with a silly red crest on top of his narrow foolish head say that we humans were deficient in *feii*? I controlled myself with an effort and asked him, "What about the Khalia? Do you mean to say they've got *feii* and we don't?"

"Yes, precisely," Otaî said. "But don't get cross with me about it. It's not my fault that things are that way. Anyhow, in the matter of *feii* the Khalia have one obvious advantage over you."

"Tell me about it," I said, tight-lipped.

"It's just that they've been on our planet for fifty years," Otaiî said. "They've had time to learn about us, what we think proper, what we consider good form, and what we don't like, too."

"Give me an example."

"Well, for one thing, you expose your entire arms like a common *horoji*. None of us ever do, have you noticed? And the Khalia not only cover their elbows, but wear the blue *anaraji* elbow-covers of rank whenever they go out of doors."

"And that really makes a difference?"

"A tremendous difference. Not just any single thing, but the cumulative effect of all of them. Not just the *anaraji* elbow-covers, but also the crimson eyelid paint which we call *tauriang*, and the other things, like *heligo-dun, vastiis, molocatia,* and there are more. The Khalia have learned them, and have adopted them. They've increased their *feii* so much that they've passed quite beyond the class of human creature, into the realm of the godlike. That's why we continue to respect them even though they're out of power. We Nedge of the Guilds do not like to betray godlike beings. It can bring very bad luck."

With Woodpecker's help I drew up a list of the things which conferred *feii.* All of them involved clothing or ornaments. The Khalia wore them, we did not. That was the explanation for our low status on Target, and for the continued prestige of the despised Khalia. Already my trip had proven of value. When I was able to tell Bar Kochba about this, I had no doubt he would make the wearing of these items obligatory for our troops.

One thing still puzzled me about *feii.* "If that's all it takes, why don't all the Nedge raise themselves in status? It seems simple enough. The orange *achiki,* for example, which confers rank in minor nobility. It's just a piece of cloth and two strips of leather tied around the left foot."

"We could never do that," Woodpecker said. "Status is either hereditary, or conferred by services to the Guild, or sanctioned by *na-aringi.*"

"What's that?" I asked him.

"*Na-aringi* refers to divine irresistible impulse. It's impossible to fake."

I didn't correct him. The Khalians had made good use of the doctrine of *na-aringi,* and so would we. Here was the explanation for our low status on Target, and for the continued prestige of the Khalia. That would change as soon as I got back to headquarters.

Just now there were other things to think about. According to Woodpecker, we were within a half-day's trek of the Khalian camp, and the secret spaceship factory, or whatever it was.

IX.

The night was dark, and a cold wind whipped over the desert floor. We had been climbing for several hours, steadily and without a stop. Little pebbles skittered and rolled under our feet as we negotiated a narrow pass between bulging boulders and came to a long sloping escarpment. We began our descent between knife-sharp ridges. I didn't ask Woodpecker how much farther we had to go. By his nervousness, evident through a constant ruffling of his tailfeathers, I knew we were close. We came to a pass, went through it, and Woodpecker searched around for landmarks. I risked using a pencil-thin beam of light to help him orient himself. He seemed doubtful, unsure of himself. Then he said, "Here's the entrance!"

It was through a maze of tumbled boulders. After passing through them, we found steps roughly hewn into the rock. They led downward.

We went down for a considerable distance. I estimated that we were some hundreds of feet below the surface. Woodpecker led me down a passageway, dimly lit with glow bulbs set into niches. We came to the end and turned a corner, and I came to an abrupt halt, because the stone ledge ended abruptly.

I steadied myself, looked outward, and then I beheld it. I was in a cavern that seemed as vast as thought itself, bathed in an eerie green from natural luminescence in the rocks. It stretched as far as the eye could see, beneath a lowering vault of stone. It was a view of boundlessness rigorously framed—an oxymoron of stone and space.

And on that cavern floor, lying there with the dignity of industrial archeology, in an awesome iconization of technological power, lay a vast grouping of spaceships. At first, I could only make out their rounded steel hulls, gleaming blue or grey, reflections winking off their surfaces. Then I noticed their disarray, for they were piled one atop another in the familiar disorder of the junkyard.

I had no time to consider the shattering implications of this find, however. I noticed that Woodpecker had stepped back, and his movement set off a faint alarm in my mind. I turned, groping for my cluster pistol. Shadows were detaching themselves from the walls, coming toward me. In the gloom, I caught the gleam of pointed teeth, and I tried to swing my weapon into firing position. Too late. Something crashed against the side of my head. I knew that I was falling, but I was unconscious before I hit the ground.

X.

When I recovered consciousness, my first emotion was one of amazement that I was not dead. My gratitude gave way to darker emotions when I remembered that the Khalia take prisoners mainly for the purpose of providing themselves with a supply of fresh meat. They are pure carnivores, and their eating habits are said to resemble Terran leopards or hyenas. They were cannibals at one time in their history, until they developed a sense of racial identity. Now they feast on the flesh of others, as do we humans. They generally like their meat fresh and bloody, just killed, for then it still contains the *mana* that makes for strength. There are exceptions to this fresh meat rule, however: as the Khalians developed their rudimentary civilization, they also acquired a fondness for meat that is "high," which is to say, rotten. They would appreciate the old Earth recipe for jugged hare, in which you keep the carcass in a jug until it comes apart at the touch, rottenness and tenderness being synonymous. I hoped that fate was not intended for me.

I was seated on the ground in a cavelike structure. A rope was tied around my ankle, the other end of which was affixed to an iron staple in the wall. Examining the knot, I saw that I could undo it without great difficulty. But I did not: I had heard that there was nothing the Khalia liked better than to find one of their animated food supplies trying to escape from the den. Our reports said that such attempts were invariably detected, and the unfortunate victim was turned over to the cubs to snack on, then tied up again half-dead from wounds, to await his fate as a living appetizer.

I sat on the ground, nursing my bruised head and silently lamenting my bad luck. After a while, three Khalian warriors came to inspect me. They were about four feet tall, and they wore short, multicolored garments that resembled kilts. The colors, I learned later, were a form of war-band identification. They wore a leather harness crossed around their narrow chests and cinched around their waists. From this harness depended a variety of hand weapons—swords and short axes, knives of various sorts, whips, a lariat, and several kinds of small arms. They jabbered at me in their barking language, then, seeing I did not understand, howled in unison until Woodpecker came running up to translate for them.

"They want you to stand up. They will release your bonds. They want you to accompany them quietly. It would be best for you if you did so, because they haven't had lunch yet and any show of resistance might set off in them a feeding frenzy. That is not a good thing to see, especially when you would be the object of their appetites."

"Tell them they have nothing to fear from me," I said bitterly. "You arranged this yourself, didn't you, Otaî?"

"Yes, Judah. But do not think badly of me. I was forced to do it because of my Guild Pledge, which is the most sacred duty of any Nedge in his capacity as a Guild member."

"I don't know what you're talking about," I said. Before Otaî could tell me more the Khalian warriors had untied me and led me away by jerking on the rope they had tied around my neck and emitting sharp yapping cries.

My guards led me through winding underground passage-ways, all the time yapping and growling among themselves; discussing different ways of serving me up, no doubt. They brought me to a large chamber hewn out of the rock. One of them, who spoke a little English, pointed to a chair with a forepaw.

"Sit!" he said. "No move! Tostig, he come."

I sat down. The guards left. I looked around, but saw nothing that could be used as a weapon. This seemed not the time to try anything. Later I hoped to have a better opportunity. If there was a later. Meanwhile, I waited for this Tostig to come. No doubt he wanted to sample me to see if I was suitable for one of their beastly feasts.

After a while a single Khalian brave entered the chamber. "Hello, I'm Tostig," he said, in clear, barely accented English. He was larger than the others. His kilt was edged with purple, his harness was studded with silver ornaments. He had a swagger to him and an air of confidence that bespoke a leader.

"I am Captain Judah ben Judah," I told him.

"Delighted," Tostig said. He threw his scabbarded sword into a corner, peeled off his gauntlets and threw them after his sword, then dropped carelessly into a couch. There he yawned, stretched, kicked off his boots and stretched out his claws.

"You know," he said, "it's damned hard to make a boot that fits nicely over a paw. The claws get in the way."

There seemed no immediate reply to that, so I remained silent. But I was interested in Tostig. It is difficult to read alien physiognomies and Tostig resembled, of course, a very large weasel. But he gave me the impression of a level-headed fighting man, gallant, even-tempered, and of a humorous and even ironic turn of mind.

"Well, Captain," he said, "your people have pulled a good one on us today. Caught one of our groups coming out of a town after a raid. They were all bunched together and singing one of their fighting songs, the silly bastards. Your people cut them down. I've told them often enough to spread out whenever there's a chance that enemies might be around. Make less of a target for a beam or projectile attack. Easy enough to understand, I think. But do they listen? Not this lot. Spreading out's un-Khalia-like, they tell me. Lessens our ferocity. The good old-fashioned Khalian way is good enough for us—in a pack, all teeth and claws. No arguing with the silly buggers. So we lost seven. A good one for your side."

From his expression and tone of voice, he bore me no ill will. He might have been announcing the score at a tennis match for all the emotion he showed.

"But I can't really expect you to sympathize with me, can I?" he went on in his good-humored way. "Hereditary enemies and all that. Our loss is your gain, eh? And vice versa, of course."

"I suppose it is," I said. "But you didn't arrange all this to discuss planetary destinies with me."

"True enough!" he said. "Time I put you in the picture."

"Before you do that, there's one thing I'd like to know," I told him.

"Ask away!" he said.

"Am I to be a main course at one of your banquets, or do

you consider me more in the category of snack food?"

Tostig exploded with laughter. "Oh, I say, that *is* good! You must admit it is rather droll, to have a conversation with snack food. But fear not, you're my guest. And whereas it's possible that in the long run I may have to kill you if things don't work out, for the present you're perfectly safe and I can assure you all the civilized amenities will be observed."

"Might I enquire," I asked, "where you learned your excellent English?"

"As it happens I was a guest for a while in the London Zoo on the planet Earth. In fact, I was the main attraction in their Horrifying Predators Exhibition. Managed to break out after a while, steal a ship and get back to my war band. But I shall never forget the kindness of the British. Yes, in a way those were good days . . . But forgive me, I seem to be forgetting my hospitality."

Tostig jumped off the couch in one effortless bound, crossed to the sideboard, lifted a bottle.

"Whiskey, Captain Judah? We picked it up last month in a raid on one of your outposts. Not to the taste of us Khalia, but I keep it around for occasions like this."

I accepted a glass. Tostig poured himself a glass of what I later learned was a kind of fermented milk from a tanned skin sack hanging from the wall.

"Cheers," he said. We drank. "Are you hungry? I could send for some lunch for you?"

"There's a Nedge here named Otaî," I said, "I wouldn't mind a bit of him, roasted, baked or boiled, whichever is most convenient."

Tostig chuckled. "I wish I could oblige you. But Otaî works for me, and he betrayed you only in order to fulfill his Guild Oath. Perhaps a nice salad instead? I understand you humans can eat green stuff without becoming ill."

"Nothing at the moment, thank you. I don't understand about that Guild Oath stuff."

"Well, that's because you haven't been here fifty years. I requisitioned the services of a Master Tinker, you see, and the Guild sent Otaî. But he couldn't do what we asked of him. They had sent me an untrained young cub who had gotten his Guild affiliation through a highly placed uncle. Yes, these things do happen here. Well, naturally, I was cross, and was about to turn him over to my chef for filleting and marination, when Otaî said he would fulfill his Guild Oath by bringing me a substitute whose skills would be sufficient for my needs."

"And that was me."

"Yes, though not you personally. Any human would have done, because your entire race is renowned as peerless Tinkers. Not bad fighters, either, I must say, but exceptional when it comes to fixing things."

"Baron Tostig," I said, "or whatever your title is . . ."

" 'Baron' will do nicely," Tostig said. "Has quite a nice ring to it, don't you think?"

I shrugged. "Baron, shmaron, it's all the same to me. If you think I'm going to help you, the most dangerous enemy humankind has yet encountered, you've misjudged me entirely."

"Well, of course, you have to say that," Tostig said, "But suppose I make you an offer you can't refuse?"

Tostig had learned a few things during his stay at the London Zoo, that much was evident. "What's the offer?" I asked.

"Suppose I can prove to you that the assistance you give me will benefit your own people as well?"

"I doubt very much whether you will be able to prove that to me."

"But suppose I can? And suppose I promise that, upon completion of the job, I will set you free, unharmed?"

"No matter what you do to me, I will never betray humanity."

"That remains to be seen, doesn't it?" He sat up and pulled on his boots. "But don't think it will come to that. Let me show you what I have in mind, and then you can decide, rather hastily, I fear, but I can give you a minute or two. But that's putting the hindquarters before the front paws, as we say in Khalia. Come with me. This will interest you."

Tostig marched to the entrance, his long cloak swirling behind him. I followed. What else was I to do?

XI.

Tostig was a credit to his race, as the goyim used to say about some of us on Earth. The same could not be said for his followers. They lounged around passageways, drinking their fermented milk and getting quite drunk, telling jokes, slapping each other on the back with loud guffaws, farting rudely whenever possible, and jeering at the hapless human prisoner trotting along at the heels of their leader. In this they behaved like troops all over the galaxy; but it tried my patience nonetheless.

For Tostig they showed a mixture of easy familiarity and poorly disguised awe. This was the only proper attitude to take with a battle leader as famous as Tostig. Like the Norsemen of old Terra, these Khalia had sworn personal fealty to Tostig, and he had led them to much glory and more booty.

He led me through a bewildering array of passageways hewn out of the rock, and then down irregularly spaced stone staircases which Tostig negotiated on all fours, and a lot quicker than I on two legs. We came out on the floor of the cavern. Ahead of us lay the colossal grouping of spaceships, and toward that we walked.

"You seem to have quite a few of the smaller ships," I remarked. "More, it seems to me, than you Khalia put into the line of battle against the Fleet, to judge by the reports I've heard."

"That's quite correct," Tostig said, leading me down the wavering aisles that ran between the masses of ships. "Nothing we could do about that, of course."

I was silent. If he believed that, I certainly wasn't going to tell him differently.

Here and there among the ships I could see parties of Khalia working. Each crew seemed to be under the command of an older Khalian, and these overseers, or whatever they were, wore silver-grey tunics and oddly pointed hats made of felt or some similar material.

"What's going on?" I asked Tostig.

"It should be obvious enough," he said, never lessening his stride, or rather, his lope, as we hurried toward some unknown destination. "Those are repair crews. We're fixing the damaged ships. I'm sure you have similar procedures."

I watched the Khalia for a while. They were removing modulized components from the ships, and taking them somewhere else. The overseer was checking the identification numbers of the modules against a master list in his paw.

"It's all quite straightforward," Tostig told me, noticing my interest. "Each ship has a status panel which identifies a misfunctioning part and gives us its location, serial number, and removal procedure. We take out the damaged part and put in a new one."

"And you get the new one from some other ship," I said. "Is that correct?"

"Of course. How else does one get parts?"

I nodded as if his method were obviously the only one that could be followed. Now I understood the significance of this graveyard for spaceships. It was the closest equivalent to a warehouse the Khalia had. We humans would have put up an automated warehouse which we'd keep stocked with freshly manufactured spare parts ready to be used as needed by the ships of the Fleet.

It was evident now that the Khalia had no warehouse system, not even for a battle as important as this struggle for Target. There could be but one reason for this: they had no industry with which to manufacture replacement parts. Nor, apparently, did they have an outside source.

This insight, later confirmed, was obviously of overwhelming importance to Fleet Intelligence. When one of the Khalian ships broke down, all they could do was replace the entire module in which the breakdown had occurred. If they could find one. Otherwise the ship had to stay out of action.

And the importance of this spaceship graveyard was now clear. Parts from this collection of broken spaceships was probably keeping a major part of the Khalian fleet in operation. Destroy this dump and who knows how far they'd have to travel to find replacements?

Fixing things—the basis of technological civilization— was of little interest to the Khalian. There was a caste among them who did do a certain amount of repair work. They might, in time, have developed into a guild of scientists and craftsmen. But they chose instead the mystical path, and became the seers and singers of a magical and poeticized pseudo-technology. I was to learn more about this from Homer Farsinger, the Destination Master of Tostig's band. But all that came later. Now I was just catching up with Tostig, who had come to a stop at last beside a medium-sized spaceship, somewhat smaller than one of the fleet's cruisers.

Tostig turned to me. "Now, my friend, comes a time of decision for you. I have a simple proposal to make."

"My mind's already made up," I said, "if your proposal is what I think it is."

"And what is that?"

"I figure you want my help in getting these ships working again. So you can fight our Fleet again, and perhaps this time come out better. The answer is no."

"I wouldn't blame you for refusing that," Tostig said. "That would be treason, and that's something no warrior of honor asks of another. But such a task would be beyond any one man's capabilities, and is not what I have in mind."

"What is it, then?"

"Behold this ship," Tostig said, "It is my own personal ship. You know, perhaps, that we Khalia go to battle under our chosen war leaders, each of whom has his own ship. Actually, we don't go to war, since that implies a contest that can be brought to a decision. We fight for booty, and above all, we fight for glory. Where neither booty nor glory are to be had, some of us, many of us, consider it no disgrace to break off an engagement and go elsewhere, where things may be more to our liking."

"I can assure you," I said, "I am all in favor of you going elsewhere."

I was speaking ironically, of course. But Tostig took it seriously.

"In that case, Judah, there should be no problem between us. Because what I want you to do is help me get this ship spaceworthy. As soon as it is, I will load up my men and we will go somewhere else. Some place more amusing than Target has turned out to be, especially in this last phase."

I turned it over in my mind. "Would you give me your word that you'd go away from Target?"

"Certainly."

"And that you would not attack humanity again?"

"Don't be silly," Tostig said. "Of course I'm going to attack humanity again. That's the game, you see. I mean, there's nothing else for a Khalian warrior to do."

"I don't know," I said, "whether that would be helpful to humanity or disloyal."

"Well, you can't know entirely, can you?" Tostig said. "But it seems to me that this way we both get to keep our lives, and who can say what the future will hold for either of us, or for either of our races? You give up a tricky situation here and maybe it turns up somewhere else. Or maybe not. The point is moot, I think. It will certainly save the lives of your men on Target. But one thing is certain. If you don't help me, you'll die in this place before I do. That's a promise, not a threat. Since I've taken a liking to you, I won't eat you, in the event I must kill you. But die you will if you turn me down. But don't let that influence you. What do you say?"

As you can imagine, I did a great deal of thinking in a very short time, there on the chilly cavern floor, beneath the steely loom of Tostig's spaceship lit vaguely by the cavern's green phosphorescence. I had a natural desire to stay alive, of course. But my decision was based upon objective considerations.

As an Intelligence Officer, or just as an intelligence source, it was necessary for me to stay alive, and to bring back this new knowledge which I had acquired about the Khalia. The lack of a manufacturing source for the ship's replacement parts was crucial knowledge. Given that fact, spaceship graveyards acquired an importance we had not considered before; they were sources of materials that kept the Khalian raiders in action. The importance to them of this spaceship depository was why they were fighting so fiercely for this planet. If I could get back, I could direct the Fleet's telemetry to the approximate location. They could blow away the spaceship graveyard here in the wilderness without risking any Nedge lives.

Finally, there was this: if the Khalia were unable to manufacture their own spaceships, as seemed now to be the case, who was manufacturing them? And why were they doing it? This was something the Fleet leaders had to ponder. And to be exposed to the question, I had to get back to tell them.

Would he actually let me go?

I hoped he was a weasel of his word.

I had to take the chance.

"I'll do it," I said.

"Good fellow!" he cried, with evident warmth. "Come along then. You'll want to meet the Destination Master. He'll tell you what's needed."

XII.

Tostig led me down to a crude building which had been set up a few yards from the cruiser. It was a one-room shack, put together from bits and pieces of metal, old doors, metal shielding. Tostig found a patch of ground to lie down in, and motioned for me to put myself at my ease.

"What's up?" I asked.

"The Destination Master is inside, talking to the gods. We mustn't disturb him. He'll come out when he's finished."

"What, exactly, is a Destination Master?" I asked.

From what Tostig told me, our nearest equivalent would be a navigator. But the Khalian Destination Masters were also in charge of maintaining the navigational equipment through prayers and meditation. Destination Masters, I learned, are always chosen from the Poet Class, since, by common consent, the Poets of Khalia understand about Travelling and Fighting, since they compose the heroic verses which are woven into the Sagas and constitute the soul of the Khalian race. Only this dedicated Poet caste can be trusted to communicate the correct messages to the ship's computer.

I was just beginning to grasp the meaning of all this when the Destination Master came out of his house. He was considerably older than Tostig, who was himself noticeably older than most of his followers. His name, translated into our own language, was Homer Farsinger. His fur was a greyish brown, grizzled white at the ends. He walked with great dignity, but with more than a hint of the rheumatism that affects so many Khalia in their old age.

His voice was high, quavering, unpleasant.

"Baron Tostig," he said, "Why have you brought this racially impure human to the Shrine of Communication?"

At first I thought he was being anti-Semitic, but then realized that he considered all humans racially impure. Perhaps from the viewpoint of a weasel that made sense.

"Now Homer," Tostig said, his voice conciliatory, "you know we discussed this. Human beings are very good at fixing things. With his help, you'll be able to sort out the computer in no time and we can be on our way to fresh booty. And glory, too, we must never forget that."

"A Poet-Bard of the Khalia is unapt to forget glory," Homer remarked. "I do not need this creature's help. I am perfectly capable of conducting the Diving Startup Procedure."

"Yes, I know," Tostig said, "But the fact is, we still can't get the damned thing going."

"The Gods of Communication will grant us passage," Homer said. "We must not try to rush them."

"I must point out," Tostig said, "that some among the Khalia have come to believe that computers are responsive to straightforward cause and effect principles rather than the purely hypothetical Communication Gods."

"Don't speak sacrilege in my presence," Homer said. "You may be Baron Tostig, the greatest hero the Inchidian Clan of the West Khalia has yet produced. But religiously, you're still a pup."

"Let's not get into a huff about it," Tostig said pleasantly. "I intend to get out of this place with my warriors. This man is the key. You can either let him be your assistant, or I will appoint you his assistant. Let's have no more discussion about this, Homer."

Homer looked as though he had quite a good deal more to say. But he must have gauged the meaning of Tostig's set expression and the way his right forepaw toyed with the tassel on the end of his laser pistol.

"Of course he may assist me," Homer said. "And if he has any worthwhile suggestions, I'll be glad to follow them. Sometimes the Gods of Communication choose unconventional ways to convey their messages."

"Good," Tostig said, "glad that's settled. I'll leave you two to get acquainted, then."

And he hurried off, obviously pleased to get away from Homer Farsinger, but not failing to give me a wink to let me know he sympathized. At least, I think it meant that. He was a good sort, Tostig.

XIII.

A Khalian baron, invariably an outstanding warrior, is in sole command of a Khalian raid. He gives the orders where to go, and when. But it is the Destination Master who actually implements those orders. The baron wouldn't dream of taking the controls himself. His business is fighting and giving orders. Someone else actually carries out the orders, doing what is necessary to take the ship from here to there.

Khalian navigation is simplicity itself, though only the Destination Masters of the Poet's Guild seem to have caught on to it. What the Destination Master actually does is this: After a long mantric chant, "New direction, pounds of torque," repeated over and over until the words made no sense (if they ever did), the Master is ready to perform. He takes from its special receptacle the Ship's Travel Disc. It is a thin plastic rectangle containing a great deal of encoded electronic information, or, as the Khalia would say, it holds much power. The Master puts that into the computer's slot, and up on the screen comes a directory of destinations. The Master selects the one desired, and punches EXECUTE. The ship gets underway. The remaining procedures are purely automatic. Unless a manual override is employed, the program will execute lift-off, take the ship off-planet by magnetic engines, switch at the appropriate time to FTL drive, and reverse the procedure for the landing at the chosen destination. In actual ship-to-ship combat, the Khalian commanders override the automatics and fly their ships personally, just as we humans do. But aside from that, the computer program handles everything.

Many variations are possible, but that's the basic routine.

A nice, simple, foolproof method, well suited to the blood-thirsty and childish personalities of most of the Khalian race. Just within their intellectual grasp.

But what happens when that simple, traditional, time-tested method of navigation fails? What happens when, as in the case of Tostig, the computer, when asked to get us out of here, flashes back, *System Error*?

The Destination Master had asked to be alone with his computer, and tried several prayers known only to him, mantras of great power. He emerged after three days shaking his head. None of his words had had the slightest effect. The machine continued to display its single-minded message:

System Error!

"That's fascinating," I said to Homer, standing beside him and looking at the CRT tube of the ship's computer. "My people, too, know what it means when God won't speak to them any longer."

"The point is of considerable theological interest," he said, agreeing with me though that wasn't quite what I had meant. "System Error is mentioned in our ancient literature, specifically in the teaching story called 'How System Error Came into the World.' Briefly, the legend tells that the Gods of Communication gave the ancient Khalia two storerooms. From one of them, they were allowed to take all good things. But the other they were not permitted to touch. But they became greedy, and impious, and opened the second storeroom expecting even greater riches. Instead, out came a forlorn little creature with a long sting in its tail, and this was the demon System Error, and it has been stinging us ever since."

"That's great," I said, "I love stories like that. Now, if you don't mind, I'll just sit down at the keyboard and see what I can learn about System Error."

"I can show you all the commentaries on the basic text," Homer said.

"Thanks, anyway, but what we need is a pragmatic procedure. That's what's recommended in the System Manual."

He looked at me with fury. "Don't pretend to knowledge

you do not have! Nobody has ever seen the System Manual, and certainly the Communication Gods would never show it to a human. But you may try to influence the machine, if you wish."

XIV.

The running of a ship's computer, even if it is simplified to a degree just short of automaticity, still requires the operator to indicate to the machine what routine he wants the machine to follow. And in indicating his wishes, the operator must communicate them to the computer in the proper order, and know how to recover if accident befalls. He needn't know what his maneuvers actually do in terms of bits or bytes. But he must know how to do them accurately.

Homer Farsinger knew many programming routines by heart, and that was a considerable achievement for a pre-technological race. He didn't call them programs, however. He called them "Stanzas of Instruction," and they were imbedded in the heart of the Sagas, mixed in with poetical stories of supernatural happenings in the early days of the Khalian race.

A typical stanza (this is from "The Murder-Rage of Destrid Crazyclaws") goes like this:

"Then Destrid toggled once,
And squeezed the mouse of destiny,
And lines appeared on the Video Machine,
And at that moment the Communication God spoke:
'Option, Shift, E, Seven!,
Do it and all will be well!'
And Destrid praised the Lord,
And reverently entered the divine computation . . ."

Good stuff, no doubt, and useful, too. As long as the actual programming instructions didn't get twisted around. If the program needed Option Shift Seven E, in that order, then not even the High Lord of Communication is going to get your program running if you entered it wrong.

The way I figured it, what had originally started as

straightforward programming instructions had become poeticized by a race that feared technology and considered it a
form of magic. Since they were not considered precise
instructions, they were always being improved upon by
succeeding generations of Poets. And the new Sagas were
being written using many of the old programming formulas,
but out of context, merely as a form of poetic speech.

In one of the old Sagas, "The Threat of Hafeld
Alieneater," the computer is threatened into obedience by
its larger-than-weasel protagonist:

> *"Hafeld Alieneater, that great warrior,*
> *Seized old Computer by the powercord,*
> *And shook it until its pixels winked in agony,*
> *And System Errors appeared in its screen,*
> *And the soul of the machine begged for mercy,*
> *Then Hafeld Alieneater said,*
> *'Take my people home, Computer,*
> *Or I'll feed you no more fat electrons,'*
> *And when Computer still hesitated,*
> *Cunningly counting the nanoseconds*
> *On its interior clock of gold,*
> *Hafeld Alieneater grew passing wroth,*
> *And signalled to his men to engage in rude laughter,*
> *So that Computer should be discomfitted,*
> *And stop giving itself airs,*
> *And do what had to be done,*
> *To bring Ostran and his brave warriors*
> *Home to the brave campfires of The People . . ."*

It worked in the poem, but nothing Homer could do would
duplicate the results.

I worked at the computer when Homer would allow. But
it was not easy, trying to deduce its programming from the
few clues available to me. He watched my efforts, but made
little comment.

During our moments of relaxation, when we paced up
and down beside Tostig's battle cruiser, trying to rest our
eyes, I prevailed on Homer to tell me legends from the old
days. He saw no harm in this. What practical concern could
those old stories be? And perhaps he sought to convert me

to his own cult of Orthodox Khalian Communicationism.

Back in the old days, he told me, back in the ancient time before spaceships (a period of about four hundred years back, I estimated through other clues he gave me), The People (The Khalia) were simple barbarians, made up of many tribes and clans continually at war with one another. Then the First Others came from their home beyond the stars, and they gave weapons to the warrior people, and spaceships to the best of the battle group leaders, and sent them out on their trips of fame, booty, glory, and death. And they gave to the Poet's Guild the task of recording these glories of the Khalian race in the form of Sagas.

This was very interesting news, pointing, as it did, to the intervention of some race into Khalian affairs, the arming of Khalia and encouraging them to raid the ships of The Alliance. Who had given the Khalia their ships? This was something else the leaders of the Fleet would have to ponder—once I was able to return and tell them about it.

After several days, I knew I was getting closer to programming the ship's computer so that it would accept and access the Destinations Disc. Yet something always went wrong. It began to seem as though there were a perversity built into the machine, something that defeated even the most logical steps, even the most intuitive leaps.

And then one day, coming back to the ship early from a solitary stroll, I came upon Homer Farsinger sitting at the keyboard, rapt in concentration.

I watched his procedure with fascination. With unexpected skill for a pre-technological, he was undoing the information I had previously put in, like Penelope at night taking out by night the work she had put on the loom by day.

"You're trying to glitz the program!" I shouted at him.

His lips curled in a supercilious smile, but he did not reply.

"You don't want this ship to work! You want Tostig and the men to stay right here and die!"

"I'm surprised that you didn't catch on sooner," Homer said.

"Tostig will be interested to hear of this," I told him. I

hefted a crowbar. "Don't try to stop me or I'll brain you, you traitorous bastard!"

By then, as was perhaps inevitable, I was identifying with the Khalia.

"Before you do that," Homer said, "don't you want to know why I'm doing it?"

Perhaps I should have gone straight to Tostig. If I had, the outcome might have been very different. But I hesitated. Inquisitiveness is a well-known Perdidan quality. "Why are you doing it?" I asked.

He smiled. In a mild voice, he said, "Tell me, human, what do you know about the requirements for writing Khalian Sagas?"

I put down the crowbar. I sat down. I was hooked.

"Tell me," I said.

XV.

"Sagas," Homer told me, "are the heartblood of our people. All of the great Sagas have certain elements in common. There is a heroic figure, such as Tostig. There is an impossible situation, such as our stay on Target, there is treachery by a trusted key figure, and there is a glorious death in battle for the leader and his men. Tostig is a fit subject for the greatest of Sagas. I have employed my skill to construct such a one. I have enumerated in glowing verses all of his great triumphs—the massacre at Eagle Station, the devastation of Star Pass, the daylight raid against Algol IV. Never in living memory has a Khalian hero performed such feats. All that remains is a satisfactory conclusion."

"Such as?" I asked.

"There is only one that is possible. Baron Tostig must fight a heroic and foredoomed last stand, betrayed by his friend, and die here upon the site of the greatest naval battle in all Khalian history, here on Target."

"Maybe that's not what Tostig wants," I suggested.

"It doesn't matter what the Baron wants. What is important is that his Saga be brought to a satisfactory conclusion, and be sung thereafter as an inspiration to the rest of us."

"It's difficult for me to see how your saga can be preserved," I said. "If you are here with Baron Tostig when he goes down to glory and death."

"That's my problem," Homer said. "No doubt I will solve it, as the great bards always have. Even if I die before finishing the final stanzas, I will manage to get a copy of my work back to the Poet's Guild. Other paws will have to finish the final verses."

"I don't like it," I told him.

"That's because you do not have the poetic vocation. But you are clever enough to know where your own advantage lies."

"I suppose you have some advice for me on that score," I suggested.

"Indeed I do. Your loyalty to your own kind should make you desire that Baron Tostig never leave this place."

Homer had a pungent way of speaking. But he had a point. I knew that Tostig was one weasel among a million, far more intelligent and flexible than is usual for his race.

"What surprises me," I said to Homer, "is why such a Khalian as Tostig was not given wider powers, more warriors."

"It is not our way. We are not a cooperative people. That is why we cannot trust ourselves with a ship larger than a cruiser. A good leader can hold together groups of twenty, fifty, even a hundred warriors. But when it comes to the dreadnaughts with their crews of two thousand, that is beyond us. Nor have The Others encouraged us to combine clans under gifted leaders. They prefer us as we are, intimidating, but not quite overwhelming."

"They sound pretty smart, these Others," I said. "What planet did you say they came from?"

"I would die before telling you anything useful about the Others. And I am spared the necessity since I know nothing about them. But tell me, human, do not our aims coincide here? You wish for a material victory, I for a spiritual one. Both of us can be satisfied by Tostig fighting his last stand here, and dying."

"That would also be a quick way to get myself killed."

He shook his head. "I myself, on my oath as a Master Poet, would see that you were returned to your friends alive and well. And the glory would be yours, rather than the shame of letting Tostig escape."

"But I gave Tostig my word," I said.

"You gave it from a posture of constraint rather than of free will. In this case, it could not be considered binding."

"When I give my word," I told him, "I consider it binding."

"Now you are arguing like a stupid Khalian trooper. Aren't you interested in furthering the concerns of your race and people? Or are you another romantic like Tostig?"

"I don't know what in hell to do," I said irritably. "Damn it, I *like* Tostig!"

"And I, his bard and companion through all the famous battles, I love him as myself. If you are his friend as well as his enemy, will you not give him the great conclusion he longs for?"

"You've got it wrong," I told him. "The Baron wants to get out of here. He's told me himself how he wants to fight for booty and glory on other fronts, in better circumstances."

"Oh, he likes to give the appearance of being a rational life-fearing creature." Homer said, "It is a foible he picked up in the London Zoo. But at heart, he is pure Khalian, and he will embrace the hero's death whether he wills it or not. It is a situation repeated time and again in our old Sagas. The hero tries to avoid his destiny, but his best friend betrays him and so the hero embraces his fate."

"I'm not his best friend!" I shouted. But he had turned away from me and was praying to his Gods of Communication. And I was left with a fearful tangle in my mind and heart.

XVI.

My last meeting with Tostig was as pleasant as all the others had been. The Khalian Captain was in his quarters, finishing his grooming. He was a little vain in this regard, and even used a hot iron to curl his chin hairs in the upward tilt so popular that year among the Khalian nobility.

"It's hardly worth trying to stay in style," he grumbled. "Just when I have my whiskers trained to go one way, I hear that everyone's wearing them in some quite different fashion. And it doesn't look very flattering anyhow. So much for my vanity. Tell me, Judah, is the ship ready?"

"It is," I told him. "I located the glitch and took care of it. With the invaluable assistance of Homer Farsinger, of course. Is there any of that whiskey left?"

"Help yourself. The bottle's in its usual place."

I poured myself a stiff one. Tostig watched me, concern showing in his brown eyes.

"You seem a little out of sorts today, Judah."

I had spent the night wrestling with my conscience. We Jews of the planet Perdido spend a lot of time doing that. We call it "arguing with the angel." This time, however, the issue was far from clear-cut. I found it difficult to define my terms, to determine just what ends I wished to accomplish, and which means I could permit myself to use. It was true, on the one hand, as the Destination Master had pointed out, that Baron Tostig and his battling weasels would be a thorn in our sides as long as they lived. On the other hand, individuals don't determine the fate of interstellar empires. It was vital to the Alliance that I returned with the information I had learned. But wasn't a man's word of honor worth something in the scheme of things?

There were good reasons, even compelling ones, which argued in my mind that I should not betray Baron Tostig, that I should act the part of a true friend, tell him about Homer's scheme, give the baron his chance to get away from this killing ground, on to further exploits, or to the little retirement cottage he once mentioned to me, tucked away among low green hills on a planet whose name he never revealed.

I had just about made up my mind to tell Tostig everything. But then I would remember the central role of the Sagas in the life of the Khalia, and how they all featured a friend who becomes a traitor, who conspires to bring the hero to his glorious doom, satisfying his deep-seated desire for a glorious death which would live forever in the Sagas of his people.

Was a true friend the one who helped the hero get away, so that he could die at last, quietly in bed, perhaps attended by pretty little bright-eyed weasel nymphets? Or was a true friend the one who assisted the hero toward his true, inner goal, the valiant death in battle against great odds?

"I'll be sorry to see you go," I told him, speaking the truth, though not all of it.

"My feelings, too," Tostig said. "Perhaps friendship isn't possible between our races. I don't know the truth of that, it is too deep for me. But this I know—friendship between individuals *is* possible. I shall miss you, Judah."

It was in my mind to say something to him then, but his guard of honor had just arrived, four piratical-looking Khalia liberally covered with weapons, one of them with a black patch over one eye.

"Let us inspect your work," Tostig said lightly, and we marched out surrounded by the guard of honor.

Tostig's men were drawn up in front of the battle cruiser. There were almost a hundred of them, since other battle groups fighting on Target had sworn fealty to him, wishing to have some share in his glory. Homer Farsinger was there, too, resplendent in his silver-grey robe, his face an unreadable mask.

After the cheering had subsided, Tostig boarded his ship, and Homer and I followed him. As we came to the pilot's section, I could hold myself in no longer. "Tostig," I said, "there is something I must tell you!"

He regarded me with a level gaze. "No," he said, "you do not. You see, I already know."

"You know?"

Tostig smiled. "I know the old Sagas a lot better than you do. Almost as well as our colleague here, the Destination Master. Isn't that so, Homer?"

"The Baron's knowledge of matters poetical is unexcelled," Homer said. "For a layman, of course."

"Of course," Tostig said. He looked over the controls, then turned to Homer again. "How, exactly, did you arrange the treachery, Homer? Something ingenious, I trust?"

"Ingenious enough," he said. "When you go to turn on the ship's computer, I've set up a special code you must enter before making any other move. Otherwise, a disabling program is implemented, putting the computer out of service once and for all. But how did you find out?"

"I had no idea," Tostig said. "I just thought I'd pretend to know and see what you said."

"So you tricked us!" Homer said.

"One good trick deserves another," Tostig said. "I've known your plans for me for a long time, Destination Master. And of course you were able to convince my naive friend here that death in battle and glory in song is what I really wanted for myself."

"I should never have listened to him," I said. "Tostig, you can still get away. The code to disarm the disabling pro-gram—"

Tostig held up an imperious paw. "No, don't tell me. I might be tempted to use it."

We stared at him. Then a grim smile crossed the face of the Destination Master.

"Then I was not wrong about you, Baron Tostig!"

"You knew me better than I knew myself. But then, he who can read the soul of the race has the key to the individual as well."

We followed Tostig as he walked to the spaceship door. The crowd of Khalian warriors fell silent as he looked at them.

"Men," he said, "the spaceship is fixed. But we do not need it. This is too great an opportunity to be missed. We're going to take on the entire Fleet and all the land forces the humans can throw against us. We are going to perform the greatest feats of arms known to Khalian history. We have lived long enough. Now I invoke the code of the berserker. I will attack, even if I must do so alone. Are there any of you who would like to accompany me?"

The resounding cheer that came up showed that the vote was unanimous. True Khalia all, they could not resist the glamour of a great death under a famous leader and immortality in song.

"We'll be celebrating tonight," Tostig said, "in prepara-tion for our attack. Go now, Judah, my friend, go home in safety and with my regard. Baron Tostig keeps his word. And take this Poet with you, because his Saga must be preserved for our future generations."

Homer Farsinger drew himself up to his full height. "No,

Tostig, I won't go. You have made the right decision, the only decision possible for a hero. But my decision is the correct one for a Poet. I will stay here with you, witness your last battle, and record it for the conclusion of my Saga."

"But, you silly idiot," Tostig said, "you're likely to be killed with the rest of us, war being no respecter even of poets. And then what will become of my great Saga?"

"I have considered the problem," Homer said. "I hoped that matters would work out in this way. I made my preparations."

From within his long robes he took out a small machine. I recognized it at once as one of our standard model cassette recorders.

"I took this piece of alien technology from the spoils of our most recent battle. On it I have recorded all of the Saga, right up to the present moment. The human has shown himself to be worthy of trust, to yourself in regard to friendship and to me in terms of the deepest poetical wishes of the Khalian people. We understand each other, Judah and I. No doubt I will survive your death, Tostig, because Bards are often lucky in that way. In that case, I will finish the Saga myself and find a way to get it back to the College of Poets on Khalia. But if I should die, then I request of you, Judah, that you find some way to get this to the Khalia, so that they can finish the story themselves."

"I'll do that," I said, taking the little cassette recorder and putting it in my pocket. I shook Homer's paw, embraced Tostig, and then I was on my way.

The rest is well known to the members of this court-martial. It took our forces another two months to bring Tostig to bay, and it cost us many lives before we killed him in the great slaughter at Deadman's Pass.

As for the Great Saga, it is a sadness for me to have to report that the Destination Master was no mastery of gadgetry, not even something as straightforward as a cassette recorder. He had managed to turn it on, and the winking little red light had convinced him that the thing was working properly. But evidently he had forgotten to release the pause button, and so, despite the spirited winking of the little red light, no words were taken down.

And Homer Farsinger did not survive the battle to be able to sing his song again.

These words which you now read are my own poor effort to tell the story of Tostig's glory. I have done the best I could for him. He was my enemy, he was my friend, and I betrayed him in the prescribed Khalian manner, and now, to the best of my ability, I have sung his song.

The rest is quickly told. Through an intermediary, I delivered this account of my meeting with Tostig to a representative of the Khalian Poet's Guild.

"It is not in proper metric form," he said, "and it speaks rather more of you than of Tostig. But we are grateful for your efforts. We accept your Saga. Let it be called: 'The Ballad of Baron Tostig.' And let it also be known that you are the only alien ever to invent a Saga accepted by the Khalian Poet's Guild."

He gave me a silver-grey cloak of office, and the pointed hat of a bard. They are too small for me to wear, but I have hung them on the wall of my study in New Jerusalem. When I look at them, I remember Tostig. If that be treason, I stand condemned out of my own mouth.

INTERLUDE

"Markedly strange," Admiral Meier agreed, looking up from the screen at the special investigator. Smythe waited for a further comment but received none.

"Even more strange," he replied to fill the silence, "is the other file I found. Completely different. Almost as if we were dealing with another race entirely, but it was definitely the Khalia."

During the hour that Meier had studied the occupation file from Target, exhaustion had caught up with Smythe. He had been pushing himself for weeks and only by dint of willpower had stayed awake while sitting in the admiral's office. The investigator's hand shook as he inserted a second file.

NARC

by Shariann Lewitt

THE TANDELEISTRASSE ON Efrichen was officially off-limits
from 9:00 P.M. to 8:00 A.M. local time, but the spacers stayed
away even in daylight hours. There was no reason for them to
do so; the Tandeleistrasse was no more foreboding than any
other street in the city, with its whimsical antique lights and
scrubbed steps and modestly closed lace curtains at every
window. The brass knockers were fiercely shiny and there was
rarely anyone abroad. Over several of the heavy wooden
doors were primitive carvings of animals, worn and grained
with most of their paint lost to time and weather. Near the
middle of the street was a door engraved with a giant snake
that looked to be the oldest and shabbiest carving in the
entire area. The colony of Efrichen was only ten generations
old, yet already it was showing signs of wear around the
edges.

Ensign Diego Bach leaned back in the webbing as the g's
increased during descent. If it had been his choice he
wouldn't opt for liberty on Efrichen, but it hadn't been his
choice and he wasn't exactly on liberty. The thin hull of the
merchanter shuddered slightly and Diego tried not to
wince. He was used to the solid ships of the Fleet, not these

ration cans that hauled junk at the very edge of safety. He'd better get used to them, though, he told himself, and the thought stung. Bad enough to be out here on the uncivilized Ridge half the galaxy away from the real action, the honor and glory and chance to distinguish himself on Target. Instead he had to pray that Ari wasn't drunk and would get them down in the pattern, that the authorizations would hold, that the snake would pass.

The thought of the snake made Diego wince internally. "Beautiful piece of work, if I do say so myself," the artist in the disguise section of Intelligence had said as he put the tattooing needles away. "You might want to think about leaving it on. I would."

Leaving it on was the last thing Diego had ever contemplated. Not that it was hideous. In a way he would have preferred it ugly and miserable, not the sinuous metallic violet creature with the sapphire eye that might have almost passed as decoration in the pits of Anares. Which was the reason above all he hated it. There was nothing in the known universe that could render that tattoo anything other than what it was, a passport to the rateri clubs of the Tandeleistrasse. It was exactly the kind of thing a Bach never did, that his father the admiral would call disgraceful, and his mother the admiral would call common.

The merchanter shuddered violently for the last time and jerked abruptly. Diego's teeth ground together under the pressure as the Tobishi Lines System interfaced with the Port, feeding in idents and registrations. He had shipped aboard *Lodestone* just before they got under way for Efrichen, his ident stating that he was an engineer, 2nd class, on the Tobishi Lines freighter *Tompkin,* and transferred to *Lodestone* when Davis was promoted. All very routine, courtesy of Fleet Intelligence which had provided documents that weren't precisely forged. He knew that, knew the documents were good, but he still held his breath as the registration went through. Palming the new ident disc and slinging his battered red flight bag over his shoulder, Diego disembarked, the perfect image of a merchanter on liberty.

"I'll take care of business," Ari had said. "I hate this place, and I'd rather be working than using up liberty time."

Imagine, orders from Tobishi himself. To come here. To pick up a consignment of bacteriological, no less.''

Ari'd winked as they crossed into the union reception lobby and checked into their quarters. No one had liked the idea of liberty on Efrichen. It had been a subject of speculation why Tobishi himself, the owner of the merchant line, should order them into this hell-forsaken place. Diego had started at least three of the rumors currently in circulation among the crew of the *Lodestone* and was rewarded by the fact that no one suspected any Fleet intervention at all.

The union hall was filled with heavy haulers, merchant liners, and skip-runners who were little better than the Khalia pirates. In the gaudy heraldry Diego had studied the few months since his assignment to Intelligence, he could pick out the uv white stripes on the haulers' jackets and the colored belts of the indies. A few turned to stare at him, and Diego felt a pang of fear. Surely they could see what he was under the Tobishi grey worksuit, couldn't miss the bearing and stride that had been stamped into cellular memory.

Keeping up the front was the worst. Aboard *Lodestone* he'd gotten a reputation as a loner. Ari had offered to share a bottle more than once and Diego had refused. He hadn't wanted to. Since leaving Port he hadn't talked to anyone and the loneliness was beginning to eat at him, but he had resisted temptation. He didn't trust himself not to talk.

It wasn't even like he'd chosen Intelligence, he thought as he passed the last of the lobby stares and dropped his kit on the floor of the tube. He'd had his whole career very carefully mapped out. Starting with Junior Weapons Officer aboard a cruiser and sticking with cruisers until he got enough seniority to really make a name in the Scout Fast Attack Wing. There wasn't any going back, and it only made things worse to dwell on the preferable. Now, today, he should have been on his way to Target with the Fast Attack Wing. Instead he was on Efrichen, the boonies of the backwater, and his assignment was just beginning.

The merchant spacer's union quarters on Efrichen weren't exactly sumptuous. Diego found his room was an oversized closet with a sleeping platform and a washroom barely large enough to turn around in. He peeled off his

Tobishi uniform and muttered to activate the lights and shower, both of which came on full force. He caught a glimpse of a stranger in the mirror and nearly broke the glass before he realized that he was only seeing himself.

On *Lodestone* he'd managed to avoid looking in the mirror as much as possible, so the change was startling. The violet snake wound from his right knee around his thigh, slithered over his back and arched down from his left shoulder. The disguise artist had also instructed him to grow out his hair, which now hung in almost colorless tendrils past his shoulders. The two earrings in his left ear had different meanings depending on whether he was being a merchanter or an Efrichen rateri addict. He'd always managed to avoid looking at them before, so the glitter of the jewels startled him. All in all, Diego thought, he looked thoroughly disreputable. His parents would be ashamed if they saw him. Even his old school friends wouldn't recognize him now as the Academy's "Most Likely to Succeed."

He glanced at the blinking green chrono over the bed. He was supposed to meet his contact at the Snake Club just before planetary midnight. If the contact was still alive. The reports had stopped coming months ago. At first Intelligence thought that a courier had been captured. Now no one was sure of anything, only that Jurgen was in trouble.

That was the only name he had been given. At the briefing he had seen two pictures, one of a young officer and one of a rateri addict. He'd memorized the second. His orders were for one evening only and were perfectly explicit. Get Jurgen and bring him in, along with any evidence.

Exactly what kind of evidence they were looking for was unclear. Diego had asked more than once, and Sein had muttered something vague about Khalia incursions into the region. Diego knew when he wasn't going to get a straight answer. It was one of the things he hated about working in this group, almost more than he hated missing the chance to distinguish himself in combat. Everyone knew that the best way to make major career strides was combat, and he cursed again under his breath that the opportunity had been under his nose and yanked away. Maybe when this was done there'd still be some mopping up to do, something where he could really show his stuff. Not this backwater police effort, that was for sure. He still wasn't certain why the Fleet should be involved at all. Two-bit drug running was a local issue. The Fleet had better things to worry about.

Maybe it was a little early, and his instructors had been very clear about being careful on site, but Diego decided that he just couldn't stay still any longer. From the red kit he pulled on silver pants and a loose jacket that opened to reveal the snake's attacking head. The outfit cost more than he could possibly afford on his salary, which was just fine. It reminded him more of his costume for the Beaux Arts Ball, where he had escorted debutantes three years ago. The debs had been silly and the party had been boring. The only good part had been the champagne, and this time even that wasn't guaranteed.

The streets of Efrichen caught him up once he left the union hall. The great stone houses seemed to soak up all sound and he could hear the light hollow slap of his soles against the pavement in the darkness. Above him, soft yellow light wound from behind the closed creamy lace curtains and occasionally he could hear muted laughter. It was quick, muffled, and then swallowed up again in the light. They used antique electric bulbs, lights that only halfheartedly pierced the blackness with a puddle of cheer, leaving most of the street cold and lonely. Inside, against the windows, it looked like a haven of warmth and company closed against the world. Huddled against the night, the rateri, the Tandeleistrasse, Efrichen vigorously barricaded its fiercely middle-class respectability behind thick walls and lace curtains.

When he turned the corner, Diego discovered that he had entered the Tandeleistrasse. Slowly, feeling some oppression from the simple knowledge that this was enemy territory, he entered and continued to walk. At this hour the street appeared no different from its neighbors. He found the club with little trouble, the wooden serpent carved in the door matched the one on his body. It was one of the rateri clubs, the oldest and most established. The inner core, Jurgen had called it in an early report, the club favored by the Khalia and the one delegated by them to handle the precious rateri trade. Softly, hesitantly, he turned the heavy brass knob and entered.

The first thing that hit him was the smell. It was a strange mixture of stale tobacco, half-washed glasses, warm beer, and furniture polish, mingled with heavy spice perfume and the faint bitterness he knew was rateri. The antechamber looked as innocuous as the rest of the street, but Diego caught the soft clicking of a telltale near the second door. The telltale would either admit him or it would trap him. Sein had never said what happened to an intruder in a rateri den.

For a moment it occurred to Diego that he could simply turn around and go back. He hadn't really volunteered for this assignment. Then his hand found the gold St. Barbara medal that had been his grandfathers' all the way back to the Fuentes who had fought for freedom and human honor at the side of Bolivar. He should have taken it off, left it back at the union hall, but here the presence called up all those generations who had served the human cause and drained all the fear and anger away. Diego placed his palm against the talelock without wavering, and without surprise when he was admitted.

It took him awhile to adjust to the extremely dim light and the haze of smoke that permeated every centimeter of the hall. Colors drifted through the cloud. There were human faces and masks, brilliant dominoes decorated with paste jewels and feathers, some painted metallic colors with quasi-Aztec designs.

A woman with glittering ruby hair brushed past him clad in red. She raised her hand on a glass of some pale green liquid and he noticed that her hands were tattooed into five-headed hydras, tipped with gold and green lacquer depicting the jaws and venom. It was beautiful. Diego slumped into a chair at an empty table full of dead beer glasses and heavily laden ashtrays.

The woman turned to regard him suspiciously. "Who are you? I haven't seen you here before."

"I'm a friend of Jurgen's," Diego answered, relaxing with some effort across the arm of the chair. "And who are you?"

She giggled and held out one of the hydras, writhing. "Then it's okay. I'm called Zoe. Jurgen won't be here for awhile anyway. Dance with me."

Diego danced. He felt silly spending so much time when

he should be gathering evidence, dancing with a succession of ladies whose only unusual quality was their makeup and hand tattoos. Intelligence had spent a lot of time and money and so far it all was just like the Beaux Arts Ball without the champagne.

The red hydra-hand fingered his holy medal light and smiled. "You're with the ship, aren't you?" she asked in a throaty voice.

Suddenly Diego's hearing perked up. "What makes you think that?"

Zoe shook her head slowly. "That won't work with me. I know. I've been around a long time. Jurgen trusts me and he knows the ships. I'm glad you've come. We've waited for a long time. Tell the friends that I'm a good friend, too. I'm ready."

Diego permitted himself a small smile. "Just how ready?" he demanded.

The hand at the chain twisted hard around his throat and cut off his breath for only a moment. A show of force. Diego's hands came up independently and broke the hold, twisted the vividly colored wrist back so far he could feel the bones strain before he even realized what he had done. Slowly he let the woman go.

As the medal fell back into place he felt a sudden tingling, as if the gold had carried some electric shock. Just nerves, he told himself firmly. His hand went unconsciously to stroke the medallion, but by the time he touched it the sensation was gone.

She blinked twice and untwisted her mouth. "I know more about the trade than you ever will, even if you are on the first ship. It's only a matter of time. And if you've had a chance to walk around at all you know that Efrichen is ripe. After dark only the rateri friends are on the streets. Go out and look for yourself."

Diego smiled slowly, unpleasantly. "I don't have to. I believe you."

Jurgen, he thought. Where the hell is Jurgen? Ships or ship? Diego was completely lost except for a single salient fact. He wasn't just a narc and this wasn't any old police action. For a moment he wished that he could get Zoe to tell him more, but it was obvious that if he tried to get more information she would begin to suspect his story. It was the contact he needed, Jurgen who was one of their own.

"Jurgen just came in," Zoe hissed, then disappeared into a swirl of bodies.

Trying not to look obvious Diego turned his head toward the door. Jurgen looked just like the picture, the midnight blue snake undulating across his body, just matching his hair in the dim light. A shadow made to work in the shadows, Diego thought, unlike himself who was a creature of light, or at least ash pale umbra.

The crowd pressed between the tables, flowing in its own patterns that swallowed bits of the room and spit them up again, reformed. Jurgen's dark presence was obscured behind tangerine and topaz, wine and lapis-studded draperies. Then the rhythms of the music changed and the rainbow horde swirled once again. Jurgen was now seated at the table just behind his. Slowly Diego's contact raised his eyes from the glass in front of him and met Diego's gaze.

Diego swallowed hard and wished he'd ordered a beer, something to quench the dryness. The eyes that had bored into him had never belonged to the Commander of the twenty-third. Slowly, casually, he made his way over to Jurgen's table and took the empty chair at his contact's elbow.

"Jurgen," he stated. No need for a question.

Indigo lights played in unnaturally dark hair as Jurgen turned to face Diego. His face split into something that Diego thought had once been meant as a smile.

"I didn't know they'd send a baby," Jurgen said softly, then frowned. "I thought I was worth more than that."

"Sein himself sent me," Diego countered.

Jurgen laughed unpleasantly. "That's because he knew nobody else would take the job, I guess. Get some stinking green ensign who can't even wipe his own butt yet, let alone bring me back. Anyone who knew better wouldn't bother trying. Good old Sein. Got to give the guy credit."

Jurgen slid his thumb over the polished wooden edge of the table, following the deeply carved snake and leaf pattern that seemed more appropriate for a monastery or a museum. Two tiny ampules appeared in his hand, flourished like a stage magician with a dove.

"It only *looks* primitive," he said, offering one of the capsules to Diego. "Go ahead, take it. The best there is, perfectly refined, without anything added. No zombie charms here."

Diego flinched and drew into himself. He'd heard plenty about rateri but had never been this close to it. Lying in Jurgen's palm the two capsules seemed very small and innocent. Pale yellow, just like the headache medicine he used to get for the migraines when he took his quals. Fascinated and repelled, he couldn't pull his eyes away.

Suddenly Jurgen closed his fist and crushed the capsules. Yellow liquid glittered against his skin for a moment and then disappeared. "It's absorbed through the skin," Jurgen said softly, smiling.

Diego swallowed hard and gripped the carved edge of the table as the room began to revolve slowly around him. The snakes of wood joined other snakes as each of the tattoos and carvings, embroideries, and paintings came to life. Even the violet tattoo on his own body began to slither across his skin, dry and soft, very slow.

He opened his mouth to speak but no words came out. Only more snakes, feeding off his own death. The woman with the hydra hands. She must have known. And Jurgen was laughing in front of him as the poison struck home, waiting for him to die.

"So I see Zoe already offered hospitality. I should have known. She has such exquisite manners, don't you think?"

The voice thundered in his head and echoed around the room. The club had expanded in at least two dimensions and it no longer seemed so crowded. Snakes, living and writhing, filled all the new space, but Diego didn't find them disturbing. If anything they were an alien comfort, each one vaguely connected to him as if they were both intelligent and telepathic. Happy, that was it. They were all happy. All the snakes and all the people. Both slithered over each other in some rateri-aided symbiosis that rendered the club, the other addicts, and the Khalia all together harmless.

Time itself yawned in front of Diego, and he looked down into the abyss of his own history. Himself at the Port Officer's Children's School, then the Academy and learning how to ski on Volkstaad and experimenting with falling in love with Emily Clarke when they were fourteen. Not looking, really, Diego decided. It was more as if time didn't make any distinction between the Diego of now and the one who was fourteen and ten and twenty and six. All of them existed at once, each one demanded attention and the clamor was overwhelming.

Diego tried to listen to them all, look at them through himself and from the rateri eyes. Together the pictures showed one single, overwhelming scene and Diego was so sad that he was tempted to cry. His whole life, everything he had ever wanted or dreamed had been dry and dull, always perfectly anticipated and predictable. Grey shot through each time frame, the storm cloud topped mountains merging with his cadet-grey uniform blending to the grey water of Lake Rememberance where he and Emily had half-succeeded in seducing each other.

Compared to Diego, to the time held in the layers of glistening polish on the wooden table, the people around him were beautifully vivid. The feathered masks came alive as quasi-human birds hovered over the club and his own metallic snake turned to catch the glitter of the scattered light. The scents that had been unpleasant moments ago fractured, and alone each was redolent of humanity and history and a vitality that seemed to have passed Diego Bach without a glance.

The livingness of it called out to him and he wanted it, like he had wanted a last perfect run down Mt. Coatl, the way he had wanted warmth and food and hot soup, waiting to be rescued. He understood Jurgen now, knew why he had gone over. Ultimately there was no choice, not when he knew what it meant to live like the dead for twenty-three years and to suddenly wake up. Eyes fully open and aware, there was no way he could turn back any more than Jurgen could. It was worth death. It was even worth dishonor. His life to this moment had been the meaningless jerking of a marionette.

In his frenzy of understanding Diego sought Jurgen, to let him know that there was no enmity anymore. But the dark man with the midnight snake had vanished.

In truth, beyond the immediate swirl of colors and the faint memory of music, the club had vanished as well. The

Tandeleistrasse lay against the grey dawn battened against
the assault of those still out on the street.

Diego was not the only one lying on the picturesque
sidewalk under the soft yellow illumination of an antique
streetlight. He watched unmoving as one by one the lights
went out as the day began. Images of the night before
coalesced in his clearing head, and his first reaction was
sorrow. It had all seemed so easy, so beautiful in the club
when all he had to do was reach out and touch the life
around him. Understanding Jurgen had opened him to an
understanding of himself that didn't dissipate with the
morning.

A soft moaning nearby penetrated his thoughts and he
turned just slightly to see Jurgen sitting with his back
against the light pole. In the harsh early light Diego saw the
plain marks of age and anguish mixed with the clear signs of
rateri addiction mixed on his face. He moaned again, this
time nearly inaudibly, and dragged himself closer to Diego.
The iridescent black-purple feathers that hung from the
shoulders of his jacket seemed incongruously jaunty, the
only hint at the gaiety of the night before.

"You're from Sein?" Jurgen asked haltingly, stumbling
over the words.

Diego nodded, unable to pronounce the words. This
Jurgen had a different voice, heavier and not so arrogant as
the man he had met at the club. Then Jurgen grabbed the
light pole and pulled himself up. "Come on," he said
thickly. "We've got to be out of here before the catchers
come." He made a weak gesture at Diego.

Bach honestly tried to get up and honestly failed on the
first attempt. It wasn't like any hangover he'd ever had. His
head felt perfectly clear and his body was absolutely limp. It
took two more tries before he was even able to sit up, by
which time Jurgen was already staggering along the wall,
hauling himself hand over hand against the rough cut stone.

"Move," he commanded sharply. "Don't care how, just
do it."

Diego never did figure out just how he managed to drag
himself to his knees, to force one palm out in front of the
other on the sidewalk, pushing with legs that were one step
removed from gel. He noticed one or two others who were

making as good an attempt to leave as he was, and a few more who lay with fearful recognition in their eyes.

The questions churned in the back of his mind but Diego kept most of his concentration on getting out of the Tandeleistrasse. Just why could wait for a minute or two, for when Jurgen was able to tell him. Suddenly he thought to wonder if it had been the same Jurgen after all, or if in the rateri dream he had seen whatever he expected to see. Only that was too simple, and that was assuming Zoe was far more than what she appeared. *Keep an open mind,* he told himself severely. Never underestimate the enemy, and never assume that because someone appears friendly he is. Or she.

They rounded the corner and passed through the wide wrought iron gate just before the star Efrin blazed over the horizon. Diego glanced back to see what looked like people in blue-grey uniforms picking up those addicts who hadn't been able to move. Only there was something wrong about the people in uniform, something that from this distance he couldn't quite define. They weren't right somehow, that much was certain.

"Let's stop," Diego gasped. "Here." He indicated a pastry shop across the street with a nod. The white and pink and brown cakes on their individual lace doilies were making his stomach contract painfully.

"Won't serve us," Jurgen mumbled without looking back. "Soon."

Soon turned out to be only half a block more. Jurgen stumbled up steps scrubbed a glistening white and fumbled with an old-style key in a brass plate. Once inside he led Diego up the stairs.

It wasn't as pleasant as Diego had imagined the night before. The building was obviously clean, reeking of disinfectant like a hospital ward, and appointed with about as much charm. Jurgen opened another door at the top of the stairs and disappeared in darkness.

There was no window in this room, Diego noted with distaste. It wasn't any larger than his own temp quarters in the union hall and it wasn't particularly more personal either. Which was reasonable. If Jurgen was an addict then nothing besides rateri really mattered.

If it hadn't been for the matter of the ship Diego would have left then and there. He had stopped thinking of Jurgen, whatever his real name had once been, as a fellow officer, an Intelligence operative. Now he was only a broken fool stranded out on Efrichen. The drug weakness was wearing off rapidly now and movement was no longer difficult. Diego almost felt good again, all the more reason to get out of this pit, get something decent to eat and report in. Then go home.

Jurgen flopped on the disheveled sleeping platform and smiled evilly. "I have a trade for you," he said thickly. "Money. I need money, maybe a new ident." He fingered a microreel card carefully. "The reports. Everything."

"I thought you'd gone over," Diego said slowly. "With their ship."

"Don't believe everything you hear." Jurgen said harshly. "They had to send a baby. You can't even keep your fingers dry. Anyway, trade. The reports, everything you and Sein and everyone else wants to know for fifty bigs. In small negotiables, jewels, collectables. Nothing in the system and nothing traceable, you understand?"

Diego nodded.

"We'll meet back at the club. You bring my payment, I bring this. Deal?"

Diego hesitated. "I don't know that's any good," he said finally. "I could pay you and that tape could be blank, or full of garbage or something. I want to see what I'm getting before I hand over that much."

Jurgen chuckled. "Maybe you aren't such a baby. But I'd need security. Because you could run off without paying me and take the goodies with you. All that word of honor shit doesn't mean I trust you at all."

Diego thought quickly, then unfastened the St. Barbara medal and held it clenched in his fist. "This for security? It isn't worth quite fifty on the open market, but it is gold. And it's worth a lot more than that to me."

"Sentimentality. What would we do without sentimentality? It's only one of our weaknesses. That's why we're going to lose in the end, you know. Not because the Khalia are smarter than we are, or stronger, or even meaner. It's because they couldn't care less."

Diego leaned forward and snatched the card at the same time he dropped the medal. It fell against the tangled sheets.

"What makes you so sure I wouldn't kill you?" Diego asked as he turned away. The question had really been directed at himself and he didn't know he had spoken aloud until he heard Jurgen answer.

"The same reason you'll come back for this," Jurgen said. "Sentimentality. And nerve. I'll bet you've never killed anyone, and you're not going to start now. Not the same as a ship. Crossing the line."

Diego left. It seemed longer going back to the union hall, maybe because he couldn't get Jurgen out of his mind or maybe because he couldn't ignore the openly hostile stares on the street. When he returned to his union cubby he tossed the reel aside and spent the better part of an hour washing the bitter memories from his skin. Then he ate a hideously overpriced sausage dish with a respectable glass of beer before he felt ready to face Jurgen's tape.

Three hours and two beers later he found what he had been looking for. And it was worth the snake and the rateri and the assignment to play narc in the backwoods. It was even worth the Fuentes' St. Barbara medal. He played the section of the tape a second time to make sure he wasn't imagining it all.

A Khalian trade ship arrived yesterday. I went down as one of the responsibles in the club. No doubt they were unloading rateri. When we got our allotment the club chief rounded us up to go. I got lost and lingered. Before the ship lifted a second consignment was brought aboard. I couldn't see very well, but it appeared to be a line of slaves. Efrichen don't deal in slaves, not in their listed economy. I watched more closely, and at least two of the consignment were tattooed with rateri marks.

Pictures followed, blurry the way they were when the camera was handheld in a concealed position. But he could see clearly the brilliant colors of the club tattoos on the people nearest the camera. And the blankness on their faces that seemed devoid of intelligence. Enough rateri over enough time, maybe on the right people with the right psychological makeup, Diego thought.

He shuddered. The rateri seduction was still close, still

clinging to him in the shape of a violet serpent that sprawled over his ice white skin. Behind those vacant masks, how many of those new slaves were dreaming of vivid colors and vital activity, he wondered. He could still feel it breathing on his flesh, the need to experience utterly, to throw off the careful shackles of breeding and ambition and lose himself in a universe of sensuality.

He keyed the board absently, losing his place in Jurgen's narrative. The face in the screen flickered, suddenly looking far more haggard than it had before, as if the other had aged years over the course of ten minutes.

The Khalian vanguard ship is due in two months. There are rumors around the club about the "friends." Some insist that they are going to liberate us from the Efrichen Bund government, others say that they are going to level the planet and take the rateri friends away. Still others are convinced that the Khalia are surveying to settle here. My analysis of the various actions of the Khalia in this sector over the past two years indicates that they are searching for a staging outpost in this region. Efrichen is particularly well suited to such use. It is already fully habitable and self-sustaining with a ready trained work force, the port facilities are relatively modern for an agrarian world and in excellent repair. There are large areas, including whole continents, of virgin land for expansion and additional facilities. Only two or three other colonies in this entire quadrant offer as much. What makes Efrichen unique among them is that it is at the Mowbrey point in colonial development, the colonists' first and most violent clash with their own value structure. At this point, the colony is now generating enough wealth for the first time to provide the luxury of dissent, and many of the young people of the colony are disenchanted with the philosophical/ agrarian goals of the colony. In two more generations, according to the normal model, the colony should have gone from primary agriculture to primary industry in an agricultural base, stemming directly from this rebellion in thought. However, at this point the younger generation on Efrichen is excited by anything new, and especially anything alien. They are unquestionably ripe for an alien drug to be introduced. There is no question in my mind that rateri is the first wave of a Khalian invasion into this sector through the corruption of the Efrichen culture and economy.

Diego drew a deep breath as the tape ran out. The enormity of it frightened him. In the back of his mind he could hear his father the admiral droning on, "Your first duty is to humankind as a whole. That takes precedence over the individual." And he could hear his mother the admiral, also, saying, "It is better to make a mistake than not to act at all."

The chrono blinked steadily in the corner of the screen. He had five hours, six on the outside, before he had to return to the club and meet Jurgen. Now there was no choice. It wasn't simply a matter of losing the medal, no matter how much that meant to him. But he was afraid of losing his soul. That was the one thing Sein had never mentioned.

He was trained to kill ships, had done so many times in simulations and didn't doubt his ability in real time. Ships were inanimate objects, enemies that were provided as targets. Faced with the shape and speed of the metal hulk it was easy to forget there were sentient beings inside, and everything encouraged them to forget. Besides, whoever was there, wasn't human. Khalia didn't look like people, Diego reminded himself. They looked and acted like malevolently animated pack animals.

This was different. Jurgen had once had a name, a full name that classmates at the Academy would remember as belonging to the Commander of the twenty-third. He'd had a family and a career, a history and a home planet. He was made of the same flesh and feelings. Diego knew that only too well. The seduction of the rateri dream lay only half-dormant at the edge of consciousness and only an act of supreme will kept him from leaning back and reliving it in all its vivid splendor.

One step at a time. Even in simple terms what he wanted to do wasn't easy. In fact, Bach wasn't sure if he could do it at all. First, he had to assume that Jurgen was leaving on that Khalian vanguard ship. Zoe had implied as much, and Jurgen had cryptically told him about the same thing. Beyond that, he had to assume it was as a member of the pirate band and not a slave. If they took Jurgen as a slave, the whole plan was ruined. Not that Diego knew all that much about Khalian ship design, but he did know that the cargo hold was not next to the main engines and that there were no delicate ships' controls down in that area. That much was just sense.

No, it was more risk than he had been instructed to take. Bring back the report and let the Fast Attack Wing move in the way they were supposed to, that was the way Sein would want him to handle it. Diego turned the thought around and it left a bitter, metallic taste in his mouth. He knew he was tasting his own fear for the very first time and it amazed him.

One step at a time. Being prepared didn't mean taking the risk, not until he was ready to throw his chips on the table. He had never gambled before. It had been strictly forbidden, and Diego Bach wasn't about to risk his career for the chance to play cards for credits. He hadn't known just how terror and excitement would mix to produce this supernormal awareness.

There was no choice but to make the assumption that Jurgen would be at least partly accepted as an ally by the Khalia. That would mean that he would be permitted to watch the FTL acceleration from the bridge, at least if the data on Khalian courtesy were accurate. That meant there was exactly one moment and one chance.

Diego surveyed his wardrobe and pulled on a mud brown worksuit that covered every trace of the snake and hung on his body like an old sack. No way he wanted to be affiliated with rateri or Tobishi Lines or anything else. He wanted to be a perfect blank in the mind of anyone he might encounter. To be perfectly average is to be invisible, so his mother had once said. He hoped she was right. His shoulder-length blond hair would be memorable on Efrichen, where it was associated with the rateri clubs, but he couldn't cut it until after the rendezvous with Jurgen that night. Not good enough. He stared at his reflection for a good five minutes until a solution came.

The microscale washroom did actually have a dispenser for first aid gel, and Diego combed it through his hair with his fingers. The result was so inspiring that he wadded together several cotton balls and inserted them between his gums and lower lip. To complete the effect he took more of the gel and smeared it on the cuffs of his pants. When he was finished and finally satisfied with the results, Diego could pass for a mental deficient. There were plenty of them in every city and they were routinely used for simple errands and routine cleaning work. Maybe it would have been more economical to use mechanicals, but this gave people work and dignity as well as a place in society. It was the sort of thing governments usually wanted to change, but the tradition was ubiquitous and no one wanted to bother finding something better to replace it.

Diego studied himself with pride. He'd never worked on disguise before. In front of the mirror he practiced walking with the slightly hunched, heavy gait he remembered from one of the assistant gardeners at home. It took more than a few tries before he was satisfied enough to leave the confines of his cubby.

The computer-generated note in his pocket had been creased and refolded several times, cash chits attached. He entered the first decent jewelry store he encountered and handed over the note with the money. A human clerk gave him a pityingly disgusted look and then set out to fill the list. While Sein had made sure he was adequately covered with the kind of negotiables Jurgen wanted, no one had foreseen the changes in plan Diego had made. No one had equipped him with the latest gadgets Intelligence had for just this occurrence, and so it was up to him to provide for himself.

Which was exactly what the Khalia wouldn't expect, Diego told himself. Or Jurgen, either, for that matter. When they expect the best, give 'em low tech. Diego didn't quite remember who had said that, but it stuck in his mind. This was going to be as low as it came.

The jeweler returned mumbling something that Diego didn't quite catch and handed over an antique-style watch. Playing the part of mental deficient, Bach took the valuable item and stuffed it into his pocket along with the note and the rest of the money, slurred a goodby and left.

A second trip to a hobby shop was similar. Here the robovendor didn't even bother with a telltale scan as it delivered up the goods. Satisfied, he headed back to the union quarters where he underwent another change back into the Tobishi Lines engineer. It was sixteen hundred

hours. Exactly right. Diego went to the union dining hall as
soon as his hair had dried.

Ari, first navigator on the *Lodestone,* was already seated
in front of a large plate of muffins and cake. Diego felt a
wave of relief. He had remembered that Ari came from a
planet that adhered to a different eating schedule than the
one he had been raised with and always insisted on a late
afternoon meal. Which was probably why he was over-
weight. After helping himself to a cup of coffee he slipped
into the seat across from Ari, who was busily wolfing down a
large piece of chocolate cake.

"You gotta try this cake," Ari said immediately. "Black
Forest cake, they call it. Traditional here. Made with
cherries soaked in brandy and chocolate."

Diego smiled politely and shook his head. The sweetness
of the cake would only make the fear on his tongue taste
worse. "I actually came to ask you a couple of questions,"
he started. "Like, when the FTL Drive commits, it signals
before the safeties are acknowledged, right?"

Ari regarded him carefully and nodded. "And it's a nice
bright green light, too. Funny about that. The Khalia use
blue, I heard. I wonder if that's physical or cultural. You
know anything about it?" A slow smile spread over his
broad face as Diego shook his head. "Mr. Bach, if that is
your name, good luck. I think."

Frantically Diego considered everything he had done in
the past weeks. He hadn't thought he'd broken cover, had
never let himself get into a compromising situation even on
Lodestone and hadn't talked to anyone. Even Ari. Especially Ari. Stunned, he said neither thank you nor goodby
before leaving his full coffee cup on the table and bolting.

Back in the comforting solitude of his cubby, Diego
began systematically pulling apart the back of the watch.
The task was far more difficult than he had originally
imagined since his hands were trembling ever so slightly.
Suppose he gave himself away tonight? Not that it would
matter, he thought. He still wasn't convinced that he was
really going to try out this idiot gambler's scheme.

Besides, it was one thing to think about killing Jurgen,
once a fellow officer who deserved at least the consideration
of a clean choice. When he was only twelve his father had

told him of an ancient custom of Earth, where a dishonored officer was locked in a room with a pistol and a bottle. He at least had the chance to restore his integrity in the eyes of his peers. Jurgen wasn't going to get even that much chance.

Beyond it, the whole plan was filthy, ugly. To blow anyone apart—Jurgen or a slave or even a Khalian functionary—was not in the confines of proper combat.

And then Diego knew that that had all been dreams and stories and school, where everything was neat and clean and all decisions came out in little boxes labeled "right" and "wrong." If Jurgen hadn't put him in this position, if Jurgen had been a proper Intelligence agent instead of a traitor, he wouldn't have to make such a decision, take such a risk. Anger at Jurgen boiled over and Diego hissed his sudden fury like a snake ready to strike.

The back of the watch came off, revealing a single chip attached to a microbattery and mostly empty space, which was exactly what Diego had hoped. The hobby store package contained several old fashioned collector's item dueling pistols, complete with shot and powder. Funny that they would sell things like that on the open market, forgetting just how dangerous such toys could be. Just because there were more accurate and effective weapons in existence didn't mean that a dueling pistol or its powder was no longer deadly. Only that people didn't think of it that way any more.

The hobby shop had also supplied an "eye" that responded to different wavelengths of light. The directions were somewhat garbled and it took Diego a bit of time to figure out how to set the thing on wide-band blue. He hoped Ari had given him the right information, and the thought of Ari brought the fear taste back to overlay the anger.

Taking a deep breath to steady his hands, Diego pried the chip of blue stone from the face of the watch and set the eye behind the hole it left. He connected the low-grade telltale to the battery and filled the rest of the space with black powder.

It was already past dinner when Diego got the watch back together. The thing looked perfect. Better than that, no scan or telltale would notice it. From the outside it was an ostentatious piece of frippery, and on the inside nothing was geared to reading anything so primitive as a powder explosion. He let out a deep breath, not realizing he had held it so long, and leaned back against the wall. Tension flowed out of his muscles and he closed his eyes and let the stress of the fine work go for just a moment. Then Diego wrapped the watch back with the other jewelry and negotiables Jurgen had demanded and changed himself back into the rateri addict of the night before.

This time it was late as he traversed the city. He was not the only addict out on the streets. In varicolored costumes the rateri lovers wandered under soft yellow streetlights. They were bleached out, bleached and black with no color except when they passed under some unconfined shard of light bled by the weary lamps. Enchanted by the flamboyant dress and sparkling chatter, it took Diego several blocks to realize that rateri club members were the only people he saw in the street. The more respectable middle class were all locked away behind their thick doors and lace curtains now. The street belonged to the rateri, which meant it belonged to the Khalia. Diego kept that firmly in mind as he made his way to the Tandeleistrasse, and to a particularly old and weathered door under the sign of the snake.

The club looked different this night. This time he noticed how worn the carpet was near the entrance and that there were burn marks on the polished table. The costumes were still lovely from a distance, the feathers and glittering jewels and filmy silks appearing rich and inviting. Only tonight Diego found himself noticing that the feathers were old and wilted, the jewels cheap glass and glitter paper, the silks and satins the cheapest synthetics and poorly sewn. It was gaiety painted over weariness. His mother the admiral would have called it "tawdry," and for once Diego had to agree with her.

He chose a table and sat, careful not to touch any surfaces with his bare flesh. One thing he didn't want was another rateri dream. One had been rather too much for a lifetime. He didn't know if he could resist two.

Luckily Jurgen appeared before he even had time to look around. Maybe the traitor had been there all along, waiting, lurking in the crowd.

"I wasn't sure you would come." This Jurgen was the

rateri addict of the night, supreme, confident, at ease.

Diego lay his package on the table and said nothing while the other unwrapped it. He was pleased to see that Jurgen seemed particularly pleased with the watch, even tried it on. "For later," Jurgen said as he replaced it. "It would make them wonder."

"Talk about wondering," Diego said, trying to stay as calm as the addict beside him, "I was wondering if you really were going with the Khalian ship the way Zoe thought. Or if it was just a rumor."

Jurgen's eyes flashed. "Why?"

Diego shrugged. "Zoe was insistent. I was curious. Forget I asked. Just give me my medal and we'll call it even."

Jurgen placed the gold St. Barbara medal on the polished wood. Using a handkerchief, Diego picked it up while carefully avoiding any direct contact.

"My, my, we are suspicious."

Diego only smiled, all innocence. "You never know what's lying around in a place like this, spilled on the table maybe. You can't be too careful."

As he rose to leave he felt a single restraining hand on his forearm. "I am going," Jurgen informed him. "Invited to report directly to the Khalian commander."

Diego couldn't decide which was worse, the fact that Jurgen was doing it or the pride that so clearly illuminated the other's face. He jerked his arm away from Jurgen's hand. The touch was burning contamination. The door and the cool night air weren't close enough.

By the time he reached the union hall he had managed to calm down enough to transmit directly to the Fleet sector duty ship, a destroyer named *Bolivar*. He caressed the medal wrapped in handkerchief in his pocket. There was something almost mystically right. Of course it was *Bolivar*. The Fuentes family had always been on the right hand of the Liberator.

The communication itself was a balm, using the proper, safe forms with something of real significance to report. It wasn't until he had washed and lay down in the dark that he realized exactly what he had done.

He had taken the gamble, the risk. In giving Jurgen the

watch he had made a unilateral decision to execute an individual, someone he had known and, in another time and place, might have even respected. That knowledge, even coupled with the fact that he believed in the decision he had made, contorted his stomach and cramped his lungs. For the first time in his life, Diego Bach didn't know whether he was going to be sick or cry.

Strange how the Intelligence Complex at Port felt so much like home. Even Sein's debriefing had been more laudatory than anything else, but Diego was glad it was over.

"Well, after fingering that pirate ship you could have pretty much your own choice of orders," Sein had told him. "I still can't get over how you managed to blast their controls just enough to slow them down so that *Bolivar* could get them."

"Too bad the Khalia blew the ship before we could really take it," he had replied. "I'd love to know exactly how they're made."

Sein, the stone-faced sub director of counterintelligence, smiled for what Diego thought had to be the first time in recorded history. "You aren't the only one. So, what'll it be? I know you wanted the Fast Attack Wing. Not that I won't be sorry to lose you, but you deserve anything I can get you. That's a promise."

Diego hesitated, not because he didn't know what he wanted, but because he was surprised to realize it. Suddenly all his careful career plans, his parents neat flowcharts of his future, took on the grim grey lifelessness the rateri had made him fear. Efrichen had been important, he had done something that really counted there. And he had been truly alive, even when it hurt. Shocked only because it was true, Diego heard himself say, "I indicated that earlier, before I had the experience on Efrichen. I think I'd like to remain in Intelligence, sir. That is, if you think you could use me."

Then Sein did a really unheard-of thing. He actually chuckled. "Ensign, I'd give my left hand to have five more just like you. Welcome aboard."

His parents weren't going to be pleased about this choice. He didn't care. He was pleased. In fact, he was elated.

"Go get yourself a beer," Sein had said then. "Unless you plan to stop by and get the snake removed first."

Diego shook his head vehemently. "I'm keeping it, sir. Unless there's some regulation against it?" And he knew there wasn't, that there was a place for the violet serpent, the signature of Efrichen.

Sein had only shaken his head. "You won't be the first."

INTERLUDE

It was over two months later when the final stages of the Recovery of Bethesda were under way. Smythe and Meier had become almost friends. Not that the Admiral ever completely forgot that Neuton Smythe was a publicly appointed spy for the Alliance Council.

Tonight they'd both worked late and the corridors glowed red. Port was tense because all that was left to be done was wait for battle reports. Half a bottle of fine Michigan wine had helped Smythe and Meier to relax; the carafe sat between them on the desk. Smythe tapped idly on the console looking troubled. Meier waited patiently for him to speak.

"Expanding as quickly as you have, a few bad apples were bound to slip in," the investigator began.

"What do you mean by that?" the Admiral of the White snapped, even though he had tried to keep his tone neutral. For him defending The Fleet was a reflex.

Smythe took a deep breath before continuing. "I'd rather show you. It's a report from one of the planetary levies, just arrived this morning."

"Levies, huh. Never did like amateurs."

"Better reserve judgment until you've seen the report,"

Smythe cautioned. "Some of those levies are pretty damn tough."

Meier said nothing, carefully filling both glasses.

When he had almost finished calling up the report, Smythe added enigmatically, "This rather supports my theory that some of the Khalia's ploys are too sophisticated for their culture."

"Like that drug business on Efrichen," Meier quickly agreed, glad to leave an awkward subject.

"Yes . . ." Smythe murmured as the images formed on the screen.

SOFT LIKE A WOMAN
by Piers Anthony

"Now IT GETS tight," George said. "We're shielded, but they can spot us if they know where to look." He glanced up. "I need a break. Whose turn to pilot?"

"Mine," Quiti said.

"Never mind, cutie," George said. "It's a man's job."

"Listen, I'm qualified!" she snapped. "I've had the same training you had! I'll take my turn."

But Ivan came up behind, his big gloved hand sliding across her posterior as if coincidentally. "Soft like a woman," he murmured. Then: "I've got it, George." Just as if he was talking only about the piloting.

Quiti masked her outrage. Even here on the mission, they were treating her with the contempt they deemed due a woman! She had smoldered under it throughout training and her tour of duty at Port Tau Ceti, clinging to the hope that it would be different on an actual mission. Now she was on it, and nothing had changed. She might as well have been a housemaid.

"Hey, make me up a sandwich, will you honey?" Ivan said without looking at her. "I forgot to eat."

The worst of it was, he wasn't even conscious of the

insult. None of them were. They all took it for granted that she was along for tokenism, if not pure decoration. They did not abuse her, or force their attentions on her openly; they simply did not take her seriously.

There was no point in aggravating anyone right now; their mission was dangerous enough without that. She opened the supply chest and made a sandwich: actually two slabs of hardtack, as it was called, of complementary flavors. Any one slab contained all the nutrients a human being needed, but was too bland for interest.

She handed Ivan the sandwich. "Thanks, cutie," he said absentmindedly, his eyes on the planet ahead. The shield made its outline vague, but made the outline of the scout ship even less clear to any observer on the planet.

"The name is Quiti," she reminded him. "Kwee-tee."

"Sure thing, cutie."

She gave up. He wasn't even listening to her. Well, it was no worse than being called "monkey," as some of her trainingmates had, because of her planet of origin. The truth was that the human species was beginning a new radiation, with subspecies forming in a necessary adaptation to the extremes of their host planets. In the three thousand years since colonization had begun, some changes had been engineered genetically, and some had been by mutation and drastic natural selection, so that evolution had leaped. Somehow all that other people noticed about her particular subspecies was its supposed simian characteristic, rather than its mental one. But her kind could still interbreed with the others, which meant it was definitely human, and no one could tell by looking at Quiti now that she was not identical to the "standard" variant of Earth. That, perhaps, was part of the problem: the men here saw her as a sex object, just because she was young and full-fleshed.

Morosely, she watched the growing planet of Formut. It was the most Earthlike of the bodies in this primitive system. Its only distinction was that it was the closest habitable planet to the neighboring system that contained the human colony of Bethesda, which the Fleet hoped to recover soon. It had two Khalian batteries that could inflict devastating losses on any passing convoy. It was the Fleet's intent to make a diversionary thrust, a decoy gesture, through this system, to distract the Khalia from the main thrust elsewhere. That would be useless if the batteries wiped out the token force at the outset.

Therefore those batteries had to be taken out. This could not be done from space without doing irreparable harm to the planet, and since the natives were not the enemy, that was out. But they could be tackled from behind, as it were: by a surprise attack from the ground. That was the present mission: two five-man ships were to infiltrate the planet and take out those batteries. Then the ships would report and wait for the Fleet to pick them up in a week, as they lacked the power to escape the planet's gravity well.

It seemed simple enough—and it was, if all went well. Each ship had small arms and one plasma weapon. Because this was technically a hostile planet, there were no reloading cartridges; it was essential that the enemy not be able to take over the weapon and use it against the infiltrating party. The three shots of its initial loading should suffice; if not, it would probably be too late.

The loaded weapon weighed twenty-five kilograms. That was why there were two crews of two men each: to haul the hefty one-point-three-meter pipe expeditiously to an appropriate line of sight with the battery, and to haul it away again without delay. Whether there would be pursuit was uncertain; it was not known whether the Khalia had full complements here or merely minimal site crews. If the former, things could quickly become, as George put it, tight.

Their chances of survival and safe return were rated at seventy-five percent. Those were considered good odds for this type of work. The men acted as if there were no danger at all, calling it a milk run (with significant glances at Quiti's bosom), but they knew the risk. They used only first names, not even knowing each other's full names, to protect their identities in case any one of them fell into enemy hands and was interrogated. They were, for all their insensitivity, good men.

Two crews of two. Why, then, was she along at all? To guard the ship. If enemy forces threatened to take it, it was her duty to push the destruct button. That would strand the men and, incidentally, blow her to bits—but the ship would not fall into enemy hands. Would she push that button? Yes; that was part of her training. However lightly the men might take her, they knew she would do that much of her job.

Still, they wouldn't let her participate in the real action, despite her ability to do so. She was by their notion merely a woman, existing principally for the entertainment of a man. The men of the two ships on this mission had a pot on for the one who first managed to, as they put it, ground her. They didn't even bother to conceal this game from her. Each day they each put another credit in the "honey pot." The longer it took, the more the victor would have. There were of course certain rules: force could not be used, and no false promises were allowed. Nine men and one woman: they figured the end was certain, with only the timing and the identity of the victor in doubt. That was her value to them: the challenge. It was all perfectly good-natured on their part. They all admired her body, and said so rather too often. They took it for granted that she admired theirs. They were, after all, men.

This was why so few women volunteered for frontline service. Even when they got it, they didn't get it. She had thought she could fight through, demonstrating her competence, and make a place for herself. So far, she had not been given the chance. Soft like a woman, indeed!

They made it to the planetary surface, and skimmed in toward the objective. The land below seemed to be solid mountain and forest, with no sign of civilization. The two Khalian batteries were a hundred and fifty kilometers apart; their companion ship would orient on the other, so that the twin strikes could be accomplished almost simultaneously. That was the ideal.

They glided to within fifteen kilometers. That was as close as they dared take the scout; they did not want to trigger any alarms. The indications were that Khalian force-field alerts were limited to ten kilometers. That might change, after this mission! From here they should be able to climb a hill and establish a direct line of sight to the battery. That was all that was required.

Jack opened the port, letting the planetary atmosphere in. They had all been given shots to adapt them to the local air, and the ship's receptors had tested for verification of compatibility. This was an Earthlike planet, slightly smaller than Earth but with a denser core, so that gravity at the surface was almost the same. There was enough oxygen to sustain them; it was the trace elements that the shot protected them from, so that there would not be cumulative damage to the lungs and blood. The plants and animal life were similar too, not in detail but in fundamental metabolism.

George and Ivan were the first team. They girt themselves with water and rations, and each picked up an end of the pipe. "Be back soon, cutie," George said. "Catch yourself a little beauty nap."

Ha ha, she thought. Catch yourself some other beauty, chauvinist!

Henry drew his laser pistol. He checked it, then pointed it at the fourth man, Jack. "Disarm yourself, slowly," he said.

Jack looked at him, startled. "What?"

"I am a Khalian operative," Henry said. "I am taking the three of you prisoner. Your mission is over."

Jack smiled. "Some joke! The Khalia don't take prisoners. Come on, we have to go, so we can get the tube back fast when these weaklings wear out."

"Second notice," Henry said grimly. "I prefer not to have to kill you. I'm not a Khalian, I only work for them. Disarm yourself."

"I don't think he's joking," George said. He started to lower his end of the plasma pipe.

Henry's laser swung around to cover him. "Hold your position!"

Jack's hand dived for his own laser. Henry snapped his weapon back and fired. The beam seared across Jack's throat, opening it as if a knife were slicing. Blood spewed out as the man fell, his eyes wide with amazement rather than pain.

The other two men dropped the plasma pipe and reached for their weapons. Henry swept his beam across both of their throats. Both fell, unconscious and dying; the blood pressure at their brains was gone.

Now Henry turned to Quiti. She, like a complete idiot, had stood aghast, unmoving, stunned by the speed and horror of the event. "Disarm," he said.

He had her covered. Slowly she removed her laser and dropped it.

"Out of the ship."

She stepped carefully across the bodies and out the open port. Why hadn't she drawn her weapon and fired while he was lasering the others?

The surface of the planet was lushly green. This was a jungle region, the kind the Khalia liked. They had landed in a long glade fronting the steep base of a mountain ridge; this provided both cover from observation by the battery personnel and a place to land comfortably.

She braced herself to run, but Henry was right behind her. "Make no sudden move, cutie. I especially don't want to have to kill you."

After what had just occurred, she had no doubt of his ability to kill her. Training had been rigorous, but obviously he had had some that was not in the manual. She stood outside the ship, facing away from him, making no move.

She knew she had only a moment before he emerged. Anything she was going to do to protect herself she had to do now.

She put her face in her hands and sobbed. Her fingers pushed up through her pinned-back brown hair.

He emerged, his pistol keeping her covered. "Soft like a woman," he muttered disdainfully, echoing Ivan's remark. He stepped away from the ship, coming to stand before her. "You know the routine, honey."

Slowly she lifted her face, her fingers sliding down across her forehead and her tear-wet cheeks. She gazed at him, her fingers actually poking into her mouth.

"Don't try your pitiful look on me, cutie," he snapped. "Just get your clothes off. Be thankful you're to be a slave instead of a casualty. I won't see you again after I turn you in, so it has to be now."

It did make sense, she knew, in his terms. The Khalia did not take prisoners, they took slaves, and not many of them. They would interrogate her, not caring what damage they did to her body or mind in the process, and use her as a slave thereafter if she remained sufficiently functional. Her self-hypnotic ability could dull ordinary pain but would not help her against the savagery of this. She had known from the outset what to expect from the Khalia; not for nothing had humans named them after the ancient Hindu goddess Kali, dark creature of destruction and bloody sacrifice. Now she knew what to expect from their human agent, whose lust was of a slightly different nature. It was pointless to make open resistance; he would only laser her just enough to incapacitate her, perhaps severing the nerves of her arms and legs and blinding her, then have his will of her body as she suffered. Some men were like that, preferring the writhings of a woman's agony to those of her joy.

She removed her uniform, carefully folding the sections of it and setting them on the ground beside her. She did not take undue time, knowing that stalling would gain her nothing. He watched, evidently enjoying the striptease show as her breasts and buttocks came into view. She had counted on that, and even moved a little more than she had to, to make those portions flex and quiver. She wanted him watching her body, not her face. Her teeth were clenched, her lips very slightly parted. Soon she stood naked except for her heavy military socks.

Henry nodded. "Cutie, I always thought your body was the best," he said. "Now I'm sure of it. You sure don't look like a monkey to me."

She did not answer. She merely stood, teeth still clenched, waiting for his next directive.

"Very docile, aren't we," he remarked. "But I'm not fool enough to take chances. Go fetch the emergency cord."

She walked in her socks to the ship. The odor of fresh blood was strong inside; the bodies of the men lay in pools of it. She used her self-hypnotism to keep her mind clear, treating the bodies as if they were merely meat, and stepped carefully to the storage compartment. Henry kept her covered from the port. She made no false move; she had seen how accurately he aimed his laser, and how quick his reflexes were.

She got out the rope and brought it back. Now there was some blood on her socks; she had been unable to avoid it. But this was no time to be squeamish about details; her own blood, and the success of the mission, were on the line. She said nothing.

Back outside, Henry made her go to a nearby copse of

young trees. There he made her form nooses and put them over her own ankles and wrists; then he had her lie down while he looped the ends of the cords around trees and drew them tight. Only then did he put away the laser and strip off his own clothing.

Quiti was spread-eagled on the turf, her arms and legs anchored by the cords so that she could not bring them in. Still she kept her teeth clenched and spoke no word. Her fit of grief as she first stepped out of the ship was the only expression of emotion she had allowed herself.

"It doesn't make any difference, you know," Henry said as he kneeled beside her and ran his hands along her body. "I never expected your desire, or even your approval; I just want your body, one time. You can sweet-talk me or curse me or just play zombie; my pleasure comes from having a lovely woman who would never submit voluntarily." He squeezed her right breast, then her left. "Soft like a woman," he said again, trying to provoke a reaction. She made none.

He built himself up to a pitch of erotic excitement, his strokes and pokes having the opposite effect on her, then straddled her. He let his weight come on her, moving his chest against her breasts, squeezing the last bit of sensation from the contact before getting into the primary act. He did not try to kiss her, evidently cautious about possible biting. The right side of his head was near her face, the outline of a vein showing as his excitement mounted.

Suddenly her head jerked up. The pin she had clenched between her teeth jabbed into the vein.

His head turned, stung—and her second thrust with the pin caught his right eye, puncturing it.

Now he screamed with pain and rolled off her, clutching at his face. The pain was in his eye, but the venom was in his vein, moving toward his heart. The pin was poisoned; she had held it dry between her lips the whole time, awaiting her chance to use it. Only a tiny weapon, a barb that projected beyond her lips only when those lips flattened against the target, but a deadly coating.

Within thirty seconds Henry's heart stopped. His body convulsed as its other functions tried to continue; then he was dead.

Quiti turned her head to the side, and carefully spat out the pin. It was deadly yet; she wanted none of its coating on her. The riskiest part of her operation had been the setting of it between her teeth; had it scratched her as she slid it down from her hair to her mouth, or had her forced tears wet it so that the venom dripped into her mouth . . .

She had survived, and even gotten through uninjured, though her body felt unclean where he had handled and kneaded and pressed on it. She would have accepted the rape if she had to, to get the proper opportunity to score on him with the pin; fortunately she hadn't had to. She wasn't prudish, but she preferred to indulge on a voluntary basis, not involuntary. Some year, when she found a man who truly respected her, she would show him what kind of pleasure a healthy woman could give.

But she still had a problem. She was securely bound, and could neither slip the nooses nor bring a hand in to untie them. She had tied them herself, but had done it right, because Henry would have known if she had not. She had done nothing to provoke him, because one slap across the mouth would have killed her, had he but known it. She had protected herself and her pin by making no other moves.

But there was one other thing Henry had not thought about. Quiti was of a variant humanoid species that had redeveloped prehensile feet. The terrain was extremely rugged on her home planet, with rugged vegetation to match; man had returned largely to the trees. Genetic manipulation had restored what other humanoids had lost: the ability to use the feet almost as cleverly as the hands. Hence the contemptuous nickname "monkey." Her kind tended to run lithe rather than fat, because excess weight was a liability when swinging in the trees. She really could climb like a monkey, and hang by one hand or one foot.

Quiti, already the butt of sexist attention because of her gender, had not cared to add to it by showing off her feet. Therefore she had worn special shoes, braced to accommodate her feet so that she could walk in comfort, that made them appear normal. She had left her socks on when she stripped for Henry, maintaining that concealment, also aware that that slight bit of coverage made the rest of her body seem more naked. So the man hadn't challenged it; he already had access to the portions of her that interested him.

The feet, unlike the hands, were set at right angles to the supporting limbs. Thus they were able to do what the hands could not: twist back to set their fingerlike toes against their own ankles. First she flexed the toes to slide off the socks; then they set to work on the nooses, loosening them. What a mainstream human could not have done at all, she did readily: she untied her feet with her feet. She could have done it before, but again had wanted no indication of her potential. The man had had to believe that she was entirely helpless. Indeed, she had been helpless enough, while he held that laser pistol!

Once the feet were free, she hiked her body up to give slack to the wrist ropes, then raised her feet to untie the remaining knots. This limberness was part of it; those who depended on trees for support had to be able to take and hold a grip with any extremity, and to exchange grips readily.

She dressed quickly, not bothering with the blood-tainted socks or the shoes; her feet were tough, and it was good to have them fully functional again.

Now she had a job to do. She returned to the ship and lifted the twenty-five-kilo plasma tube. She wiped off the blood that was caking on it, then had an idea. This thing was intended to be carried and operated by two men, but there was a harness so that one man could do both in an emergency. She made her way to the supply chest and brought out that harness. It would add to the total weight of the package, but she needed it.

She put it on the tube, then hefted the assembly to her back. It was an awkward process, but she was in fit condition and could handle it.

The plasma pipe had to be fired line of sight. She was close enough; all she needed was elevation. So she headed up the mountain before her, using hands and feet to draw herself up efficiently. The men had never given her a chance to prove herself; she regretted that they could not see her now.

That reminded her, in a moment when her guard had dropped, of their brutal deaths. A choke formed in her throat. They had been, for all their unconscious snobbery, decent men; they had not deserved to be so casually slain. She had not been close to any of them, and not just because of the sexism; she simply preferred not to mix duty with pleasure. After she proved herself in combat, and had credits of her own, she could consider romance. She could have accepted a secretarial or maintenance position, as many women did, but had insisted on frontline duty, partly because of her need to prove herself and her planet. Now at last she had her chance to do that duty as it should be done. But how terrible that this chance had come only because of the brutal murder of the rest of the complement!

She was soon panting and sweating. The air was pleasant, but the loaded climb was more than enough to compensate. That tube weighed half as much as she did!

She persevered, and soon reached an outcropping of rock that overlooked the relatively level expanse beyond. And there was the battery! There was no mistaking the huge laser cannon, that could score on anything that passed within a light hour and farther if the target was stationary in space. The fleet dared not pass within range of that monster!

She eased the tube to the ground. She removed it from its harness and set it up against a split rock, wedging it into place. She put her eye to the scope set along its top, and nudged the tube until the distant cannon came across the cross hairs. That was all that was necessary; there was no recoil as such, only a blast of light-swift plasma blasting through the air.

She fired and there was a crack of thunder, not from any detonation of the weapon, but from the heat of the bolt's passage through the air.

The cannon disintegrated, and a fireball formed.

Quiti smiled. She had taken it out!

She started to put the harness back on the tube, but then hesitated; it was still too hot. Maybe she didn't need to carry it back to the ship anyway; it was for one purpose only, and that purpose had been fulfilled. She had better get herself back to the ship as fast as possible, for the hornets could soon be buzzing. It depended on how solid an establishment this battery was; if it was a full complement, there would be auxiliary forces patrolling the region, and these would be

searching for the source of the attack. Let them find the
plasma tube, much good would it do them now! Even if they
figured out how to fire it, where was their target?

She hurried away as the sound of the explosion reached
her. What a satisfying noise! It made up in part for the
losses her mission had taken; these were now echoed by
worse losses for the Khalia.

The return was much faster than the trip out had been.
Now she was able to use feet and hands to full effect without
the enormous burden of the weapon. She could clamber
along branches that were too weak to support her loaded
weight, and leap from tree to tree instead of trudging along
the ground.

She hesitated as she approached the ship. Henry's naked
body, its mouth open in the rictus of the agony of death,
reminded her of the slaughter within. But she had to enter,
because she had to make contact with the other ship. They
were supposed to coordinate after their missions were
accomplished, and compare notes on the outlook for avoiding capture by the enemy during the coming week. It could
get pretty tight. The broadcasts were coded; if the enemy
ever broke the code, there would be real trouble. But of
course if the enemy had cracked the code, this mission
would never have made it to the surface of the planet. The
ship's special radio would be a real prize for the Khalia!

She nerved herself for the blood and entered the ship. She
stepped over the bodies again and went to the radio
chamber. She activated it and gave her message: "MISSION
ACCOMPLISHED. FOUR LOST. STATUS? QUITI."
Then she touched the Send key, and the radio fired out a
compacted blip of coded information that only an alert and
properly tuned receiver could catch, and that only a Fleet
receiver could interpret. On a primitive planet like this,
with its nearest base a smoking ruin, the chances were
excellent that the enemy would never even realize that a
message had gone out.

In a moment the radio gave the response, in its machine
monotone: "MISSION DITTO. NO LOSSES. STAND BY
FOR UNION. GOOD JOB, QUITI. LUTHER."

She slumped with relief. She had feared that something
similiar could have happened to the other crew. Soon they

would be here to clean up the mess and make the necessary reports, and she could go back to being innocent, ignored "cutie." Then she could relax the hypnotic block that kept her sane and functional during this crisis.

Cutie. Something bothered her about that. Of course she resented that demeaning nickname, but that wasn't it. There was something else.

She wanted to get out of the ship, away from the horror it contained. But she delayed. What was nagging her? Her intuition, supposedly a foolish female trait, was operating, and she had learned never to ignore it.

Something about the message. She reactivated the radio. "Replay message," she told it.

It repeated the message, exactly as before, concluding with "Good job, Quiti." And of course the signoff of the mission leader, Luther. It was the first time he had complimented her on her work; he was just as bad as the others about her status as a participant. But of course she *had* done a good job; she had completed the mission when the men could not. The compliment was in order.

So what was bothering her?

She played the message back another time. Then, abruptly, she had it.

Luther had given her name correctly. Luther wouldn't have done that. None of them would. To them she was "cutie" and nothing else. Except "honey," or possibly "monkey." That alone was irrevocable, because it was unconscious.

Luther had not sent that message.

That galvanized her. She almost leaped into the "tack" chamber and grabbed several slabs of hardtack. She gulped down water. Then she took a survival pack, stuffed the hardtack into it, and another package of water, and slung it over her shoulder.

She almost danced over the bodies, heedless of the tacky blood her toefingers encountered. She plunged out of the port and ran across the glade, adjusting her pack. She flung herself into the foliage at the edge of the slope.

She continued on up the mountain, her ears alert for the approaching scoutship. It should take it a while to arrive, since it had to orient on her ship, and its crew might not

have been ready for an instant takeoff. But she had to cut
the risk as much as possible.

She made it to the ledge where the plasma tube lay, in half
the time she had taken before. The weapon was undisturbed. There was no sign of activity at the defunct battery;
evidently it was after all only a minimal complement, with
no reserves for the unexpected. That was a break for her.

She hefted the tube in its harness; it was now cool. She
carried it back toward the ship, but not along the precise
route she had taken. She located an outcropping that
overlooked the site of the ship. The ship itself was not
visible; they had of course parked it under the cover of
overhanging trees at the far edge of the glade. The lengthen-
ing shadows covered any other evidence of the landing. But
she had a fair notion where it was.

She set up the tube, aiming it down toward the ship. Then
she waited.

After about fifteen minutes she saw it coming, flying low
and somewhat clumsily. It came in for a landing some
distance from her own ship.

As its motion ceased, she reoriented the tube and touched
the firing stud. The arriving ship went up in a fireball, and
the sound smote her. The range was almost too close for
such a weapon!

Now, belatedly, she experienced doubt. Suppose she had
misread the situation, and Luther really had used her
proper name? Had she just murdered the rest of her
mission?

Feverishly she descended, leaving the tube behind again,
and her pack of supplies with it. She was tired, but the route
was now familiar; it seemed only a moment before she was
there.

The first thing she saw was part of the body of what
looked like a monstrous weasel, evidently blown from the
other ship.

She had not been mistaken. *That was a Khalian!*

Obviously there had been an enemy agent on the other
ship, too. Not only had he stopped the mission, he had
contacted the Khalia and turned the ship over to them,
together with its invaluable radio. That was why they had
been able to answer her coded message. Had she not been

tipped by that single failure of sexism, she would by now be captive again, or dead. Instead, she had reversed the ploy, and taken them out.

She was, then, the only survivor of the mission. She would have to pilot the ship herself, and try to do the job the other ship had not done: take out the second enemy battery.

Well, she was a qualified pilot, and she knew the approximate location of the battery. She could do it.

Or could she? That battery would not be caught offguard; the destruction of the first one would have alerted it. Any alien vessel approaching it would be vaporized in short order.

She considered a moment. Then she got into her ship, went to the pilot's cubby, and activated the system. She started it moving, and taxied it out into takeoff position. She set the auto-pilot for the destination, with a two minute delay before implementation. Then she got out, and ran for the mountain again.

The ship took off without her. In moments it was airborne. It rose to low cruising height and oriented; then it flew directly toward the battery.

Quiti climbed the mountain. She had hardly made progress before she heard the boom of the exploding ship. The battery was alert, without doubt.

With luck, the Khalia would assume that that was the end of her. It would seem that she had lured them into a trap, destroyed the other ship, then set out to finish the job in her own—exactly as she had considered doing. They might send a crew to clean up the mess in the glade, but they would not set out in pursuit of her, because they thought she was dead. She hoped.

Now she was alone, without a ship, stranded on a foreign planet. What was she to do?

She knew the answer. She had a mission to complete. She had to take out that other battery, before the Fleet passed this region. She had one charge left in the plasm tube.

But the battery was a hundred and fifty kilometers away.

She sighed. She would simply have to walk.

First she slept, for night was closing and she knew better than to waste her strength traveling blind. Then she walked. She hauled the plasma tube down the mountain and through the jungle at its base. Away from the glade the vegetation closed in solidly with brambles, spiked yuccas, and thorny vines. She had to don her shoes to protect her feet, but then it got worse and she realized that she could not make progress of the kind she had to, through this mess. She had no more than a week to reach that battery and take it out with her final plasma charge; that meant she had to cover at least twenty kilometers a day. On a flat plain, carrying only her travel supplies, that would be a significant hike. On that plain, carrying half her weight in the mass of the awkward plasma weapon in addition to her supplies, it would be a savage workout. Across this tangled, ragged morass of jungle, it was practically impossible. She was healthy, not superhuman.

An enemy aircraft flew over. She ducked under cover. That was another problem: the closer she got to the battery, the more enemy surveillance there would be, hindering her progress.

She rested, panting. There had to be a better way! She would have to eat ravenously just to maintain her strength, and her supplies were far too limited. She should have brought out all the hardtack, before sending the ship on its doom flight. She was making mistakes, and she couldn't afford them! She would have to forage—and she had not been briefed for that for this planet, as no such trek had been contemplated by the brass.

The brass spent too much time on their fat posteriors, and not enough in the field! Foul-ups and emergencies were always possible; she should have been briefed for every contingency. If she had been in charge—

She shrugged. Such speculation was pointless. They would never let a woman be in charge of anything. She was here, and she had a job to do. How was she to do it?

If she couldn't trek to the battery in time, was there another way to take it out? Yes; all she needed was to establish a line of sight. From the ground, that meant getting close, but if she fired from an elevation, she could do it from here. All she needed was a suitable mountain.

The trouble was, there were too many mountains here! She would have to climb the tallest, so as to see over the lower peaks. She had taken out the first battery from the lower ledge of a mountain close to it, but the farther one was much more of a challenge. She dreaded hauling that heavy tube up the steep slopes! The added weight of her supplies made it that much worse.

But if the vertical distance was small, she could make separate trips for supplies. And if there was a spring or river in the vicinity, she could go frequently to it for drinking water. And if there were edible fruits, or animals she could laser and cook, she could forage. There was an advantage in operating in a set location; foraging would be much easier. She could even make temporary trails, or at least she could memorize the local characteristics of the terrain, so that she would not blunder into anything bad.

There would still be a lot of work, but at least it was feasible. She felt better. Now she could afford to eat and look about.

That afternoon she found her mountain. It was not the tallest in the vicinity, but it was taller than most, and had a fairly nice ridge along the side away from the direction of the battery. That meant there would be few brambles or tangled masses of foliage to drive through. At the base was a spring; she had found it because of a faint animal trail leading to it. That meant that the water was potable, and that no civilized creature used it. (She was assuming for this purpose that the Khalia and their minions were civilized.) Near it was a tree bearing unfamiliar fruit; the presence of scattered rinds and seeds near it suggested that animals ate the fruit, which meant it was unlikely to be poisonous. Nothing was certain, of course, on an alien planet, but the odds were in her favor. At any rate, it was a gamble she had to take. The fruit was fleshy and juicy; she would eat it here, and save the dry and solid hardtack for the upper reaches, as it was structured for traveling.

Next day she hauled the plasma tube to the base of the mountain, not too close to the spring. There was after all no sense in making her presence obvious. Then she returned to the region the ship had been, because she needed the cord that Henry had used to tie her with. It should come in handy in the difficult upper region of the mountain. Also, it occurred to her that the less evidence of what Henry had tried to do to her, and how she had escaped, the better. She doubted she would ever have occasion to use such a pin again, but others of her sex might.

She knew by the smell when she got close. The rope was there, as was Henry's body and that of the Khalian. Flies were feeding, very like the ones on her home planet, and indeed, like those of any planet; the little winged predators seemed universal, with only their insignificant detail differing. She got the rope first, untangling it and coiling it about her arm and shoulder, then went to inspect the enemy more closely. She had seen mock-ups of the Khalia in training, but this was the first actual body she had encountered. She was surprised to discover that it did not look like a monster, but more like a slaughtered pet. Only the hind section was here; the head and forelimbs had been torn off in the explosion. It was furry, with short legs, like a magnified weasel, and about one small ankle was a metallic bracelet.

Military identification? Or jewelry? Could this have been a female, like herself? Soft like a woman? That bothered her, and she turned away. She felt no grief for the traitor Henry, who had mercilessly killed her companions and tried to rape her, but the concept of the alien female got to her.

She knew better than to bury the bodies, of either species, or even to disturb them. That would only make evidence of her survival, and the lack of such evidence was her greatest protection. So she left them, breathing easier as she got away, and not merely because of the clearing air.

Then she heard something. She ducked under cover and waited.

It was a party of creatures, not wild ones. The enemy was coming to this site!

She drew her laser pistol. If they discovered her, she would have to fight.

They passed close enough to alarm her, but evidently were not aware of her. One Khalian, walking somewhat awkwardly on its short hind legs, and two of what were evidently the natives: man-sized humanoid bipeds with feathery scales. The Khalian was clothed only in its fur, but the natives wore uniforms of some sort. But the only one to carry a weapon was the Khalian; that made the relationship clear enough.

For a moment she was tempted to laser the Khalian. She could so readily kill it from this ambush! But she refrained, partly because she didn't like one-sided slaughter—she had seen too much of that recently!—but mostly because she intended to do nothing that would give away her existence. She would kill if she had to, but not unprovoked.

The party went on into the glade. there was a burst of alien chatter. Evidently they had found what they sought: the remnant of the violence here. They were simply an investigatory party.

Quiti used the opportunity of their distraction to remove herself from the vicinity. The encounter was reassuring, actually; it seemed to confirm that the enemy had no awareness of any human survivors. Her ploy with the scout ship must have been successful.

She brought the rope to her mountain base camp, then ate some more fruit and settled into a tree for the night. That was one thing about this perilous mission: the nights made her feel right at home!

Next day she started the hard work. She hiked up the ridge, carrying her supplies and rope. She used hands and feet to grasp the projections of rock, and to get her safely across a fissure that had a solid fallen trunk as a natural bridge. She was not merely climbing, she was scouting out the best route for her next trip. When she was uncertain of a particular path, she climbed back down and tried another. What she could do when lightly loaded did not necessarily establish what she could do with the heavy load. How glad she was for the bug repellant in the survival kit; a cloud of flies followed her constantly, now.

When she found a suitable landing that she deemed to be at the reasonable limit of her hauling capacity, she fixed its location in her mind. Then she left her supply pack, and started back down, carrying only her laser pistol. She did not intend to be caught defenseless again.

Back at the bottom, she ate more fruit, drank deeply, and curled up in her tree for the night. She had to conserve her strength for the next day's effort. She had used three days getting properly set up; she hoped to complete her mission in three more, with a leeway of one. It was always best to have a margin for the unexpected.

In the morning she hefted up the plasma tube in its harness and set out. She had planned well, and made good progress at first. Then the heat of the day and her own exertions caught up with her, draining her strength. She sweated profusely, but had no water; that was in the spring below, and at the camp above. All she could do was rest briefly, cooling a little, then go on.

The tube had been heavy at the start. It grew heavier as she went. It overbalanced her, making her steeper ascents dangerous; she was afraid she would reel and fall and injure herself, ruining everything. Sweat made her hands and feet slide, and her grip weak. She felt like an ant carrying a spaceship up a vertical cliff.

Then a storm came up. At first this was a relief, for it brought down gusts of cool air. Then the wind intensified, as if trying to pluck her from the slope and hurl her down. Then the rain splashed across, making the entire mountain slippery. But she plowed on, knowing she had no alternative.

She reached her camp behind schedule; it was almost dark, and her fatigue had drained her of hunger. She forced herself to eat a little, and to drink a little, and slept. Perhaps an hour later she woke, and ate and drank a little more. She had to restore her body for the next day's effort.

Somewhere in the night she decided to take a gamble. She needed to find the final site on the next day. That meant she could leave the pack here, because she wouldn't need to worry about eating after she fired the plasma tube. Food was just to sustain her for the great hauling effort. She could travel faster without the pack, and would save more strength.

At dawn she woke, ate quickly, and moved her sore body on up the slope, making the next path and carrying her supplies up. Her stiffness eased as she got into it, but another thing developed: itching eyes, blurring sight, and frequent sneezing. She was allergic to something growing here!

No, it was probably worse. All this hard exercise and complete exposure to the planetary atmosphere was causing her shot to wear off sooner than otherwise. She was losing her adaptation to this environment. It struck first in the breathing system and the eyes, most exposed to it, but it would progress inevitably into her system and do more damage there. If she rested, that might slow its progress— but she couldn't rest, because she had to complete her mission.

So she gritted her teeth, this time for real, and plowed on. The implacable slope continued, never ending, always draining her diminishing energy—and she hadn't even started carrying the plasma tube yet on this stretch. The very thought of it increased her fatigue; why couldn't they have made it weigh five kilos instead of twenty-five!

She spared her eyes by looking ahead, noting the situation, and climbing through it with her eyes closed. But she couldn't do the same with her breathing. She had less trouble when she breathed exclusively through her mouth —but what was she doing to her lungs? She didn't know, but decided to operate the best way she could for now, and damn the consequence. If she got—*when* she got the tube in place and completed her mission, then she could relax into terminal asthma. Not now.

Tomorrow was her last scheduled day, to haul up the tube. Today she had to find a suitable site. If she couldn't get the tube there tomorrow, then she would use her reserve day. If that wasn't enough . . .

The afternoon was progressing, and there was no sign of the top. She was climbing pretty slowly now, conserving her strength, trying to take the very best route. But the mountain loomed monstrously before her; she could not possibly reach the top today!

But maybe she didn't have to. If she circled to the other side, and looked, she could ascertain that minimum elevation required to sight the battery over the mountains between them. That would prevent her from wearing herself out trying to climb higher than she needed. She should have realized that before; evidently her thinking was suffering, too.

Yet her thinking had not been all that great before. Why had she stood idiotically frozen while Henry lasered down her companions? If she had only acted properly then!

But further thought absolved her somewhat. She had reacted as any person would have: stunned by the suddenness and awfulness of it. The men had thought Henry was joking; had they realized the truth, all three could have gone for their weapons together, and one of them surely would have gotten him. She had been no worse than they. The difference was that they had been immediate targets, because they were competent males, while she had not, because she was an incompetent female. Had Henry respected her ability, he would have whipped his laser around and sliced her throat too. So it was contempt that had saved her—and perhaps her sex appeal. Soft like a woman. A justified epithet, it seemed.

She found an almost level ledge and followed it around. What a relief to stop climbing!

She had made progress. The mountain was smaller here, so that she circled it much faster than she would have at the base. Soon she was looking from the other side.

The way to the battery was blocked by an adjacent mountain. Its peak rose high enough to cost her another two days of climbing. That was hopeless.

But this mountain was not only taller, but broader than that one. Maybe she could see around it, if she continued to the side. She went on—and realized that a third mountain was overlapping the second, its slope rising as the slope of the second descended, blocking off the necessary line of sight. Damn! The two might be many kilometers apart, but the effect was solid.

But she kept on. When her compass indicated that the bottom of the effective cleft between the two other mountains was in line with the battery, she resumed her climb. Every few feet she blinked the allergetic tears out of her eyes and made another sighting. How much farther did she have to go?

On the third such sighting, she spied a glint. With wild hope she climbed just a few more meters, squinted desperately, and verified it. She had sighted the barrel of the huge laser cannon! How nice of the Khalia to keep it polished! The slanting sunlight highlighted it; otherwise she could have missed it.

Her tiredness receded. She set down her laser pistol to mark the exact spot, and started back down. She wanted no extra weight at all on the morrow! She would barely make it to the tube before dark, but now she knew she could do it. She could take out that battery!

When she slipped and started to fall, and barely caught herself, she realized that she was pushing too hard. Her vision was blurry, and her nose was running so persistently that she had simply stopped wiping it and was letting it drip on the ground. But she had to pay attention to where she was going, and not assume that what she didn't see couldn't hurt her. She had to make sure of every grip, for this was no cakewalk.

She slowed, and darkness did indeed catch her before she reached the tube, but it hardly mattered because her vision was so bad. She pounced on the pack and gulped water and gobbled hardtack and dropped almost instantly into sleep.

All too soon dawn intruded. Quiti consumed most of the rest of her supplies, and slapped on more repellant. This preparation would have to do; she would not be back here unless she completed her mission.

The last day's tube haul had started with a mass half her weight that had seemed to grow to double her weight. This time it started at double. She staggered, and doubt assailed her like the forming swarm of gnats. It was as though each tiny fly was a formulation of doubt: could she make it? "Yes I can! I will!" she exclaimed, making a small snort of determination—and mucous dribbled from her nose. She would have laughed, had she had the energy, had it been funny.

The harness settled into the accustomed sores on her back and sides, and she plodded on. She was proceeding on hands and feet, like a pack animal; the angle of the slope facilitated this, and so did the weight and balance of the burden. So did her dripping eyes and nose; the drops fell cleanly to the ground now, instead of down her chin. She was making progress; that was all that mattered.

But her strength was fading. She knew that she wasn't going to make it to the necessary site; the seeming heaviness of the tube was crushing her steadily down.

She would have to do what she had hoped not to do: draw on her last remaining reserves by hypnotizing herself. In her weakened state it wasn't safe; her body might function, but her mind could start going, perhaps hallucinating. But it was that or failure.

She did it, and in a moment slipped into a semitrance. Now the weight of the tube diminished to its proper amount, and she picked up speed. She felt better, but she knew it was illusory. She dared not squander any of this energy; when it was gone, she would be done for.

She reached the ledge and started the horizontal trek. This should have been easier, but it wasn't; her muscles were reaching toward the point of absolute fatigue that even the trance could not overcome.

Then she heard voices, and knew that her mind was starting to go. It was as if the protein required for her physical system were being drawn from her brain, depleting its sanity. She listened; there was no way not to.

"So you fell for our little charade, eh, cutie? Too bad for you!" It was the voice of her superior officer, the one who had assigned her to this outfit and this mission. "I never did have much faith in you, sweet thing, but the regs say I had to give you a chance, so I did. I sent you out on what we call a sheep-and-goat mission, wherein we ascertain which is which, if you see what I mean."

The trouble was, the voices would seem increasingly real as her strength diminished, until finally she believed them. Then she would do what they told her to do, and that might be anything. For the sake of her mission, she had to hang on to the single shred of reality that guided her to the completion of her mission.

"So here's this soft li'l thing, all dulcet and rounded, and they made book on how and when she'd catch on. They were all in on it, of course; only one can be proven at a time, for obvious reasons."

She didn't believe the voice yet. That was a good sign.

"So when they land, they go into the act. The designated Spy draws his mock laser pistol and makes his move. Will she react in competent military fashion, or will she go to pieces, woman fashion? Alas, she does neither; she merely stares. So he shoots them, and they twitch their chins and open up the catsup vents. Does she act now? She does not. She just stares."

She was rounding the mountain. She still knew reality from illusion, but her certainty was diminishing. The mission—a mere test?

"So he gives her one more chance," the voice continued. "He goes into the Rape Sequence. This is so phony she *has* to catch on. A real spy would immediately radio his cohorts, of course . . ."

Quiti grimaced. She was starting to believe. What was she doing here, hauling the tube up the mountain, when she had failed her examination at the outset?

No! That blood had been real! That attempted rape had been real! She had to believe that; otherwise . . .

"The radio, cutie," the voice said. "How do you explain that? Why didn't he call?"

She didn't answer. Once she started answering, she would be locked into the phantom reality, unable to extricate herself. That was another trap of a deteriorating mind.

Then she reached the apparent cleft between the other peaks. It was late afternoon; the day had passed in a seeming instant, but she was close, very close. The voice had tried to distract her from reality; it had succeeded to the extent of distracting her from the horrendous struggle of the climb.

Now came the hard part: climbing the last short distance. Her arms and legs were leaden, and the voices were yammering at her. Was it worth it to continue? Why *hadn't* he radioed? Obviously the other agent in the other ship had; at least one Khalian had joined him. He should have radioed; that way he would have had the other ship there before he raped her, and—

There it was! He had said he would not see her again, after he turned her in. So he had waited to make his report, so as to give himself time to have his business with her. The Khalia would not have cared one whit for his illicit passion; he had to take it first. And that had cost him his life. Then, when she had blithely radioed, they had realized what had happened, and tried to catch her anyway. The Khalia would have used a translator to speak, not knowing her nickname. So he, too, had lost the gambit.

And now she was there; she saw her laser pistol marking the spot. She eased herself down, so tired despite the hypnosis that she had to do it slowly lest she collapse and not be able to recover. She removed the harness and propped up the tube. The last glinting of the sunlight reflected from the laser cannon in the distance; she knew her target.

"Of course you realize you are stranded," the voice said. "We aren't going to waste a good ship trying to pick you up. Everyone thinks you're dead, anyway."

Maybe she would be, soon. Certainly she lacked the strength to climb back to her pack, halfway down the mountain slope. She had no supplies, no water, and sweat had dehydrated her. She had taken a calculated risk, and she had won: she would complete her mission. She would also lose her life, but she had known that. Better to sacrifice it this way, than by having to blow up her ship and herself with it!

She oriented the tube, blinked her eyes madly to clear them for just this moment, and caught the cannon in the cross hairs. "Let them explain *this*, spook!" she exclaimed. And pressed the firing stud.

She remained conscious long enough to see the fireball form. It was a direct hit! Then she faded out.

"Suck on this, cutie," the officer said, putting a free-fall drink-tube to her mouth. "Slowly; don't choke on it." Then, after a moment. "Uh-oh, I shouldn't call you that, should I! My apology, Quiti."

"Call me what you want, spook," she muttered. "I may be dying, but I completed my mission. You can't hurt me or it, now."

"She's delirious, sir," another voice said. "But we got her in time; her vitals are good. She's one tough lady."

The restorative fluid was acting on her. She opened her eyes. She was in a ship, on a bunk, and her superior officer was holding the squeeze bottle for her. Therefore she knew it was a terminal fantasy. But she liked it; phantoms weren't all bad.

"I don't expect you to assimilate this right now, Quiti," he said. "But I feel obliged to tell you myself, before I go, because I have some culpability in the matter."

She sucked on the bottle, content to listen to the spook as

the strength of the phantom elixir flowed through her. Her dream would have it that she had slept a day or so and recovered somewhat, and that now she was recovering faster. Anything was possible, in illusion.

"It was a setup, but not the way you may have supposed," he continued. "You see, the Khalia were able to convert some of our personnel to work for them. We don't know what inducement they used; that's part of what we wanted to discover. We didn't even know whom the agents were. But we had narrowed it down to a few units, and this was one of them. So we put all our suspects on this mission, and—"

Even for a vision, this was getting outrageous. "I was a suspect?" she demanded.

He nodded. "Not too many from your planet in the Fleet; we weren't absolutely sure of your fundamental loyalty, or of the pressures or temptations you might have. Also, the matter of being an attractive young woman in an all-male complement—there are those who might get resentful."

He had scored there! She shut up.

"Every one of you was bugged. Even Ivan, the only one on your ship who was in on this. When the spy revealed himself—or herself—Ivan was to activate the stun box in his pocket and render all of you unconscious until he disarmed and confined the spy. But as it happened—"

"He never had the chance," she finished. "Henry fired too soon. Ivan was holding the plasm pipe when—" She stopped. Now she was believing the vision!

"None of you had a chance," the officer agreed. "On either ship. Except that one of them did wound the spy, there, so that he had to be put away by the Khalia when they arrived; they have no use for spies whose work is finished and who are likely to be a burden."

"Bugged?" she asked, catching up to an earlier reference. "You heard it all?"

"We heard it all—up to your broadcast," he agreed. "The bugs fed into the radio unit, and it was programmed to emit a coded ball at the same time as it was used for any other purpose. So we got your whole story up until that time." He smiled. "Once the second battery blew, we extrapolated the rest, and came for you in a hurry. It was safe after that, you see; they had no battery to hit us with. Had we tried before—" He shook his head.

"You mean—this is real?" she asked, amazed.

"And I'll tell you something else, Quiti," he said. "Off the record, until it's official. You did a man's job, no affront, and restored the viability of the whole plan. You'll be getting a double promotion, and next time there's a mission like this, you'll be in command. They already have a code name for it: 'Soft Like a Woman.' Others won't know exactly what that means, which is part of the point. There's a new respect for your planet spreading through the higher echelons, and for the capacities of women in the service. No one will call you cutie any more."

She lay back dazedly. "Oh, I think I'll keep it. I don't mind it now."

He stood. "I have other business; got to go. But you know, you are awful cute. I never saw a prettier recovery of a lost mission; it will go down in the textbooks."

"Oh, I thought you meant—"

He winked. "That too. Now get some sleep."

"Soft like a woman," she repeated, liking it. Then she did sleep.

INTERLUDE

Meier was in his office reviewing terrain of the Alliance's landing zones on Bethesda's north continent when Smythe burst in.

"Something's just come in. It either destroys our theories or will amount to nothing." The normally calm investigator seemed upset. "The Khalia have agreed to a peace conference."

"How was it worded?" Meier had his own theories.

"The translation is rough, but basically it says that the house of the Bent Fang will meet with representatives of the Fleet at a neutral location."

"Has it been arranged?" Meier considered requisitioning a gig and attending himself. He had never seen a Khalian, not even one of the rare prisoners.

Smythe passed him the report. The affair had been arranged on the sector level. Two lines later Meier read that Admiral Esplendador was heading the Fleet delegation. His only impression of the man had come from being subjected to an intensive bout of lobbying designed to get the former hero assigned command on Klaxon. Esplendador hadn't seemed much of a diplomat then.

The date at the bottom of the report was the worst news of all.

Vacuum BLAST couriers and bureaucracy, the meeting had already started! It would be over long before anyone with any knowledge or authority could arrive from Port. Idly Admiral Meier wondered if Esplendador had delayed the news to ensure just that.

Then again, if the theory he and Smythe had arrived at was true, this would come to nothing . . . particularly with Esplendador in charge.

KING OF THE BLUE PLANET

by Mike Resnick

LIZARD O'NEAL LEANED back on his straw chair, folded his dirty hands across his grubby shirt, and surveyed his empire.

The empire, such as it was, extended for some two hundred feet in all directions from him, as he sat at its very epicenter. To the right were six small huts, each and every one (or so he liked to tell his customers) serviced by a reborn virgin; no one had ever asked exactly what a reborn virgin was, so he hadn't quite gotten around to defining it yet. To the left was the bar, a huge tree trunk imported ("at considerable expense") from the forest some sixty yards away, framed by wanted posters of the most notorious outlaws of the Rim, each of them personally autographed. Behind him was his royal palace, all two rooms of it, kept together by spit and bailing wire and held in place by pile upon pile of unwashed laundry. In front of him was the Royal Spaceport, a burnt and blackened strip of ground barely large enough to hold six two-man ships at a time, and right next to it was the Imperial Fuel Station.

Beyond the perimeter of his empire there were forests and mountains, rivers and streams, and ultimately the enormous ocean that made his world glow like a blue gemstone in the night sky. There were also placid furry aliens who might or might not be intelligent. Word had it that there was even a desert out there, waiting for someone even crazier than him to try crossing it.

O'Neal ran his fingers through his thick, uncombed shock of red hair, stretched, sighed, and finally turned to the carefully groomed man who looked so out of place in these surroundings.

"You've got your answer," he said, flicking a blue and gold insect away from his neck. "What are you waiting for?"

"The answer is unacceptable," replied Reinhardt.

"So is your proposition."

"Mr. O'Neal, the Alliance absolutely must have—"

"Look around you," interrupted O'Neal, "and tell me what you see."

"Absolutely nothing," said Reinhardt contemptuously.

"Right," agreed O'Neal. "No banks, no lawyers, no tax collectors, no police—and no Alliance," he added pointedly.

"That's precisely why the Alliance needs this planet," insisted Reinhardt, wiping a little trickle of sweat from his left cheek.

"Well, this planet doesn't need the Alliance. We're two thousand light years from Tau Ceti. We mind our own business, we enjoy ourselves, we get a lot of sun and sex and fresh air, and nobody is bothering us—except for you, of course."

"The fact that you're in a totally unpopulated area of the galaxy is precisely why we must have the use of your world for a few weeks."

"No."

"I could *order* you to acquiesce to my demands."

O'Neal shrugged. "Whatever makes you happy."

"This planet is within the Alliance's sphere of influence," noted Reinhardt.

"This planet declared independence five years ago," replied O'Neal.

"There is no record of that."

"Maybe you don't have a record of it, but we do." He gestured to the huge cash box behind the bar. "It's in there somewhere with the receipts."

"Totally illegal."

"Fine. Take me to court."

"In point of fact, we can take you to court over a number of matters, if we so desire," said Reinhardt calmly. "Lizard O'Neal," he quoted, "wanted for gunrunning, smuggling, pandering, swindling, consorting with known—"

"A series of misunderstandings," replied O'Neal with yet another shrug.

"We can let a court of law decide that."

"As a matter of fact, you can't," replied O'Neal. "We don't have any extradition treaties with the Alliance."

"Then I will speak to the ruler of this world."

"You're looking at him," said O'Neal with a lazy smile. "King Lizard the First."

"You are an alien here. I am speaking about the lawful leader of the native population."

"That's me. We took a vote. I won."

"*Who* took a vote?" demanded Reinhardt.

"The planetary population."

"How many ballots were cast?"

"Just one," answered O'Neal. "But it was an absolutely open election. You can hardly blame me for voter apathy."

"I can see that we'll have to add enslavement of a sentient race to your list of crimes."

"It'll take you five hundred years to find out whether or not they're sentient," replied O'Neal. "I thought you needed the world next month."

"We do—and we will have it, one way or another."

"What's so special about this world?" asked O'Neal curiously. "Uranium? Gold? Platinum?"

"This world is valuable to us precisely because it has no value," responded Reinhardt.

"What have you been drinking?"

"Whatever your barman served me," was the distasteful reply.

"Well, you can't be drunk; we water our liquor down too much." O'Neal paused and stared at Reinhardt from beneath half-lowered lids. "So why is a little dirtball out in the middle of nowhere so important that the Alliance is making threats to me, a peaceable businessman who never caused any harm to anyone?"

Reinhardt stared silently at him for a moment.

"Well?" persisted O'Neal.

"I was just trying to envision you as a peaceable business-man," he said. "And believe me, it isn't easy."

"Use your imagination," said O'Neal easily. "And I still want to know: Why do you need my planet?"

"It should be obvious to you."

"I'm sure it is," replied O'Neal. "But suppose you tell me why it's obvious to *you.*"

"Have you ever heard of Switzerland?" asked Reinhardt, leaning forward intently.

"Nope."

"It was a little country, back on Earth, that was never conquered."

"Tough sons of bitches, huh?" asked O'Neal without much show of interest.

"Not especially."

"Well, it's probably better to be lucky than tough."

"Switzerland was never conquered because it was far too valuable as a neutral country." Reinhardt paused. "Warring nations had to have a place where their diplomats could meet, where international banking could be done, where . . ."

"Spare me the details," said O'Neal. "What you're trying to say is that you want to set up a meet with the Khalia and that you want to do it on my world."

"That is correct."

"Well, why didn't you just come out and say so in the first place, instead of making all those threats?"

"Then you'll agree to it?" asked Reinhardt, surprised.

"No—but think of the time we could have saved."

"O'Neal, I have been assigned to procure the services of this world for a secret meeting with the Khalia. I really can't return with my mission unfulfilled."

"And I really can't agree with my pockets unfulfilled," replied O'Neal.

"So it comes down to money?"

"Doesn't it always?"

"Have you no concept of loyalty at all?" demanded Reinhardt. "You have an opportunity to be of inestimable service to your own race!"

"I belong to the race of capitalist beachcombers," said O'Neal, "to whom I am intensely loyal. As for you and the Khalia, you're just a bunch of guys with money for beer."

"All right," said Reinhardt. "What are your terms?"

O'Neal shrugged. "Make me an offer."

"The Alliance can spend up to two hundred thousand credits for the use of your planet."

"Come on," said O'Neal. "You'll spend more than that just getting here."

"Two hundred fifty thousand."

"Forget it."

"And a pardon for all previous crimes."

"I'm never going back. What do I need a pardon for?"

"What *do* you want?" demanded Reinhardt in exasperation.

"Got a pen?"

"I have my pocket computer."

"All right," said O'Neal. "First, I want one million credits."

"That's out of the question."

"Second, I want the pardon you offered me."

"I told you, the amount is—"

"Let me finish," said O'Neal. "Then we can negotiate." He leaned back comfortably. "Third, I want it—in writing —that the Alliance can't erect any competitive bars while they're here. Any soldier who wants a drink has to come to the Devil's Asshole."

"The Devil's Asshole?"

"That's where we are."

"We simply can't have that name, O'Neal. You will have to change it."

"I like it."

"Nevertheless."

"Who's making the rules here, anyway?"

"This is to be the site of a diplomatic meeting. We can't have you calling it the Devil's Asshole!"

"I'll think about it," replied O'Neal. "Fourth, if any special buildings have to be erected for the Khalia, the Alliance has to pay for them."

"Is that all?" asked Reinhardt dryly.

"Nope. I can't seem to get vodka out here. I want

twenty-four cases of top quality vodka. And finally, I want official recognition as King Lizard I."

"Surely you're jesting!"

"Not at all."

"Your conditions are totally unacceptable."

"Well, as I said, they're negotiable. I'll take sixteen cases of vodka if I have to."

"You'll take two hundred thousand credits and nothing else, and be glad we don't blow your planet right out of orbit."

"You'll give me what I asked or I'll mine every inch of this place."

"You can't mine an entire planet," said Reinhardt confidently.

"Maybe not, but I can make the air and water awfully dirty."

"We'll go elsewhere," threatened Reinhardt.

"Fine. I wish you would."

"Damn it, O'Neal—we've only got a month!"

"So you said." O'Neal grinned. "I've done a little math, and according to my figures, if you've only got a month the Khalia are already on their way."

"Only in this general direction."

"And your engineers must be within a day's flight of here if you want the Khalia sleeping anywhere besides grass huts." O'Neal took a long sip from his drink. "I'd say this is a seller's market."

"I'll have to contact my superiors and get back to you."

"I've got all the time in the world," said O'Neal pleasantly.

Reinhardt stalked off, hoping that O'Neal couldn't see the trace of a smile forming at the corners of his mouth.

The Alliance approved O'Neal's terms within three hours.

"Oh dear, oh dear," said the little diplomat. "This won't do at all, Mr. O'Neal. Not at all."

"What won't?" asked O'Neal.

"We can't have our men sleeping in a . . . a *whorehouse*. It would do terrible things for discipline and morale."

"As a matter of fact," contradicted O'Neal, "it would be

the best thing in the world for morale. They'd wake up smiling every morning."

"No, it just won't do, Mr. O'Neal. I'm afraid your female employees will have to go."

"Go? Go where?"

The little man stared at him. "That's hardly *my* problem."

"They stay right where they are."

"Then I shall advise the Alliance that you have broken the spirit if not the letter of your agreement, and that payment not be made."

"Fine," said O'Neal. "You do that. And while you're at it, get the hell off my planet."

"I have every right to be here, Mr. O'Neal."

"I'm the king, and I said Scram!"

"Allow me to refer you to Section 19, sub-section 3, paragraph 21 of your signed agreement with the Alliance . . ."

"Why don't you just tell me what you think it says?"

"It gives me permission to survey the construction sites and—"

"Sites?" repeated O'Neal. "You mean there's more than one?"

"I hope you didn't think we would permit our troops to sleep in thatched huts, Mr. O'Neal!" said the little diplomat, quite shocked. "And of course, we shall have to erect a dwelling fully commensurate with the needs of the Khalia."

"What has that got to do with my girls?"

"Really, Mr. O'Neal, I've no time for levity. And of course the name of your establishment must be changed."

"It already has been."

The little diplomat looked severe. "Satan's Sphincter has to go. If you won't change it, one of our people will be happy to come up with a new name."

"You've knocked down all my trees!" complained O'Neal.

"We can't have the Khalia thinking we have any men hidden out there," said the General, who was supervising the defoliation.

"There's nothing out there! I've been here for three years, and I've never seen anything but a few birds!"

"You know it and I know it, Mr. O'Neal," replied the General, "but the Khalia may not believe it, and I won't have the conference fall apart over a trivial matter of a few trees."

"Do you know how long those trees have been standing there?" demanded O'Neal.

"I haven't the slightest idea."

"Centuries!"

"Then they'll be glad to have a rest, won't they?"

"You're desecrating my planet!" complained O'Neal.

"It's *our* planet for the next few weeks," replied the General. "And by the way, you're going to have to come up with a new name for your establishment."

"I already did."

"I don't know who approved of Lucifer's Rectum, but I assure you it's totally unacceptable."

O'Neal glared at him and began wishing he had put an escape clause into the contract.

"Reinhardt! Where the hell have you been?" King Lizard I demanded.

"Around," replied Reinhardt calmly. "I've had numerous details to look after."

"I want to talk to you!"

"Well, here I am. Start talking."

"This isn't working out," said O'Neal.

"Nonsense," said Reinhardt, staring at the cold grey steel structures. "Construction is actually two days ahead of schedule."

"That's not what I mean."

"Then please explain yourself."

"There are too damned many people here, and your buildings are eyesores."

"Most of the people will be gone before long, and you can decorate the buildings any way you like once we've finished here."

"I plan to tear them down."

Reinhardt uttered an amused laugh. "They're made of fortified titanium with a tight molecular bonding."

"What the hell does that mean?"

"It means that they're virtually indestructible. After all, it wouldn't do to have a saboteur try to blow them up during the meeting, would it?"

"You mean they're going to be here forever?"

"You'll get used to them. And I'm sure your—ah—ladyfriends will appreciate them come winter."

"We don't *have* any winters here!" yelled O'Neal.

"So you don't. My mistake."

"Then what am I going to do with them?"

Reinhardt grinned at him. "War is hell, O'Neal."

"Ready for your physical?" asked the Major.

"What physical?" replied O'Neal suspiciously.

"The Khalia are due to land here in just six more days."

"What the hell does that have to do with my health?"

"It's not *your* health we're worried about," answered the Major. "But they're mammals, and very likely subject to many of the same diseases that afflict humans. What if you have a cold, or a minor viral infection? For all we know, it could kill the Khalia—and we can't have them all dying on us, can we?"

"I thought that was the whole purpose of going to war with them," muttered O'Neal.

"What a refreshing sense of humor you have!" laughed the Major. "Now be a good fellow and report to Building 4 for your physical, won't you?"

"You go to hell."

"You can report voluntarily or I can call the guard, but you *will* report, Mr. O'Neal. Allow me to refer you to your written agreement with the Alliance, page 7, paragraph . . ."

"Now breathe out."

O'Neal, his face a bright red, exhaled and began gasping for air.

"We're just a bit out of shape, aren't we?" asked the doctor with a smile.

"We didn't realize that holding our breath for ten minutes was a prerequisite for being king," replied O'Neal caustically.

"Come, now, Mr. O'Neal," chuckled the doctor. "You held it for barely thirty seconds."

"What does that have to do with carrying some disease that can wipe out the Khalia?" demanded O'Neal.

"Nothing," replied the doctor. "On the other hand, we don't want a reigning monarch to die during our occupation. It wouldn't look at all good back at headquarters."

"I have no intention of dying."

"Well, we seem to be in total agreement on that point."

"You bet your ass we are."

"Therefore, I'm certain you won't mind going on an immediate 800-calorie-per-day diet."

"What?"

"Just until you've lost twenty-five pounds or so," said the doctor. "And of course, the tobacco and liquor will have to go."

"They're not going anywhere!" snapped O'Neal.

"Really, Mr. O'Neal, a man with your blood pressure should try not to get so excited. I think a brisk three-mile walk every morning and evening is also called for."

"Then *you* take it."

"Please, Mr. O'Neal—your health is my responsibility."

"Not unless the Khalia can get high blood pressure by visiting my planet, it isn't."

"This is most awkward," said the doctor. "You are calamitously out of condition, Mr. O'Neal. I really *must* insist that you follow my instructions."

"Not a chance."

"Then I shall have to use my authority, under Section 34 of—"

"You have no authority! I'm the goddamned king!"

"Under Section 34 of the Occupying Army Specifications," continued the doctor doggedly. "'If, in the opinion of the presiding medical officer,'" he quoted, "'there is just and ample cause for . . .'"

"Never mind," said O'Neal wearily.

"It's for your own good," said the doctor. "Some day you'll thank me."

"Don't hold your breath," muttered O'Neal.

"I won't," said the doctor agreeably. "But with luck, and a considerable amount of self-discipline, you may someday be able to hold yours."

* * *

"What now?" demanded O'Neal as Reinhardt approached him.

"It's time for you to leave," replied Reinhardt. "The Khalia are expected within the next ten hours."

"So what? It's *my* planet. I'm curious to see what they look like."

"We can't have you representing the human race dressed like *that!* When was the last time you wore a pair of shoes?"

"What's that got to do with anything? For all you know, the Khalia don't even wear clothes."

"*They* may not, but *humans* do," answered Reinhardt severely. "You're simply not presentable."

"Then I'll get a pair of shoes."

"And a whole new outfit."

"Right," muttered O'Neal wearily.

"And a shave."

"What? No manicure?" said O'Neal sardonically.

"I was about to suggest that," agreed Reinhardt.

"Somehow I'm not surprised."

The Khalia came and the Khalia went, accusations were hurled back and forth, and nothing very much was resolved, to nobody's great surprise.

"Thank God *that's* over!" muttered O'Neal thankfully as the last of the Khalian ships departed.

"I should think that you, of all people, would be delighted," remarked Reinhardt. "After all, you made a million credits."

"I also lost sixteen pounds, I haven't had a drink or a woman in three weeks, my feet are covered with blisters, my suit is too tight, and I don't recognize my home."

"Well, one can't have everything."

"I *had* everything a month ago. Evidently one can't *keep* everything as long as you military bastards continue to play your idiot games. Which reminds me," added O'Neal, "when are you clearing out?"

"I'm afraid I don't understand you," said Reinhardt.

"What's to understand?" snapped O'Neal. "When are you taking your men and going away?"

"I have absolutely no idea. It depends on headquarters."

"But the meeting's over, for all the good it did you."

"True," admitted Reinhardt. "But we do have an option to renew our lease."

"What the hell for?" demanded O'Neal. "You're never going to make peace with those bastards."

"Probably not," agreed Reinhardt. "Still, I don't see why it should bother you in the least. You'll get a renewal fee."

"I don't *want* your money! I just want to be left alone!" He stood up. "Look at me. I'm in danger of turning into *you!*"

"Then you shouldn't have leased us the planet in the first place."

"*You* came to *me,* damn it! I didn't come to you!"

"I can't see what difference that makes."

"Look," said O'Neal desperately, "why don't you just buy the damned world from me?"

"Oh, we couldn't do that," said Reinhardt. "Then it wouldn't be a neutral planet any longer." He paused. "No, we're quite pleased with our present arrangement."

Reinhardt was sitting in the bar of the Angel's Anus, sharing a drink with the General, when the speaker on his wrist beeped twice.

"Yes?" said Reinhardt.

"He's gone, sir."

"He took all his possessions with him?"

"Yes, sir."

"Did you remember to put a tracer on his ship?"

"As you ordered."

"Good. Let me know where he winds up." Reinhardt deactivated the speaker and turned to the General. "A pity that we're going to have to freeze his account. One could almost feel sorry for him, if he hadn't tried to hold us up." He allowed himself the luxury of a smile. "I do love dealing with an amoral man!"

"Where do you suppose he'll wind up?"

Reinhardt shrugged. "Who knows? Wherever it is, it'll be as far from us and the Khalia as possible." He grinned and leaned back comfortably on his chair. "The perfect place for another Switzerland, once this world has outlived its usefulness. I look forward to negotiating its use with him."

INTERLUDE

Rank has many privileges. Among these is the right to hear first both the good and bad news. It also carries with it responsibility, often over events for which the officer in question has little or no control. After Admiral Eronica's sudden resignation, Isaac Meier found himself the newly appointed Chairman of the Strategy Board. It was after his election that Meier realized who would be holding the bag if the relief of Bethesda turned into a fiasco . . . him.

Two sleepless days later Meier hurried into his old office. Smythe, bent over the computer console, looked up as he entered.

Smiling nervously, the Admiral held up a memory chit.

"The first battle reports from Bethesda," he announced. "Thought you'd like to view them with me."

Smythe gestured for him to sit down. To Meier he appeared frustratingly unimpressed.

"The battle report," Meier repeated for emphasis. Smythe had to be as anxious as he to see the report.

"Yes, I know," Smythe agreed, still entering something into the computer. "Here, I've analyzed some bits of it. Let me show you, supports our theory completely."

197

It took a moment for the Admiral and Chairman of the Strategy Board to realize Smythe must have had access to the battle report for several hours in order to analyze it. He was about to say something when the image of a Khalian cruiser appeared on the screen.

TACTICAL INNOVATION
by Bill Fawcett

THE KHALIAN WARRIOR was sprawled over the partially melted barrel of a plasma cannon. Whatever killed him had torn a fist-sized hole in his back. The short, tan fur was scorched and, near the wound, matted with blood. The alien's lips were drawn back in a snarl. The teeth in his short muzzle were impressively long.

Cadet Officer Auro Lebaric found the image made him uncomfortable. Even dead the creature reminded him of the Khalia's vicious efficiency. He had studied too many recent battles the Khalia had won with sheer ferocity for even a dead weasel to be anything but threatening.

Even listening to Buchanon's lecture was preferable . . . maybe.

"To defeat the Khalia, I have created a new tactic. One so innovative, so unique in military history, that it will revolutionize warfare."

Senior Tactician and Fleet Captain Ginga Buchanon was obviously enjoying himself. At the start of the session he had literally bowed, swinging his arm in a wide arc. Since then, every phrase and gesture the staff officer made included some sort of theatrical flourish. Those primarily inspired by the overblown antics of Omni gameshow hosts.

Ensign Auro Lebaric was unimpressed. He slouched lower in the heavily padded, acuform seat. It murmured, adjusting to his new posture. Might as well be back at the Academy, the cadet grumbled to himself.

For the last hour Auro's reflexive boredom had been battling with growing nervousness. In navigation class they had worked out the estimated location of the ship. Auro's pleasure at obtaining the correct answer had been balanced by the significance of the location itself. They were now in a sector occupied by the Khalia, and decelerating.

A few meters away Captain Buchanon finally had reverted to his normal style, a sleep-inducing drone, only occasionally remembering to emphasize some pronouncement with a new gyration. Auro wondered how so many great battles could be made to sound so dull.

The lecture hall was laid out in the traditional sloping half-circle. Each officer candidate sat or reclined in a workstation complete with terminal, an array of recording devices, and a small food dispenser. Every conceivable comfort or device needed to maximize learning had been provided, except a teacher who could hold his audience's attention.

From where Auro sat there was no indication of how this particular classroom was part of the *Hamilton,* a Fleet battlecruiser. It alternated as the briefing room on those rare occasions when there was time for the captains to gather before an action.

Never an outstanding student, Auro had chafed badly under the strict requirements of his fifth year as a Fleet cadet. With two years still remaining until graduation, he had concluded the situation was intolerable.

As the son of an Alliance Senator, he had learned young how to handle people. As a boy the cadet had absorbed negotiating techniques through the same osmosis all children employ to adapt to the alien culture of the adult world. Returning to Novo Veneto he had presented his father with a "decision" to leave the academy. They had spent a long night in heated discussion. At the time Auro was sure that facing his father was the bravest thing he would ever be called upon to do. Finally, his father had consented to use his influence to get Auro an assignment to the field.

Auro had been proud of this negotiating success. Next time he'd read the fine print.

He was reassigned, all right; to a command intern's billet with Admiral "Dynamite" Duane. He had escaped from Port over a month ago, but the drudgery continued, made worse by Buchanon's constant harassment and Duane's volatile temper. The only other change was that he now had to share quarters with three other interns. Neither situation could be judged in any way an improvement over his life on Port.

Buchanon's voice rose several octaves in another pronouncement.

"I have found, therefore, that we have a totally new tactical situation," he paused for a long five count. Taking the hint, Auro stabbed the "notes" button and the last two minutes of the lecture were stored for review.

"The Fleet has never faced an enemy like this," the officer continued. "By their very disorganization and reckless courage, the Khalia thwart most traditional tactics. You will no doubt remember from my last lecture how Admiral Harrigan collapsed the defensive globe of the Abruzzi Federation through the use of a locally strong penetrating attack. A similar tactic was employed by Admiral Stone three months ago."

Auro tensed, he had heard about this battle. Forgetting he was already recording, he stabbed the notes button a second time.

"As future admirals yourselves, you should realize that even negative information is important. The survivors of the battle recovered the command recorder from what remained of Stone's bridge."

The Omni behind Buchanon was suddenly filled with ships clawing at each other. The subliminal murmur, the type generated by any group of bored students, died. On the screen the image skipped from one ship to another as the flagship, the *Morwood,* automatically scanned each nearby vessel visually.

The generally smaller, but more numerous, Khalian vessels were firing constantly at whatever target or targets were closest. The ships of the Fleet carefully coordinated their fire to overwhelm a single ship at a time. This stream

of pictures was occasionally impaired by waves of colors
slipping across the images. This was the *Morwood*'s screen:
only inches above the cruiser's cameras.

In the lower left corner of the projection was a reproduction of Stone's command display. Little blue sparks represented ships of the Fleet; red, the Khalian. Every ten
seconds symbols appeared briefly by each blue spark,
identifying the vessel and giving its condition. On this
display Admiral Stone's tactics were obvious. The Khalia
had formed into a very rough plane, obviously hoping to
envelope the more compact Fleet formation. As they approached, it began to break down with individual Khalian
ships accelerating ahead of the line and rushing past the
Fleet ships, firing rapidly. These did little damage but were
each in turn subjected to the disciplined fire from the Fleet.
Some survived, more were transformed into drifting hulks,
their spark vanishing as they became irrelevant.

Stone had formed half of his command in a similar plane.
The rest of his flotilla was tightening into a cone whose
point faced the Khalia. At the tip was Admiral Stone and
the *Morwood* herself.

"You will note how the late Admiral showed admirable
courage, if less than sound judgment." There was no
soundtrack to the recording. Even if there had been, sound
was not carried through the vacuum of space. The most
violent explosion spread and faded in total silence.
Buchanon's voice seemed loud. Auro wondered if he would
have had the courage to lead such an attack. The war had
seemed more appealing back on Port.

"Stone led the cone into an area where Khalian command
signals were most frequent. Correctly deduced this to be the
location of their flagship."

A dozen ships were suddenly visible as the cone drove
into a tightly formed swarm of Khalians. The *Morwood*'s
screen threw off waves of darkening sparks as the combined
firepower of three dozen ships slammed into it. The vessels
of the Fleet returned fire and the screens of the largest
Khalian ship glowed brightly, and then the ship simply
wasn't there anymore. More Fleet ships entered at point-
blank range and concentrated on half a dozen targets. A
second, smaller Khalian raider disappeared in a flash so

bright the overload blanked the screen.

On the command display the cone of blue sparks slid into the wall of less densely packed red sparks and passed through. It took less than a minute, but no red sparks were left where it had passed.

The Khalian commander's ship was either dead or too badly disabled to register as anything but debris. The ensign waited for the Khalian formation to collapse outward and regroup: the tactic Auro would have followed in a similar situation. Instead, the Khalian formation simply dissolved, each ship attacking those closest to it. The cadet suddenly found his seat uncomfortable and squirmed unconsciously.

"By destroying the command vessel, Stone may have defeated his own strategy," the Tactics Expert pronounced with the sure wisdom of hindsight.

By virtue of being a smaller target, the densely packed cone attracted relatively few attackers. The other thirty Fleet warships were swarmed by over three times their number and began to take serious losses.

On the Omni the visual scan resumed, stars arced wildly as the flagship turned at full emergency acceleration. On the display the cone dissolved into individual ships scrambling to reverse their direction.

Stone's carefully orchestrated engagement had devolved into a swirling melee. In this type of free-for-all the Fleet's superior fire discipline and training were less important than the Khalian's greater numbers.

The Omni filled with the sudden image of the flagship's bridge. Evidently the missile that wrecked the bridge struck somewhere behind the camera. Waves of debris washed past the camera and then hurried back carried by the air rushing out through the hole it had made. As the air thinned the torrent slowed. An arm torn off at the shoulder, its staff officer's patch apparent, floated toward the lens.

The Omni went neutral and Buchanon used his central control panel to increase the lights over all the workstations. His own face passive, the training officer watched the reactions of his cadets.

Auro dragged himself mentally back to reality. He was surprised to discover his palms moist and fingers sore from being clenched in a tight fist. By the time he felt oriented, the Tactical Officer had begun his analysis.

". . . sustaining losses of over forty percent, almost entirely in the chaotic fighting immediately following the portion of the battle you observed. This can only be described as a defeat. We simply cannot afford to trade the Khalia ship for ship.

"Strategically, the battle fares better. The Khalia did retreat without raiding Castleton's World, the only inhabited planet in the system. A strategic victory, but a tactical defeat."

The Captain's voice deviated from its accustomed drone and was suddenly heavy with emotion. "Among those who died valiantly were Admiral Ernest Stone and the entire crew of the *Morwood.*"

Auro made a mental note to sneak a look at Buchanon's service record. He'd bet a month on half-pay in Port the Tactics Officer had served with Stone. Buchanon recovered, and reverted into his typical lecture-voice drone once more.

"I have spent the last weeks studying this and other battles." Once more he paused.

"Out with it," Auro demanded under his breath, "or we'll all be at Bethesda before you let us in on the secret." The thought brought with it a new tensing of his stomach muscles. He realized that he needed to use the head. Perversely, his mouth felt dry. He took a sip of water, realizing that it could only aggravate his other discomfort. Buchanon wasn't ready to give his conclusions just yet. He was obviously enjoying the attention too much.

"Simply put, most of the battles the Fleet has fought to date, and often lost, were conducted as if the Khalia were a traditional enemy. They are not. Their fleets cannot be defeated through any tactic with which we are familiar.

"Through the aid of computer-assisted analysis and hundreds of simulations, I have evolved a novel tactic. Here is its basis . . ." The equations hovered behind him on the Omni and Buchanon's voice settled once more into a monotone. Surprisingly, the cadet found he could follow the logic. Auro had to admit it might even work. That it might, but that he wouldn't want to risk his life on it, was side by side with the chilling realization that they were on their way to do exactly that.

Suddenly there were glaring errors obvious in the Tactician's logic. Only the officer's notorious dislike of contradiction kept the cadet from voicing them. He looked around and the other ten youths in the room looked equally uncomfortable. Somehow Auro found this reassuring, though he would have been unable to say why.

Buchanon rambled through a qualitative analysis of the tactic using the Allisen hypothesis. Even with his life depending on it, Auro still wasn't able to follow the convoluted logic the fabled Allisen had brought to the "science" of tactics. Lost in higher theory, the lecture rolled on to the not very surprising conclusion that Buchanon was right.

The ensign still had his doubts when a Navigation chief burst into the lecture hall and hurried up to the podium. Buchanon paused to read a printout passed him and for a brief instant looked concerned.

"Gentlemen, on the last dropback," his voice was calm, but the singsong cadence that marked his normal delivery was missing, "we received a message torp from an on-site agent on Bethesda. The place is swarming with Khalian ships. She cites a force of no less than one hundred and fifty Khalian warships.

"Dropout at Bethesda will be in three hours ten minutes. Report immediately to your briefing stations." Then he looked up and there was a slight quaver in his voice.

"This means they must be expecting us. May She look after us all."

The command display was anything but encouraging. Even to Auro's inexperienced eye, it was apparent they were in trouble. There were too many red sparks and too few blue ones. Nervously he fingered the communications console, wishing he were back in Port. Annoying, boring, safe Port.

At first Auro had been afraid that people would notice his fear. Then when his stomach had revolted and he had ducked into the head, he found three other men also puking. One had been a chief with stripes indicating fifty years of service. It didn't make the acid aftertaste more pleasant, but the young cadet felt less alone.

The Khalian ships were still sorting themselves out:

several scurrying up from the surface, one large ship that had been in the process of landing had reversed itself with impressive speed and was streaking to catch up with the others. They had to do something about that port facility. One like it on Target had been a center of Khalian activity for months during the cleanup. Between them and Bethesda red sparks swarmed in a seemingly random pattern, a very large number of red sparks. For the moment Auro watched the sparks and was reminded of Windling Bugs swarming on his native Novo Veneto. Uncomfortably Auro remembered the bloated body of a dog which had disturbed a Windling nest. To be stung once was annoying, but rarely fatal; a swarm could kill in seconds.

The cadet kicked the scanner to max range. Bethesda was the only major planet in the system. Through some quirk of evolution the others had failed to coalesce, leaving instead six asteroid belts circling the sun at intervals. This limited approaching the system to above or below the plane of the ecliptic. Their task force was approaching from below. Even here the scan was cluttered with junk. This was, the Ensign decided, a lousy place to end his career. Particularly as he had yet to begin it. His hand shook as he reached out and checked the settings programmed into his com-unit for the third time.

When he looked up again the Khalian horde had begun accelerating towards them, angling away from the green ball representing Bethesda. Trying very hard to look relaxed, Auro wondered how many Khalia manned the ships. With a start Auro remembered that the Khalia often took prisoners for use as slaves. How many colonists would die in the holds of those Khalian ships, destroyed by their own side's fire?

Auro's duty assignment was on the starboard auxiliary command bridge. Should something happen to both the main and port bridges, command of the entire fleet would devolve onto him, Lieutenant Neiburger, four officer cadets, and two Comm chiefs. The ship itself could fight from controls adjacent to the battlecruiser's power room. If they were hit hard enough to make even those controls inoperative, there was a high probability the ship would also have been destroyed. There was a similar cold consolation in that it was unlikely that the main and port command centers

would be put out of action without this one being crippled
as well.

Glancing at the internal monitors lining the wall high
over his head, Auro watched the activity in the main control
room.

Every officer on the bridge appeared to Auro to be a study
in calm assurance. Even Admiral Duane, leaning on the rail
around the main battle display, seemed to be speaking in
hushed tones. His hands moved in a wide arc, emphasizing
some point of tactics to Captain Al-Hakyim, who would
fight the flagship, leaving Duane free to command the fleet.
The ensign had the brief urge to scream into the intercom,
illogically feeling that breaking the silence could somehow
prevent the battle from starting.

Instead he contented himself with grinding his teeth
while trying to count the red blips. He found it was easier if
he thought of them as just blips, not heavily armed ships.

The estimate of one hundred and fifty was visibly overly
optimistic. Either that or Khalian reinforcements had arrived within the last few hours. It was hard to be sure as the
Khalian ships tended to drift about rather than keep
station, but the Ensign finally reached an estimate of one
hundred ninety-three Khalian ships. He was relieved to see
that most of them were about the same tonnage as a small
corvette. As usual, there were no ships larger than light
cruisers in the Khalian formation. The readout popped on
and promised that there were less than twenty as large as
that.

Curious, the Ensign allowed himself the luxury of inquir-
ing of the command console at his side the actual number of
aggressors. For a brief instant the number one hundred
ninety-one appeared. There were less than seventy-five
ships in the Fleet flotilla, the only modern battlecruiser
being the flagship. Suddenly the readout was replaced by
Captain Buchanon staring up at him. The instructor was
frowning and shaking his head in correction. Behind him
Auro could see the walls of the lecture hall. Buchanon was
also visible on the bridge in the monitor overhead.

It was against regulation to use a command console when
not actively giving orders, Auro realized. Old Buchanon
must have programmed that image in; somehow knowing

that he would disobey. Not until ordered to, or after the
other bridges became inactive, was he supposed to input
anything. There couldn't be the slightest chance of contra-
dictory orders being sent out. An error like that could lose a
battle. When Buchanon reviewed his console's tapes, there
would be dark vacuum to pay.

Auro glanced over quickly at the command center, and
there was Buchanon now talking hurriedly with a dark-
haired commander. She was Al-Hakyim's Executive Officer
and kept nodding her head solemnly. Still considering the
size of the approaching Khalian fleet, Auro found it difficult
to become concerned. Demerits lacked the power to fright-
en when there was a good chance neither he, nor Buchanon,
would live to see his next fitness review. The thought gave
the cadet a sort of giddy relief, almost as if their fate was
preordained and he had been released from any responsibility for it.

The muted clamor of the klaxon broke Auro's euphoria.
Both fleets had been slowing as they angled away from
Bethesda, determined to maximize their contact time. The
actual battle would be barely visible to the unaided eye on
the planet they were about to risk their lives to recover. Just
as in the battle against Stone, a few of the smaller Khalian
warships accelerated ahead of the rest. They were just
entering into extreme range. With a sinking feeling Auro
realized that Stone had lost nearly half of his fleet. And he
had faced much more even odds.

The thud of the battlecruiser's forward plasma battery
churned bile up from the ensign's now otherwise empty
stomach. It burnt in his throat. Behind him Auro could hear
Lieutenant Neiburger draw in and hold her breath.

The two fleets approached each other, the Fleet task force
cautiously withdrawing into the defensive formation
Buchanon had outlined a few hours earlier, the Khalia
rushing forward in no formation at all, their eagerness
obvious. Remembering his briefing Auro switched to the
system display once more. For a moment he couldn't find it,
then he found a lone blue spark diving into the system from
above. There were no red sparks left to meet her.

Uneasily Auro realized that was because they were all

hurrying to attack the formation he was in.

Buchanon didn't approve of the captain of the *Haig*'s often unorthodox methods, but the destroyer's exploits were famous even back on Port. The cadet tried to console himself that at least she would have a free run for her secret mission, something had gone as planned.

It didn't help.

After a while the Fleet formation solidified and the *Hamilton*'s guns fell silent. The Flotilla had formed itself into two globes, one smaller and inside the other. Being part of the inside sphere, the *Hamilton* couldn't fire without endangering ships in the outer echelon.

For the next fifteen minutes there was nothing for anyone in the auxiliary control center to do but watch the displays. Except for an occasional curse when a blue spark died, no one spoke. Auro was a bit surprised that nobody cheered when a Khalian ship was destroyed. Then again, he didn't feel much like cheering either.

At this point the cadet was even willing to admit to himself that he was scared. He'd even begun a childhood invocation to Her, but couldn't remember all the words.

Encouragingly the Khalia were losing several ships for each Fleet vessel lost. Then again, there were a lot more Khalian ships. As ships in the outer sphere were damaged, they were withdrawn into the center where emergency repairs could be made in relative safety. Fresh ships replaced them, having an edge on the depleted Khalian ships which hung near the Fleet formation.

Even though it was apparent once it began to move, Auro failed to notice when nearly half of the Khalian fleet and most of their heavier vessels began converging towards one part of the sphere.

Alarms rang as the *Hamilton* and three older cruisers accelerated to support that section of the globe. When Auro felt the throb of acceleration, he realized what was happening. The *Hamilton* herself was being engaged.

The flagship was Duane's last reserve. If they failed to stop this attack, if for any reason the outer globe burst, the formation would split open. There were still two Khalians for every Fleet vessel left, and the Fleet ships were completely surrounded.

Speed is relative. The *Hamilton* was already travelling in orbit at many thousands of miles an hour. Engines strained to change her vector so that now she was racing toward the outer globe. It took less than a minute for them to take up formation just behind the outer sphere. Auro would always remember it as taking at least half an hour. The *Hamilton* and her fellow cruisers were in position seconds before any of the Khalian thrust hit.

For the next several minutes Auro contemplated the near perfect frustration of being aboard a ship engaged in mortal combat and being unable to do anything about it. Twice he felt shudders as the Khalia managed to overload the shielding long enough to slip a small missile through. Both times he waited for the alarm that would announce the cruiser's thick hull had been breached, but it never came. Finally the Khalia's temporary burst of organization gave way under the force of the cruisers' heavier guns. Over twenty Khalian ships, and two Fleet destroyers, had been destroyed in less than four minutes.

The *Hamilton* was actually backing slowly away from the perimeter when it happened.

Following the battle on the display Auro noticed that one Khalian had begun accelerating directly toward them. He switched his attention to the screen showing the command bridge, primarily out of curiosity as to how this comparatively small attack would be handled.

Many of those ships which had first withdrawn to repair damage had now returned to the battle, and a steady migration continued as damaged ships were ordered to safety and replaced by more battle-worthy vessels—a process that had to continue uninterrupted or they would all be overwhelmed.

Later, records would show that what occurred was that the first missile to reach the Khalian ship hit dead center. Rather than destroying the Khalian outright, this split the ship into five parts.

Two parts were blasted into minor debris by other missiles. Another was split off on a vector which carried it away from the battle. The last two, the smallest, continued on the course they had been following. They plunged on, and ripped along the hull of the *Hamilton*, slamming through the magnetic shield by sheer force of weight.

In itself, neither fragment was large enough to destroy the battlecruiser outright, but each was large enough to gouge jagged ditches in the ship's hull.

One of these ditches cut through a netting of cable laid inside the outer hull. This severed the primary and backup circuits connecting the main bridge to the rest of the ship. To Auro's astonishment his monitor on the bridge was suddenly illuminated by crimson emergency lights.

The second fragment hit at a deeper angle and tore through the bulkheads of half a dozen compartments. No one in them had the time to put on and seal a safety suit. Forty-seven men died immediately of explosive decompression.

Seven of these men had manned the port control center.

In the minute it took for control of the *Hamilton* to be switched to the auxiliary bridge, the largest ship in the Fleet flotilla accelerated at a random angle, taking it beyond the perimeter of the outer globe.

Realizing the battlecruiser's temporary vulnerability or perhaps sensing her weakness, a dozen Khalian ships converged upon her. The first few were shredded by the ship's still functional plasma cannon and swarms of missiles, fired from now independently controlled turrets.

The combined force of the ten remaining overwhelmed the *Hamilton*'s shield four times in the next two minutes.

Lieutenant Neiburger was concentrating on the battle display when she heard Auro's hoarse exclamation. As per procedure he tried to call the Port auxiliary bridge and verify it had taken command of the flotilla.

When after thirty seconds the Port bridge had still not answered, the lieutenant began throwing the switches which would give them command of the sixty-one Fleet warships remaining.

It was none too soon. Without command control the exchange of ships between the protected inner and the outer sphere had broken down. Ships ready to return to combat waited, unable to know where they were needed most, while nearly crippled vessels were forced to fight on unrelieved. Buchanon's carefully planned tactic was about to disintegrate into chaos.

With no time to be frightened, Auro also had no time to feel pride for those around him who were responding smoothly to sort out the remaining Fleet ships and reestablish control of the battle. By the time the success of their efforts was apparent the *Hamilton* had begun hurrying back toward the comparative safety of the outer globe.

The missile which struck the side of the *Hamilton* was fired by a Khalian ship which stood between the flagship and her companions. It failed to explode. Because of this it entered the ship nearly along her line of travel and disintegrated as it tore through several bulkheads.

In the starboard auxiliary control room the effect was that of a shotgun firing buckshot.

Auro, at the panel closest to the bulkhead through which the fragments entered, felt several sharp stings, no worse than Windling Bug bites, but Lieutenant Neiburger and the others were all killed or mortally wounded. One ensign moaned and writhed in agony, clutching where a jagged piece of shrapnel had torn away half her abdomen.

It took Auro only a few seconds to accept that there was nothing he could do for the others, and to realize, too, that he was now the sole person capable of giving the orders needed to maintain the strict discipline of Buchanon's battle plan.

The next ten minutes rocketed by on an adrenaline high. Even under hypnosis during debriefing, all that Auro could remember was a feeling of unreal clarity and purpose. The ship's records show that in that ten minutes Cadet Auro Lebarie gave over a hundred commands and doing so was able to maintain some semblance of order in the formation.

At some point he remembered seeing the indicator telling him a second control panel had joined in. Glancing over, Auro was surprised to see Captain Buchanon hunched over a second panel, wiping away splattered blood with one hand while entering orders with the other.

The tactician's uniform was torn and his back was bleeding. Auro was to later learn the wound was caused when the training officer had to crawl through the jagged remains of a collapsed corridor to reach the auxiliary control room.

At about the same time, Auro became aware that his left

hand hurt. He looked down and there was a sliver of metal, perhaps a quarter-inch wide, embedded in the back of his hand. A trickle of blood oozed from the edges of where it had penetrated. When he passed his hand too low over the control panel and it snagged, the cadet was painfully informed that the sliver stuck out on both sides.

He forgot about it again while directing assistance to a cruiser being hard pressed by four of the larger Khalian ships, these being nearly all of the larger ships the weasels had left.

The splinter was still in place when the relief team from the bridge cut its way in.

It hurt like hell when the medic took it and three others in Auro's back out.

By the time the cadet was able to return to the bridge, it was apparent the battle had ended. The throb of emergency power and thud of plasma cannons had been replaced by the hum of well-tuned sub-light engines.

Auro didn't need a battle report to know they must have won.

He was still alive.

It felt good.

INTERLUDE

"The Khalia are definitely a classic barbarian culture." Smythe scanned the faces of the Strategy Board. More than half of the admirals gathered at the table looked surprised. They had expected a speech by the Special Investigator for Fleet Affairs, but this wasn't it.

"As you know, I have spent the last five months examining the records of nearly every contact we have had with the Khalians." Smythe paused for emphasis. "During this time I have also consulted with experts from half a dozen planets."

At this Meier looked surprised as well. He had no report of Smythe receiving any off-planet communications.

"The conclusions are inescapable," the investigator continued. At the head of the table Admiral Meier offered a supporting smile.

"The Khalian culture is incapable of creating the ships or weapons they currently employ. We are not even sure how they manage to service or repair what they have."

"They most certainly can fight them!" protested an admiral who had once lost half his command.

Smythe nodded knowingly. "The number of ships the Khalia operate is limited to a few types but number in the thousands. Their design is based on technology similar to ours, obviously derived from that of the old imperium. The question then, is, where did they get them?"

"Or where *do* they get them?" Meier interjected.

This time Smythe nodded approvingly. Around the table, admirals muttered suggestions, most impossible, one obscene.

When silence had returned Smythe finished with a flourish. "We don't know how the Khalia gained their ships. Finding out may be the key to victory."

His voice softened. "Let's hope that the landings on Bethesda furnish some answers. That is, if they succeed . . ."

NEEDS MUST

by Janet Morris

As THE ALLIANCE destroyer *Haig* braked through ASD toward a flyby of Bethesda, Lieutenant Tolliver English was receiving the worst briefing of his life.

Everybody in the *Haig*'s situation room knew the score, so neither of the others was really shocked when Toby English stood up, his blue eyes blazing and said, "You call this a situation report, Commander Padova? The whole Ninety-Second Marine Reaction Company's going to drop onto that weasel-infested shitball of a planet, and this is all I can tell them?" He crumpled the single sheet of hard copy on the conference table before him and leaned over it, toward the destroyer's commander, the situation report lost in his fist.

Jay Padova looked back at his line officer emotionlessly, then turned slowly to the ship's intelligence officer. "Johanna, have you got anything else for him?"

Johanna Manning slapped down the lid of her porta-base decisively. "Not for general distribution, sir," she told the commander, her sharp face showing strain under its short-cropped hair.

English looked at the woman who outranked him by a full grade and said, "Map number, flora and fauna, spaceport coordinates, and hit orders—that's *it?* No target acquisition data? No topo scans? No tech parameters? You don't even know what the enemy troop strength is down there, and you call yourself an intelligence officer?" His voice was so dangerous that the woman pushed back her chair and came out of it.

"Mister," she said wearily, "marines aren't supposed to think; they're supposed to fight. You want guesses? I'll give you guesses—*off the record,* and not for dissemination among your troops."

"Great," said English, crossing his arms, still holding the crumpled situation report. "Let's hear 'em."

"Fine, Lieutenant," said Manning, her lips pinched from the effort it took to keep her temper. "Enemy strength may be four to one over the indigs, where you're going. Khalian ships at the port, ground intelligence thinks, number about twenty scramble fighters, plus three destroyer class. Electromagnetic/optical shielding over the port makes spaceborne reconnaissance unreliable, Mister. You hear it, don't count on it. What I'm telling you is all there is that's verifiable—all we've got that's worth hearing."

"It ain't enough, not when we're risking—"

The woman interrupted him with all the skill of a winning desk jockey. "What JCSOPSCOM wants is for you to get into that port. Blow the small stuff if you can, even though they're reveted, if you're looking for brownie points, or as a diversionary action if it seems appropriate. But *before you leave the area,* you take care of those three destroyers—get one of their fusion bottles to cook off maybe, with a delayed-fuse, shaped charge—we'll give you whatever we've got. Or find another way; how you do it, lieutenant, is up to you. But if you want off that drop zone, you *do* it. You've got an extraction point and a two-hour time-coordinate fuck-factor. Better than that, you oughtn't to need."

Manning had outright threatened him—on reflection, not him alone, but his entire company. English had only two choices: reach across the table and strangle the briefer in mute protest, or sit down. With Padova there, he sat down, telling himself he must have misheard her, or misinterpreted what she'd said.

His mind replayed her words: *But if you want off that drop zone,* she'd said—a pure and mortal threat. He'd never dreamed that JCSOPSCOM—Joint Chiefs of Staff Operations Command—would be that overt. His men weren't convicts or conscripts, they were highly trained reaction marines—fifty of them. English could feel the flush creeping up his neck as he considered formally protesting the mission on the grounds that it was suicide.

He'd have to do it anyway, of course—or his men would, with a different line officer. Now English knew why the Ninety-Second's task force commander wasn't present at the briefing. Nobody at Alliance HQ wanted nonparticipating witnesses, or more privy parties than absolutely necessary, in case something went wrong.

So it was just English in the situation room tonight, with the lady officer named Manning, and Padova. And Jay wasn't saying word one.

There were good reasons to lodge a protest—go on the record, so that any casualties his company sustained had a better chance of recourse, higher disability pay, or pension credit. If anybody ever saw the record on this one.

But since English was pretty sure nobody ever would, especially if his boys never got extracted, he didn't try it. He said instead, as scathingly as he could manage, "Let me get this straight. You want me to drop with fifty marines onto a hostile planet where the Khalia have a major base, with no logistical support whatsoever, take out a whole spaceport, if possible by causing a nuclear explosion that'll trash everything within a klick, and hike ten klicks to an unmarked extraction site in pitch dark with *two hours leeway?* You sure you *want* us to come back?"

"I'm not sure that's a relevant question," said the briefer, still standing, who picked up her porta-base and turned to Padova. "With your permission, sir? I've got other work to do."

"Dismissed, Manning," said Padova, and reached for a cigar as Manning charged the door. Its electronics scrambled to move the panel from her path before she bashed into it. After two deep puffs, Padova looked through curling blue smoke at English and said, "Well, Toby, this is your big chance. Anything special you'd like from the non-regulation pool?"

Padova's eyes glittered when he mentioned the "special" equipment that the *Haig* carried. Because of Jay Padova, the *Haig* was the fightingest destroyer in the Alliance flotilla; she had electrointelligent mods that were so aftermarket as to be borderline illegal. But it made the little destroyer one monster of a fighting machine, and every man aboard her was as proud of their regulation-skirting commander as of the things their vessel could do.

"This is my big chance at what?" English's head came up defiantly. "A posthumous medal? I already *got* the longest coup-coat in this outfit, and another few weasel tails ain't worth what this go's going to cost."

"Chance at promotion. You're functioning at task force command level on this one; pull this off, and I'll see you get the paycheck and the rating to match."

That was nice. English had to admit that Padova was one hell of a psychologist. English knew better than to ask how come the regular task force commander wasn't in on the briefing for this one. In this outfit, you didn't ask questions if you knew the answers, especially when the answers were affirmations that the *Haig* was way out on a limb all by her lonesome again—so far and so lonely that she'd either get a commendation or a condemnation in the aftermath of the operation on Bethesda.

These kinds of missions were Jason Padova's stock-in-trade, and English had known that when he'd jockeyed for a berth with the paunchy, cigar-smoking, tactical genius who was still waiting for a relevant response from English to his offer of promotion.

"You know, sir, six months ago I was standing down on Budweiser, and some guy in a bar was telling me how he'd been out here in ASD, dropping a dozen hardware specialists and some penetration agents. How come, you think, that wasn't in Manning's report?"

"You know, if you weren't so damned useful where you are, English, I'd desk your butt. You're too smart to be a marine. I was about to explain that . . ."

"Hold on." English raised a palm to politely forestall the

part of his briefing so secret that Manning wasn't privy to it.
"Before we get to the ears-only, I want to take you up on
your 'special tech' offer. I'd really like a no-see-em for the
drop, sir. And a matching APC to get to the extraction
point. Ain't no need to have every weasel on Bethesda
running around the woods with their nostrils open, looking
for air-dropped marines. How about you make this look like
a high recon overflight, and let us coast in on the diversion
cone?"

"I was going to suggest it myself, if you didn't ask," said
Jay Padova, turning his cigar in his fingers. "And as for
whatever else you think of later, you'll find blank, signed
requisition orders waiting for you with the pool sergeant."

That way, Padova could always claim, if things went bad,
he hadn't known what English was doing—not really. The
more Toby English found out about this mission, the more
he disliked it. If he'd had living kin, he would have made a
will.

But he didn't, and Jay Padova was telling him about the
"infrastructure" of infiltrators that shouldn't have been on
Bethesda, a whole bunch of on-the-spot (o.t.s.) agents who'd
get with him on the ground with ready support, guidance,
and maybe some diversionary capability.

"Diversionary?" Toby asked Padova. "Shouldn't infiltration agents be conserved?"

"These are, I'm told, expendable," said Padova bluntly.
"More expendable than your marines."

"Nice to know somebody is. Want 'em lifted out, if we
can, before the cook-off?"

"No. The Fleet's coming in, full strength, after we take
out the spaceport and its big guns. They'll need the o.t.s.
contingent right where they are."

English left that meeting wondering whether he, a poor
misguided marine lieutenant from Eire, hadn't been leading
his whole life under mistaken assumptions and false pre-
tenses. He was feeling like a babe in arms, a naive kid from
the sticks; he'd been exterminating weasels for most of his
adult life, and he thought of himself as a hardened, sea-
soned veteran—until now.

What bothered him wasn't just that the Ninety-Second
Marine Reaction Company had suddenly become overtly

expendable; it was the brass's willingness to cash out their groundside agents, rather than boost them. They must want that spaceport something fierce, back at JCSOPSCOM, to be willing to sacrifice agents put in place at such great risk and cost. Because that was what would happen: once the port was blown, whatever humans were left on Bethesda were going to bear the brunt of weasel wrath. And weasel wrath was a whole lot worse than dying of a big bang.

As English was riding the elevator down alone from the command pod to the requisitions bay, it hit him: this wasn't just about destroying a spaceport, it was about pisspoor performance on the part of penetration personnel. It was about intelligence failure on a pretty massive scale. And whatever screwup this mission was covering up, nobody really wanted those penetration agents, those poor o.t.s. people and the OPSCOM agents running them, back alive —or back any way at all. It had been clear as targeting data in Jay Padova's eyes.

And it had been clearly missing from the single page situation report he'd uncrumpled and now had in his pocket. As far as JCSOPSCOM was concerned, those fools on Bethesda were already dead. Or ought to be. Nobody was going to thank the Ninety-Second for opening a closet full of spook-type skeletons. One thing English had learned about this man's Corps was that when they didn't tell you something, they meant just what they hadn't said.

So Padova giving him so much off-the-record leeway had to mean that the old man didn't agree with his own orders.

Damn, this one was going to be lots more complicated than point and shoot.

The no-see-em was just what its name implied: a troop transport with onboard countermeasures including electro-optical shielding and signature suppressors. If it was true that the Khalia couldn't detect light cones from a planetary source, and had no spaceborne snoopsats, then maybe the Ninety-Second didn't need to risk their ultra-secret, non-reg, tricked-up APC hauler. But you never knew what was true about the enemy's capabilities.

You didn't even know what was true about your own. The

no-see-em AI ate any waveform bounced at it, and substituted whatever an unremarkable response might be: if there was an expected return signal that the no-see-em was blocking, it would simulate that response. So if you were coasting down between mountain ranges, the no-see-em showed the mountain range it was blocking to any questing source.

The one trouble spot was heat from plasma burns, and theoretically the no-see-em could fake up enough data to fool anything but the naked eye. If nobody was watching, the no-see-em transport in glider mode would be invisible to surveillance until it burned on out of the atmosphere of Bethesda, long after it had dropped its no-see-em APC with surgical precision, nine point nine clicks from the targeted spaceport.

Overflying the spaceport itself was just crazy enough to work, and the Ninety-Second was doing it for a good reason: their own AIs needed target acquisition data that wasn't hearsay, and with the electromagnetic shield up over the port, they were counting on the blindband swath the Khalian shield created at one hundred thousand feet, where the shield's effect arc was polarizing.

It was a weird feeling, flying a silent, non-burn glide arc right over the enemy's head, in so close that cameras could see what looked like gun positions, when a half-mile above, you couldn't see a damned thing, and a half-mile below, you'd be auto-tracked, acquired, and blown out of the sky in less time than it took to realize you'd dipped too low.

Nobody so much as breathed in the APC's bay. Every one of English's men was clamshelled and helmeted and locked and loaded. The dropmaster had his checklist in hand, but wasn't checking anything. The first sergeant was ready to hand out plasma launchers and smart shoulder-borne missile tubes, but he wasn't moving either.

Everybody watched his chronometer; the recon-helmeted dozen had their faceshields down, monitoring the transport's progress in the same way English was doing.

If you lived with this gear long enough, you learned how to use it to its fullest advantage. English was seeing everything the pilot up front was seeing, and a split view of what the photo returns were picking up: close-in shots of the spaceport below.

No photo could tell you if the guns were real or cardboard or papier-mâché, though. Signature-seekers would have alerted countermeasures in the port area, the way tickling a weasel's whiskers would wake him up.

So they didn't do that. They snuck over the port in their glide pattern and acquired their hilltop DZ on scope.

English was about to warn his non-recon soldiers to hold tight when the dropmaster beat him to it, punching up the drop light. The guts of the sixty-place APC flared red, and the heads of fifty-two men turned toward the dropmaster, the single eyes of their helmets noncommittal.

There was a wrenching, silent moment of free-fall as the transport dropped the Ninety-Second's APC, and the quiet was shattered.

The red light went off; the burners, then afterburners fired as attitude stabilizers kicked in, then out, then in again. Men could talk if they wished without worrying about blowing everything with some errant soundwave that got caught in a standard scan, because now the APC was alive and its own countermeasures powered up.

Veterans of countless drops sat still, making desultory webbing checks; newer marines unbuckled their harnesses and staggered over to the dropmaster to get their heavy weaponry and put their helmets together for private comments.

English stayed where he was, fiddling with his hand-held command scanner. In it were loaded the beacon codes to summon the o.t.s. support he'd been promised. He hadn't integrated his gloves into his suit system yet, because he hadn't automated the beacon yet. Because he wasn't sure if he needed to do that.

But when the dropmaster signalled him that he had one minute to go, he ran up the sequence and enabled it. He couldn't start worrying about somebody else's soldiers. He had to take care of his own.

Landfall was harder than it ought to have been, and the jar of it nearly knocked the scanner from his hand. He didn't need it swinging from its strap, enabled as hell, initiating any damn message it happened to bang out against his ceramic armor.

He safed it and swore into his open com channel, which brought his boys on line.

Insect-eyed heads turned again and he said, on his heavily shielded channel: "Don't shoot the first thing that moves out there; we've got human agents coming through with milk and cookies."

Somebody sighed like he was relieved; English's display showed him it was Tamarack, the first sergeant. "Don't fraternize with 'em, neither. And don't trust your back to anybody who ain't got a unit patch. Can't tell what kind of pressure these agents are under."

Then the dropmaster took over, readying the queue and slapping the bay door's servo. Through the widening portal, English got his first sight of Bethesda, green in his nightscope.

Green as Eire and in full flower of summer. It was going to be a shame to cook-off the spaceport. All these pretty trees. . . . He'd issued everybody with breathing equipment, and antiradiation armor to boot. He said, "I know it smells good, and it's pretty, but breath through what you brought. Something goes wrong, you don't have the two point one seconds it takes to engage that gear from a cold start."

There were groans at that, but nobody flat refused. The only thing you got on the ground that you couldn't get in space was fresh air and fast action. The Ninety-Second was going to have to settle for the action, this time out.

And out they went, past the dropmaster whose gloved hand was raised to English in an eloquent gesture, and whose com channel sputtered: "Get back on the mark, Lieutenant. I got strict orders."

"So do I," English answered, and neither of them wanted to explore the matter further.

The dropmaster closed the APC tight as a clam when everybody was out, and all the shoulder launchers and explosive ordnance off-loaded. Then English ordered the visual cammo-netting spread over the APC. When that was done, and the company moved away from the no-see-em

APC, the dropmaster engaged its countermeasures. English could hear the hum right through his com helmet and his breathing gear, as if the vibration had come up through the soles of his feet.

He was about to give his sergeant an order to move the unit out along the preplot on his scanner, when he saw a movement in the bushes. And then another.

"We've got company," he said on his open channel, and men brought up weapons as they scuttled for position or dived for cover, all as neat as a training exercise.

English had his scanner to deal with, and his helmet locked on to the targets he'd acquired, those in the bushes. He had three red blips and he was sending six of his recon specialists after those blips when one blip made a beeline for him.

Pitch-black night, so there was no use going to visual, but he dialed up his starlight intensifier and was able to ascertain the humanity of the blip approaching. Weasels weren't that big, or that stupid.

"Unless you don't wanta meet and treat, I'd like recon to give this fool an escort," crackled Sawyer's voice in his helmet.

"I'm in no hurry here, go ahead," English told the recon sergeant. "And disarm all of them, if you please, Sawyer," said English in his laconic command style.

Never hurt to let the boys know how they ought to be feeling.

Except English wasn't sure how he was feeling about meeting three strange humans too close to his only ride off-planet, in the middle of the night in hostile territory.

In reality, he only met one.

As the moving blip slowed in the face of two marines, and the recon boys bore down on the other two blips in the bush, both the straggling targets bolted in opposite directions.

English said, "Hold the one, let the others go. Close ranks," and left the rest to his sergeants.

When the prisoner was brought before him, both the additional blips were still hovering at the edges of his visorscope. He said into his com channel, "Proceed to Bush One," to get his company moving and away from the APC before he really looked at the body his recon helmet still insisted on treating as a blip.

The human hadn't said a word until now. It was dirty, ragged, and wild-eyed in the green tones of his helmet nightscope. And it was female.

He motioned to the periphery, while the men moved by with their machine guns and their rpgs and their plasma weapons, and said, "You're coming with us. If your friends don't come in or disappear, I'm going to take them out. You've got sixty seconds."

He raised his gloved wrist and looked at the chronograph there steadily. His voice, coming through his helmet's speaker grille, had been pretty much stripped of inflection.

The woman didn't panic, or shout to her companions, or even argue. One of the recon group stepped forward and held out hardware: "Her weapons."

A knife. A fifteen-round pistol, badly worn; two clips for it in a magnetic belt rig. A nasty little fragmentation grenade. Primitive stuff. He was beginning to wonder if perhaps she and her two companions weren't simply a piece of walking bad luck, and not his contact at all, when she said, "Weasel tails are soft and so are these locals."

That was the recognition phrase that Manning had come by to give him, with a sour look on her face, just before he'd deshipped into the transport.

So he said, "Not as soft as a woman," which was the rest of the call-and-answer. Then he added, "What about your friends?"

"They'll tag along. They're indig; they don't need to know much about this." So he told his boys not to shoot the outriders. Yet.

The woman was one of the materiel specialists who'd been dropped here six months ago, then. He had an impulse to take off his helmet, but he resisted. You wanted to give these people something to hold onto. She was brave, living down here waiting for someone like him. And foolish, because he wasn't going to give her what she most wanted—a way out.

"I need your report. Fast." He hauled out his scanner and punched up its transcribe mode. "Shoot."

"Your Bush One route is too dangerous." She spat coordinates like a tactical officer. "You go that way, and you can come into the spaceport from the big ship side. They moved their toys around last month. We're a little bit hot, so I don't want you doing much with the group."

"A little bit hot?" English moved instinctively away from her, but the two big men just behind her elbows stayed close. The company was still moving toward Bush One. He didn't change their orders. He wasn't sure yet that he was going to. A code phrase didn't make this woman trustworthy, or even prove she was the woman he was supposed to meet. There were human collaborators all over the occupied worlds, and the weasels were consummate interrogators.

"Hot: two cells have been destroyed, some of our people may have been captured. We're using counterinsurgency rules, so no cell knew the whole picture, but I don't know what may have leaked. Or who may have been compromised."

"You don't trust the people you brought? Why'd you bring them?"

"Look . . . you sound angry. That helmet's making it hard for me to talk to you. I've been waiting a long time. I could use a bit of eye contact, maybe a little positive reinforcement. I'm Milius, and I really want to be glad to see you, Ninety-Second."

"English. Sorry, I gave them orders for full kit—" He slapped his toggles and hit his shunt button, so that his helmet's data would come up on his scanner. Then he shut down his recon camera and put his breathing gear on hold and took off his helmet altogether. Holding it under his arm, he said: "Satisfied? Human as the next guy. Now, what's this about you not trusting your agents?"

"Field officer's responsibility. Handler's blues. They're good enough, these. Committed. We can offer you better basing than Bush One, if you're brave enough to take it."

"This looks like a quilting bee to you?"

"I mean, in houses, with the locals. The weasels are sweeping for transients tonight—they do it every third night. Somehow your drop got scheduled for the wrong—"

"I get you. I've only got twenty-eight hours to do this job, lady. You think you can simplify it, I'll bite. But if it looks funny to us, or it smells funny, all your indigs are dead in the water."

"Understood," said Milius, and he thought she smiled in the dark.

He lifted his helmet, hesitated, and said apologetically, "You'll have to bear with me. I need my com system. When we get where we're going, you and I can go off for a quiet talk. Unless there's something urgent?"

"Not beyond keeping from walking into a weasel patrol at Bush One, there isn't."

"Yeah, thanks," he said absently, reinstating all his connectors as he settled his helmet once again over his head. If anyone had overheard them, beyond the electronic ears of the scanner, it would be only the two recon boys right behind Milius.

He began disseminating the coordinates she'd given, and finally said, "Tamarack, you can call your own shots once we get to this village. Anything funny, shoot 'em all and set delayed det charges with electro overrides. If this is any kind of trap, I want it to cost them. And Sergeant Tamarack, get with Dropmaster and tell him what's up. He might want to keep his finger on the burn button."

"Affirmative. Recon's flanking those two blips, still."

"Agents, so the contact says. Whose, we'll see—supposed to be ours. Tell Sawyer to stay on them, though. Now you know everything I do. Make your own calls, Tam, if it gets to it."

"Yessir. I'll tell APC its a no-say-again situation, if you concur."

"Yeah, you better." Because it was, even though putting the APC on its own recognizance was the last thing English wanted to do. From here on out, it went perfectly, or nobody went home. Which, he consoled himself, was the general nature of his business, o.t.s. agents or no o.t.s. agents.

When he got to the "village" that Milius and her outrider friends called home, he wished he hadn't made contact.

The huts were poor, small, and stinking, with dirt floors and shuttered windows. Even through his starlight intensifier, the poverty was painfully sharp-edged. There were sick or wounded humans in every hut, and there wasn't a single hut big enough for the whole company.

It kept feeling more and more like a trap to him, but if the woman called Milius was right—and there were going to be weasel sweeps and anybody found out during curfew shot on sight—he didn't have much choice.

He put five men in a hut and tried to spread the group so that each hut had a plasma weapon, a shoulder launcher, a machine gun and a recon-ready specialist. That left him by his lonesome, in the woman's own hut.

Sergeant Tamarack didn't like that one bit, but everybody stayed com-ready, and they set motion detectors disguised as rocks with photo-return around the village's perimeter. So it wasn't that bad. It just felt bad.

The hut Milius called home had an old woman in it who was shot to shit and half-crazy. She kept talking to a spot on the wall she thought was some relative, and now and then she'd moan with pain or call Milius, who ignored her. Next to the woman, on another pile of ragged blankets, was a kid with a blown-off leg who was obviously dying of gangrene. The smell was enough to insure that English kept his helmet on, except when the woman insisted that he have a drink with her.

The drink was a watery tea, and he watched her prepare it, and then took her cup after she'd taken a swallow. No use in not being careful. He kept his back against the tied branches of the hut's wall, but it didn't make him feel any safer than he'd have felt in his clamshell alone.

He was hot and he was tired and he didn't like this twenty-odd hours of hiding one bit.

But he knew he could take his boys out and blast his way into the spaceport in broad daylight, if he felt like it. There were lots of ways to die.

Milius was intent on telling him more than he wanted to know about the "resistance" here. After they had tea, she begged him to leave his helmet off, put on a long, loose robe to cover his armor, and come with her to meet the other villagers.

He did it because he had the time to kill, and because he wasn't a good man for sitting and waiting, and because he could check on his company that way. So he told himself it was a surprise inspection he was about, and went with her from hut to hut, a hunchbacked, misshapen figure in a mouldy coat which was no more than holes cut in a blanket.

"This is Andy," she said in the first hut, where one of the recon specialists had a medkit out and was trying to scrape abcessed tissue out of a teenaged boy's flank. The boy was biting on a piece of wood, but he nodded. "Andy got that trying to get his mother out of slave coffle. He's killed three weasels, trashed a supply truck of theirs, and sugared any number of gas tanks." She ruffled the boy's hair and English said to the spec, who'd stopped doctoring when his lieutenant came in, "Proceed, soldier."

The other marines in the hut were protection enough from a wounded kid and three women of indeterminate age who weren't anywhere near as good-looking as Milius.

They quit that hut, visited another, and left it before English asked, "How come so few men?"

"Dead. We use 'em; we lose 'em." Milius reached up and tugged loose her hair; it had seemed dark brown in the huts; here, it was black and fell around her face like a wave. "I'm really glad to see you, English. I've done all I can here. These people can't hold out much longer. It's not any better further north, either. I've talked to the other handlers twice. How're you going to do this?"

"Do this?"

"Get us out—the rest, I mean. I know I'll go with your unit. I'm good enough with whatever weapon you've got to spare. But the rest of us—there's a dozen in all. Are you picking them up too? The extraction procedure's never been—"

"I don't have those orders," he said bluntly. Maybe he needed her, but he'd just been in those huts and he really hated to see weasel damage on people. Milius wanted out. He didn't blame her. She had a right to expect it. But she'd obviously been planning the missions that put these folk down, and the rest at risk.

Anyway, he couldn't give her the answer she had a right to expect.

"Oh, so you're just taking me and then, when the strike force comes in, the others will get out that way?"

"I'm not even sure we'll get out ourselves, before the

strike force comes," he said. "You know they need the o.t.s. agents. Look what might have happened tonight . . ."

It satisfied her. He was relieved it did. It didn't satisfy him. Or it didn't satisfy her, and she was too proud to rail at him when it wasn't his decision.

He wished to hell it hadn't been a woman, with all these casualties to tend, who'd risked her own life after curfew to get him and his to safety. Weasels were at their worst with human women.

He found himself reaching out to turn her face to him, so she'd look at him instead of the darkness. His clamshell grated on the bundled sticks of the hut against which he leaned. He said, "I've got a floorlength coup-coat and a bedspread to boot, if it makes you feel any better. Done better than two hundred weasels, personally. My company's got an aggregate kill record of better than three thousand. The Alliance may not be outright winnin' this damned war, but the Ninety-Second's holding its own."

"I'm here to scrub that spaceport. That's all I want," she said in a voice so cold his hand fell away from her. "There are lots of planets, lots of people, who've had it worse than it is here. But that's not my problem. I want those guns out of commission and I don't care, English, if it kills every boy scout in your company to do it. Is that clear?"

"I thought you wanted to go home?"

"Home being an Alliance ship?" Her voice lightened then. "Sure, I want to know the job's done. That's when we go, right? If you guys can't do the job, nobody's going anywhere, so it's fair to speculate about that day coming."

An odd choice of words, her last. He heard them but he didn't understand what they indicated until much later, when the night was done and she went to sleep curled around an old assault rifle.

He left her in her hut and found his first sergeant's. "You know," said Tamarack, "I was talking to the two outriders that o.t.s. officer had with her, and they said she's bad news. A fanatic. Killing weasels is a religion with her. Seems one of the other cell leaders came down here and they had some kind of fight over turf and protocol, and she shot the guy for a traitor. Thought you ought to know."

"Right," said English, and made a sign meant to prompt

Tamarack to wipe the last bit of digitized log that contained those comments. When they'd synchronized their edit, both men took off their helmets.

The other marines were quiescent, perhaps sleeping. You learned to sleep any way you could, anywhere you could. Tamarack said, "She'll try something if she finds out things aren't going her way."

"I'm not sure I'd blame her," said English, and pulled a ground ration bar from his belt. He wasn't a bit hungry, but he was well trained.

He was counting on that training more than ever now, because there was something about the woman and her committed casualties that made him feel more and more rotten about the orders he'd gotten.

He was so cranky he kept wishing that the weasels would pull in here in their trucks so that he could shoot something —the sort of something that had shot an old lady and a kid, and kept these people in the kind of fearful poverty that was all around him.

In that instant, if anyone had asked him, he'd have said that Milius was the bravest single soul he'd ever met, fighting her heart out with these doomed bastards day after day, in this kind of grinding misery, and knowing it wasn't going to do a damned bit of good to anybody alive here, even if her wildest dreams were realized and the Alliance took out the spaceport. .

Sunset was fast on Bethesda, like the dropping of a smoke bomb. He had everybody in position, thanks to Milius, who'd found them a rickety bunch of wagons and jeered them into action when they balked at the audacity of her plan.

Or jeered him into action. English couldn't quite fathom how he'd ended up taking orders from that crazy lady, but he had. She knew the weasel mindset on Bethesda better than he could ever hope to, and her little band of indigs supplied milk to the spaceport, as well as fresh eggs.

So in went the unit, behind the milk in the ox-drawn carts, under the eggs in a false-bottomed lorry, and every other way but shooting.

The trick was getting the equipment out and emplaced, and getting back in the wagons, before Milius's indigs had to leave.

She'd said to him, when he worried over it, "Don't sweat it. I have a . . . relationship—" She grinned without humor at him, and there in the port, under the arc lights, she was pretty in a tortured way. "—a relationship," she repeated, "with the weasel port commander, and with some of the human trustees. I usually stay late."

He didn't understand. "You mean—"

"They all like whiskey, fool. And you know they like party games. This convoy'll hold until twenty-three hundred hours, or I won't be alive to wonder what went wrong. If you can't set your charges by then, well . . . that's what the auto-weapons are for, right? Fighting your way out's got to be easier than fighting your way in *and* out."

"No arguing with that," he'd admitted. Off she'd gone, scrambling up through the false bottom of the truck he was hiding in. He'd heard her heels on the boards above, then switched on his electronics to amplify what he could of her conversations with the trustee guards.

Then he'd heard the damnedest thing. A weasel must have joined them; Milius greeted somebody with a name that had to be barked. Her bark wasn't half-bad, considering the nature of the language she was trying to speak. Anyway, it was answered by a longer series of barks from somebody who'd been barking from birth.

And she responded. It had never occurred to him that she might speak Khalian. It had never occurred to him that any human did, although of course, among the intelligence services, somebody must, or you couldn't do signals or communications intercepts.

Then he was damned sure she walked away with the barking weasel—he could get enough isolation/amplification from his scanner to verify that.

It made him queasy, but he kept telling himself that if she'd been a collaborator, he and his men would already be prisoners—or dead. There'd be no reason for the weasels to wait.

The Ninety-Second waited until the mark was reached, dark was everywhere, and it was time for recon to do what its specialists did best.

Milius had given them coordinates and design specs for the power grid. Blowing it wasn't going to be the hardest thing they did tonight; the auxiliary had to blow with it.

While the recon specialists did that, Tamarack and English eased out of their hidey-holes and headed for the big ships by the route Milius had suggested—back alley stuff, skittering from shadow to shadow, getting as close to the destroyers as they could before the power went down.

While he and Tamarack went for the destroyers, the rest of the unit, in groups of three, were detailed to the twenty fighters. Slap a charge under a fuselage, or in a thruster pod, and keep going.

English could see every one of his soldiers on his visor's mapping display, and it was damned difficult on strange terrain, keeping track of them and his own mission, and counting weasel-parameter blips as they came up into critical mode.

Tamarack saw the first blip of real concern, while English was too busy worrying about Beta team and their exposed position to be covering his own ass.

He was telling Beta, "Six o'clock, and kill 'em quiet, please, if they scope you," when Tamarack's grunt on the dualcom made him realize that the sergeant wasn't in front of him, but behind him.

English turned just in time to see the broken-necked weasel go down, and Tamarack already had his knife out, severing the tail for his coup-coat.

"Thanks," English said into his helmet.

"Welcome," Tam said, stuffing the bloody tail in his belt. "We gonna take the lights out, or what?"

"Only when I say so," English told the sergeant very slowly, and waved Tamarack on ahead.

He was embarrassed about letting the weasel sneak up on him. Luckily, it hadn't been a full-kit weasel; it had had no electronics on it that English could see; it had sounded no verbal alarm.

But the moment when he'd have to call the power-down was rapidly approaching. He really wanted to hold off until he'd buggered his destroyer. Those ships had their own lights and they could lift off at the first sign of trouble. It would be crazy to lose the targets after going through so much to get this close to them.

So English stalked among the hangars and the trucks and the repair gantries and the fuel wells, and watched the progress of their soldiers on his visor.

When half of the Khalian fighter craft were successfully mined, his Beta got into trouble. His helmet display threw up the typical confused blip patterns, and audio shunted him a clear call for help from one of the corporals.

English was, by then, scuttling toward his objective, a destroyer, magnetic-shaped charge in hand. He did what he felt was right: he called the power-downs; he sprinted for the destroyer closest; he jumped for its main exhaust well. As his gloved hands hit the rim and he slapped his magnetic charge into place, he hung there, verbally empowering his shift video. For some few seconds he was blind to his own situation, seeing through the camera of one of his embattled corporals.

Then he shouted into his all-com channel for Sigma to help Beta. The lights went out, all over the base. He got his shift video disengaged and went back to real-time display as he let go of the exhaust well's rim and dropped to the ground.

He couldn't see Tamarack, not even with starlight intensification. He searched through his com bands, and his video bands. Tamarack's camera was blacked out—either shattered, disabled some other way, or taking a good picture of nothing at all.

He yelled on all-com, "Tamarack's out; Recon, find his charge and set it; Sawyer, you've got Tamarack's files."

Sawyer slipped smoothly into the first sergeant's duty slot and English relaxed as he ran, rifle on, hot and ready, toward the second destroyer.

When English got there, he met weasels. Weasels came at him out of the dark, jumping down from fins overhead, illuminated by a sudden burst of automatic fire. He hoped to hell the fire wasn't coming from his own men.

"Sawyer," he shouted as he dropped to the ground, rolling, shaking off a weasel who had a slippery grip on his clamshell, and shooting another as it hurtled toward him out of the air, "can you make sure you guys ain't shootin' at me? I'm at T-2 with Tamarack, who's real dead. Where the fuck are you? I'm covered with weasels!"

And he was. They were coming at him like attacking insects, out of the dark. Weasels in coveralls, with wrenches and knives. He kept rolling and shooting and kicking and trying to dodge the occasional ricochet or burst that came too close.

"Right here," said Sawyer, a figure looming suddenly. "Don't move, okay?"

English was still saying, "What do you mean, don't move? You're not going to shoot—" when Sawyer, with a clip of low-penetration rounds slapped into his auto, shot the weasels gnawing on English.

It was the most terrifying moment of English's life. He could feel the rounds slam into the weasel bodies, and *ping* against his armor. Point-blank range, yet.

But suddenly there were no moving weasels on him, and Sawyer was helping him push the weasel corpses away and get to his feet.

"No weapons," Sawyer said, and English realized that the recon sergeant's voice in his com referred to the weasels, who'd been mechanics or maintenance personnel of some sort. But there were other weasels, others with weapons. The darkened spaceport was flickering with auto fire and plasma blooms now, like myriad flashbulbs going off between the ships.

English sprinted for Tamarack's corpse and picked up the dead sergeant's platelike magnetic charge. "Let's set this and blow this place," he said to Sawyer through gritted teeth, finally feeling weasel damage where his arms and legs had taken it.

But there was enough adrenaline in him to hold off the worst of the pain. When he came down from the exhaust well of the second ship, Sawyer was right there, weapon ready, standing guard over him. And he had tails from dead weasels in his belt. There must have been a dozen.

English wasn't about to argue over whose tails those were going to be. He had a company to care for. He was going to get lots of grief for going into this action the way he had, instead of staying in the damned egg truck. He could hear it now. But then, to hear it later, he'd have to live that long.

He let Sawyer run point for him, and they did the last

destroyer, while the recon boys formed up there and held off what was beginning to become serious opposition: weasels in gun trucks, weasels with plasma rifles.

The only break the Ninety-Second got was that the weasels were afraid to fire on their own ships, here where there was so much fuel around.

"Time for a diversion." English didn't know he'd spoken on the all-com; he was thinking out loud.

"Let's blow one fighter, and run like hell toward the other end of the line," Sawyer replied. And, suddenly on a private channel: "It means leaving Tamarack's body, but they don't get any deader. We'll give him all these tails you and me got today. Dumb ass, stopping to count coup in the middle of an op like this."

"Yeah, well, we did that too. Okay, let's let him stay." The privacy channel wasn't monitored for the record. "Call roll and form up, while you're movin', guys. Blow 13-Zed, once everybody's accounted for. To X point, now!"

Everybody moved. On his visor display, it was like watching a space battle. The blips that were the ninety-second found their way around the blips that were the enemy, and the ones that weren't moving, well . . . they were dead.

You had to play it that way, in the dark against these odds. English gave a five-second warning when the fighter was going to blow, and everybody hit the deck. He could see the results on his scanner.

The blow was hotter than he'd counted on. It shook the ground and taxed his helmet's polarizing capability. His breathing apparatus went up a notch in tone, and began to filter in earnest.

There was no time to worry about what was happening back there, among the enemy ships. There was only time to pray that everybody alive made the X point, and to call the APC.

That APC was going to move a hell of a lot faster than they were, summoned on the emergency freq English was using: "Dropmaster, this is a Nonstandard Pickup, Immediate. X Point precalibrated. Move!"

If they got out before the burning fighter blew, and ignited another, and then another, English would call it a win.

If they were still running for cover when that chain reaction caused one of the destroyers to blow prematurely, English wouldn't be counting anything.

God, this wasn't supposed to happen. It shouldn't be happening. But those damned weasels left their fuel tanks too close to—

English almost stopped running, despite the display grid on his visor which told him he was just keeping up with his men, and plotted the relative times to the X point of every moving blip in his company. He almost stopped, because he'd just realized that those fighters were being fueled up for something, loaded and armed and being readied for some kind of scramble.

Did that mean word of the Alliance strike had leaked? Were the big guns pointed skyward with nukes up their spouts? If so, it was going to be one hell of a bang before the smoke cleared.

He could hear his own breathing now, labored despite his respirator, as he charged toward the X point, the place where recon had melted the fencing once they'd taken down the power grid.

It was an easy out, and he was halfway through it before he stopped. Panting, holding a plasma rifle that read empty, though he couldn't remember shooting it anywhere near that much, he froze there. As if he had all the time in the world, he counted his remaining corpsmen.

Besides Tamarack, they'd lost three others, one from recon. Not great, but pretty damned good.

He said, "Sawyer, it's all yours. Get 'em on board the APC. I'll catch up if I can. But don't wait more than five minutes, and not that long if it starts looking like a cook-off to the AI."

And he started walking away, then trotting, back toward the egg truck.

"Sir? Hey, English—what the fuck?" Sawyer was coming after him.

English didn't turn or slow. "I forgot my o.t.s. agent," he said into his privacy com channel.

"The hell you did," said Sawyer, and clipped him in the small of the back with the butt of his rifle. "Sir," Sawyer added as English fell, stunned, and the other man gathered him up.

Consequently they were both facing the landing pads when the fighters began to blow, spewing purple and gold and orange fire in oily clouds full of radioactive filth from their weapons.

English's antiradiation meters began to beep, telling him to get the hell out of there before his suit couldn't handle the load, and throwing up numbers as to how long before his equipment overloaded, and blacking out his faceplate. Then his weapon began to heat so badly in his hands that he had to drop it before it melted, and the shock wave hit everybody, knocking them to the ground.

It was a crawl-for-your-life situation, and the Ninety-Second did just that, English bringing up the rear. He'd wanted to go back for Milius, he really had. But without a suit in the kind of firestorm this was shaping up to be, she needed more than a friendly marine to assure her safety. She needed an act of God.

INTERLUDE

Admiral Meier stared out at the landing field. Ships of every
size rose at careful one-minute intervals and disappeared
into the purple sky.

The Khalia, still far from beaten, had already reappear-
ed in other sectors with even bigger fleets comprised of
new ships. The Alliance's neighbors were also mobilizing
seeing the opportunity to take advantage of the Fleet's distraction.

Most of the Fleet was either defending the frontier or
searching for the Khalian home worlds. Every other ship
that could be found was busy rallying every Alliance planet
to the cause. The scout corps had been doubled and the
search for lost colonies had taken on a manic air. Their first
reports were on his desk. Some pretty strange planets had
already been discovered, many capable of valuable contri-
butions. The Alliance was going to need every resource it
could gather.

As he watched a wing of exploration scouts rose in
unison. Statistics said one of them would not return, would
be lost among the countless unexplored stars within the
three-thousand-light-year sphere claimed by the Alliance.

Grand Admiral Meier lifted his glass of Michigan wine and saluted them. Smythe had given him a case the day before in honor of the victorious action off Bethesda. The admiral offered to the dwindling ships the traditional toast of his home world. "Good luck and may the gods guide you."

DURGA HAJIT
by *Chelsea Quinn Yarbro*

FROM THE TIME that the Celestial River carried us from the Source to this place, we have lived in the ways of our ancient laws, revering the Books that were given to us for wisdom and our welfare. We have kept to the ways from the Founding, and adhere to them as we have been instructed to do, for to do less would endanger our lives, every one of us.

The days of our coming are lost in antiquity, but there are High Caste families on Durga who count back their station for more than a hundred generations, and whose Founders are listed among those in the Sacred Passenger Manifest. It is that sacred writing, those telling of the years of the Founders, which shows that they were yet older than their venturing on the Celestial River, which flows from Janja to Durga and to the Realms of the Gods. The sacred writing states that at the time of setting out, the number of years was counted at 2144. We know that we have been here, on Durga, longer than we lived at the Source, nourished and sustained by the holy waters of Janja. We passed a short time in that holy place, and then were sent out on the Celestial River.

While some have insisted over the centuries that those were mystic numbers, not intended to relate to actual years, there are others who say that they must be regarded as accurate, for accuracy is stressed in the Sacred Maintenance Codes. Others have debated that in that most sacred of places, a year was measured in other terms than what we use now. There has never been debate over the numbers, for they are A. D. numbers, and therefore known to be Above Doubt.

It was stated in the Contracts that there would be Visitors from time to time who would aid and guide us in our work here; sent out from the Source, they were to be our inspiration, avatars of the High Gods who would mark our progress on this world and judge our acceptability to return to the Source, for the Oldest Text has promised us that we will all return to the Source.

Over the generations, many have despaired and taken to strange worship because time went by and no Visitors came. No avatar approached us to show us our way. Those of High Caste said it was because time was less important to Gods, and that the battle which has raged among them forever must still continue. The Oldest Text, the *Beved Hajit,* tells of wars and more wars fought among the Gods, Who are in eternal conflict. It was known that we were sent upon the Celestial River in a time of crisis and that Janja sent out thousands of her children on similar voyages, though what became of them only the Gods know.

Thus, when Visitors finally arrived, three years ago, there was delight and consternation among all the Castes of Durga. These Avatars landed near Kel, which is one of only three cities that must be rebuilt. Most of the High Caste said it was because Kel was their principal city, but those who serve in the temples of the Gods were not as certain, and spent hours in meditation and trials to determine the import of this momentous event.

The Scribe of Ajna set down all that he heard, which was spoken through a spirit kept in a box; this spirit knew the tongues of all places, or so it claimed. The Visitors learned from this spirit many things, and informed the Visitors of the things the Scribe revealed.

Thus the Visitor who held the spirit-box addressed the Scribe in this way.

"We are from"—there followed the name of a God we

had not heard before, the God Fleet, or a similar name— "and we're looking for lost Earth colonies."

The Scribe replied, "We are not lost. This is Durga, where the All-Mother Janja sent us."

"They look human, Commander," said one of those Visitors accompanying Him. He had two Attributes in his hands, but neither were as yet familiar to any of us.

"Can we get a fix on the language?" the Visitor addressed as Commander asked His underling.

"We can try," answered the underling. "We'll get some representative recordings and see what they can do with it back at Records Central."

Now the Scribe of Ajna realized that the title of the Visitor was significant, for only an avatar of the Highest Gods would be addressed as Commander. He also sensed that the wars between the Gods was part of the issue, for the protective garments these Visitors wore was surely armor. He knew it was not acceptable to ask questions of these great beings, and so he waited in respectful silence until they would once again address him.

"What place is that?" the avatar Commander required to know a short time later.

The Scribe of Ajna knew that he was being tested, for surely the avatar Commander was aware of where He was. "This is the city of Kel, which was rebuilt but three years ago. It is the two-hundred-ninth rebuilding of the city."

"That's a city?" the underling inquired.

"Kel is one of the three great cities that must be rebuilt," said the Scribe.

"Must be rebuilt," the Commander said, stressing the importance of what the Gods command. "What are the others like, do you think, Spandril?"

"I wouldn't like to guess, sir," he answered.

"I suppose we'd better find out," the Commander said, and once again addressed the Scribe of Ajna. "There are six of us. Is there someone here in charge?"

"There are High Caste living here at Kel, and there are the servants of the Gods in the temples. Any of them would be honored if you spoke to them, Commander." The Scribe touched all seven of his fingers together at the fourth joint, raised them to his forehead and bowed, showing the greatest reverence.

"Weird-looking, isn't he?" asked the underling of the Commander.

"Are you Zivi or Vizna?" the Scribe dared to ask, then bowed over, his head touching his knees in shame for the great error he had made.

"I am Horder. I have five men with me other than Spandril here," said the Commander, looking about at the walls of Kel. "Can you imagine living like this?"

"It looks like a pretty harsh world, Commander," said the underling.

"Better stow it, Spandril. We may need help from these . . . people." The Commander calling himself Horder stepped nearer to the Scribe, who trembled at His presence, for he had read of the caprice of the Gods when they change their Aspects in their dealing with men.

"Tell me, O Commander, O Horder, what I am to do, and I will obey at once." He remained bent over, hoping that the avatar of the God would not strike him down for his insolence. He did not recognize the name of the avatar; this meant that either a new God had risen or there were other faces to the Gods than the ones in the sacred texts we have preserved.

"I need to speak with whoever's in charge here." The spirit-box made sounds like our carrion birds, but continued to take in and give out words. Clearly the God manifest in the spirit-box did not want to encumber itself with a more usual incarnation. This puzzled the Scribe who had never known a God to choose such an unlikely form.

"The High Caste assemble each day at sunset to make offerings to Durga so that She will favor us while we are under her Dark Face." The Scribe regarded the Visitors and waited once more for them to make a decision.

"It's bound to be a couple hours, sir," said Spandril. "We could check back with the Fleet, tell them what we've found."

"Good idea," seconded the Commander. "You," he addressed the Scribe. "Tell your superiors that we will be back shortly. We have to . . . make our reports."

The Scribe did not quite understand what this meant, but he knew he would not be permitted to question a God again, and so he raised himself up and bowed again. "I will do it, O Horder."

"Why does he act like that?" Commander Horder asked.

"You know what primitives are like, sir," Spandril said, indicating the chariot in which they had descended from the Celestial River. "They're apt to misinterpret everything."

"Do you think we're in any danger?" Commander Horder asked, watching the Scribe closely. The Scribe kept himself bowed and submissive through this scrutiny, trusting that he would not be struck down at the God's whim.

"I doubt it, sir," Spandril answered. "This guy looks too respectful to cause you any harm." He motioned toward the Scribe with one of the mysterious Attributes he held.

"Maybe," Commander Horder said, taking a few steps back. "You tell them; we'll be back shortly before sunset."

"A most auspicious hour," the Scribe was bold enough to reply, his bow deeper than ever.

"Yes," said Commander Horder uncertainly. "Watch the rear, Spandril." He turned back toward His chariot, His assistant coming behind him. Just before He entered the chariot, He looked at the Scribe once more. "There'll be four of us."

"You're going to leave someone behind?" asked His assistant.

"Just in case," the God Horder replied enigmatically. "We don't know what we're getting into in this place and—" The rest was lost as the spirit-box was taken within the chariot once more and Its accommodating flow of words was cut off.

The Scribe hastened away from the chariot and went to his temple where he prostrated himself before the largest of the statues of his God Ajna. He kept at his prayers and meditations for some little time and then went, as he had been ordered to do, to tell the Highest Caste what he had learned.

Admih was the one who met the Scribe and received him with interest. "What God has come?"

The Scribe raised his head and addressed Admih. "He

has named Himself Horder and is called Commander. He is clearly of the High Gods. He has said He is from the Fleet."

Admih looked to his fellows, the Thirty-one Highest Caste who were descended in direct line from the Founding. According to the Sacred Passenger Manifest there had been well over two hundred at the Founding, but Durga is not an easy place and many of those lines had been lost with time. These of the Highest Caste were all that were left in Kel; they were terribly aware of their diminishing numbers. As all of us could remember a time when there were more, those of the Highest Caste felt this more keenly than any. "This God," said Admih. "What does He offer us?"

"He has not said," the Scribe told them.

"Surely we must not ask until His identity is known," said Derir, who was growing so old that he could no longer sit upright but was curled over in an ever-increasing bow. "To do otherwise would court disaster."

"Derir is right," said Kazei. "Whoever this God is, He will not reveal His gifts until we have learned His rightful identity." He wore his four crisscrossed strands secured at the front of his chest with an ancient medallion which had been in his family since the Founding. Its purpose had long been forgotten, but it was venerated for its origins.

"You may be right," said Admih, who would serve as head of the Highest Caste until the year. "We must not act too hastily or we will have cause to regret it."

"There is also the matter," said Gazili, who had seven children and was considered the most fortunate of all the Highest Caste, "that we are of Durga. Durga has many faces and we hope that She will keep only her most pleasant toward us, for She is unforgiving."

All of the Highest Caste nodded, and the Scribe of Ajna bowed his head, knowing it would be wrong to speak unless in answer to their questions.

"This God, this Horder, what, again, did he say was his origin?" Muthali asked, raising up his grizzled head to look at the others of the Highest Caste.

"He said he was from the Fleet," answered the Scribe.

"The Fleet," mused Muthali. "If we understood that word, we would know what we deal with." He looked at the others and they shared slow nods of agreement.

"Fleet means swift," the Scribe dared to say.

"Yes. So the God is from swiftness," said Admih. "Swiftness. A strange Attribute to select, and therefore a telling one." He approached the altar by the door, prostrated himself before it, and began to recite his prayers, for even the Highest Caste have Endless Prayers which they chant all through their lives.

"Fleet. Swift. Speed." Derir ticked off the words on his seven fingers. "What God would select those Attributes for His avatar? It is not what we expected."

"Gods are not expectable," Muthali said, reminding them of their shared puzzle. "To expect Them to be is to make Them less than Gods."

The others gestured agreement.

"When are they to return?" asked Gazili. "We must be prepared to receive Them when they return."

"Shortly before sundown," said the Scribe. "They will speak with you."

The Highest Caste were more apprehensive than they cared to admit or reveal. One of them joined Admih before the altar and the drone of two Endless Prayers filled the room.

"Sundown is growing near," announced the youngest of them, the frail youth Telo, who had kept his place at the far end of the room. "What must we do?"

"Prepare," answered Bezin. "We are honored by the God Who is Fleet, and we must show our understanding and appreciation."

"Provided we do not offend Durga," they were reminded by Gazili. "This is Her place and we are Her people before all other Gods. She is Mother of All."

Again there was solomn agreement among the Highest Caste. They made their ritual gestures of understanding and acceptance, ignoring the Scribe until finally Bezin spoke once more.

"We must send for the priests. We need their guidance." He was purposeful now, and we of Durga will eternally venerate his memory for his insistence that priests would be needed. Without their inspiration for guidance, we might have chosen wrongly then, and would be forever beyond the favor of Durga in all her forms.

"You—Scribe." Admih addressed the Scribe directly once more, and there was a look of boundless determination in his face, for he was certain that now there was an opportunity for the people of Durga to show their devotion to the Goddess. "You are to go to the temples, all of them. You are to summon the priests to speak with us, for doubtless they will know more of these Visitors, this Commander Horder, than we do. We of the Highest Caste keep the knowledge of our people, but it is the priests who bring us nearer the Gods."

The Scribe bowed double before he hastened away, first to his own temple, the largest erected to Ajna. Then to Zivi's temple, where statues of demons flanked the walkway to the altars. Then to Zivi's other self, Zakti. This temple was built on the same ancient foundations as the first of Zakti's temples and was regarded as a temple of great power, second only to the monumental temple to Durga and all Her forms. In each place he summoned the priests of highest rank and greatest wisdom, and told them of what he had learned. At last twenty-four priests came to the Highest Caste, an hour before sunset.

"We have little time," said Admih, indicating the shadows that fell through Kel, rendering many of the streets as dark as night. "The Visitors will return, and we do not yet know who they are or what they want."

"It was spoken that the Gods would send avatars from Janja to us, to show us the way," said the revered priest of Yaneza, the God of Learning, Whose Head was monsterous with all He knew. "There are many writings to confirm this."

"Yaneza is powerful in knowledge," said the priest of Engri, who wore vestments painted with exploits of his God. "Yaneza is more powerful in knowledge than all others. But He is not able to read the hearts of men as Engri can, for Engri has more of man about Him than does Yaneza. For that reason, we must also appeal to Engri to guide us."

"But these are not men; the Visitors are avatars of the Gods." Admih was distressed by the way the priests bickered, though he had seen it often enough before.

"Even then, we are men," said Engri's priest stubbornly.

"I know we are in need of His council if we are to deal with these strange beings."

"We must remember," said the formidable priest of Zakti, "that Durga is the Unapproachable, and we must regard the circumstances that bring these avatars to us as significant. We have been left alone for so long, it cannot be anything less than another great battle of the Gods that would bring them to us now."

There were buzzes and mutters in response to this: Admih was annoyed at the priests for confusing them. "I am a man who must regard all this as suspect," he declared at last. "As long as I am serving as head of the Highest Caste, I must keep my senses no matter what the provocation to lose them."

The priest of Yeimei scowled at him. "You do not know what you are playing at, Admih, to say that. This is Kel, and those of us who serve Yeimei know that our God serves Durga in all Her forms, as all Gods must. As long as Yeimei judges us, He will do so at the behest of Durga."

Admih folded his arms. "And what do you intend by that?"

"I intend only to remind you that each of us will account not only to all of us of Durga, but also to Yeimei and the All-Mother. These avatars, no matter what God they are, must be secondary to Durga Herself." He lowered his eyes. "Durga created Zakti as Her son and Her lover. She created Yeimei to judge men. All Gods are Her children, and we are the children of the Gods."

"And therefore what?" Admih asked, seeing his own puzzlement reflected in the faces of the others.

The priest shrugged. "If we do not serve Durga, we cannot serve the others."

The Scribe of Ajna, who had been commanded to remain, had been watching by the larger of the two windows, and he now bowed to the Highest Caste and the priests. "It is nearly sundown and the Visitors are returning."

"We must go and meet them." Admih was more resigned than pleased.

"Listen to what he says," suggested the priest of Yaneza. "Listen and learn."

There was a brief clamor of other suggestions as the

group prepared to leave the chamber for the gates of Kel where they would meet the Visitors who were from the Fleet.

As a last reminder, the priest of Vizna spoke up. "Recall that Vizna encompassed all of Janja in three strides. It may well be Vizna who comes to us, for He has always chosen strange guises for his avatars."

"And if it isn't Vizna, then who?" challenged one of the other priests before Admih motioned them to silence for their procession.

As with every sundown, gongs were sounded from the four corners of the city of Kel, and the people of all Castes came into the streets to say farewell to the light. It was a restless, apprehensive time, and many of those who called out the praises of the Gods watched the Highest Caste and the priests from the tails of their eyes.

Commander Horder was waiting impatiently at the southwest gate. He was accompanied now by three attendants: Spandril and two others.

After the Highest Caste had bowed and made ritual gestures of welcome, the priests showed their respect. That done, they waited for a sign from the Visitors.

"We're grateful for your welcome," said Commander Horder through the spirit-box. "We hope that you will listen to what we have to say and be willing to aid us in our work."

"The work of the Gods is the duty of man," said Admih for all of them.

"Ah . . . yes." Commander Horder glanced at the others. "Do you really think the records were right? I find it hard to believe that they came from Earth, I don't care how long ago."

"We came from the Source, from Janja—" began the Scribe of Ajna, only to be interrupted by Spandril.

"There were over three hundred colony ships sent out of India at the time of the Great Famine," he said. "It's all in the records. There's enough to link them with that expansion."

"Still . . ." Commander Horder said, then sighed. "I guess we need all the help we can get."

"Yes, sir," said one of the other two.

Commander Horder addressed the Highest Caste once

more. "We come to you for aid."

All the Highest Caste bowed double.

"There's . . ." he looked at Spandril and his other men, "hell, how do you explain the Khalia to people like this?"

"Khalia?" asked the High Priest of Durga, who had been called Lallin when he had had a name.

Commander Horder turned back toward the Highest Caste of Kel. "Yes." He wore a wide belt with three Attributes hanging from it, and though he had no twisted cords crossing his chest, there were mystic markings on his clothes that fascinated the priests. "They're . . . they're hostile. They're destructive."

All the Highest Caste listened attentively while the priests nodded their agreement.

"These . . . Khalia?" began the fortunate Gazili, "What do you want with them?"

Commander Horder straightened up. "You've got to understand that they started it. We're not like they are."

Again the priests nodded, one of them singing out his Endless Prayer.

"Does he have to do that, Commander?" asked one of the men with him.

"Leave it alone, Ecrilla," Horder warned. "We need these people on our side. They're too close to the Khalian area of influence." He looked back at the seven-fingered men before him. "I can't get used to some of these colonists. You know what I mean?"

"Yes, sir," said Ecrilla at his most wooden.

Horder sighed and looked at the Highest Caste once more. "I wish we had better records about those early colonies. We don't know winkles about them."

"True," agreed Spandril, who continued recklessly, "but if we stayed here a while, arranged for a study team, we could find out—"

"A *study team?*" Horder repeated. "Out here on the edge of Khalian territory? That would give them the excuse they need for another Target." He stared at Admih. "You're in charge, aren't you?"

"I am the Speaker for the Highest Caste, yes," said Admih with great dignity. "But each priest speaks for his God and not for the Highest Caste." He pressed his fingers together and bowed lower than any member of the Highest Caste was ever expected to bow.

"The ones with the crossed ropes are Highest Caste, right?" Horder went on, feeling his way.

"It is the mark of the Caste, as the Gods have required of us since before the time we set out on the Celestial River." He glanced at the Scribe of Ajna. "We have kept to the ways of the Gods."

"There are records from the time of the Founding," the Scribe confirmed.

"We'd like to see them, if you'll permit," said Commander Horder.

"Whatever the avatar desires we are here to fulfill." Admih showed respect again. "You have but to tell us."

The priest of Zivi bowed before speaking. "You of the Fleet, what are your Attributes, that we may know how best to serve you?"

Those with him were astonished by his audacity even as they admired his acumen, for we have long known that to address the Gods in any manner other than submissive is to court great harm. All waited to see what misfortune the avatar Horder would visit upon the priest of Zivi for such disrespect.

"The Fleet . . . well, it's a little hard to explain it to people like you, who've been out of touch for so long, but we have established quite a . . . a group of connected planets out there. Many worlds are . . . within our influence." He struggled to find the best way to describe the purpose and function of the Fleet. "We help to keep it all connected. We try to give protection and—"

"Ah," said the priest of Vizna with a smile. "Protection. Given swiftly."

Horder listened to the words of the spirit-box. "Ah . . . no, not that, it's—"

"Commander," Spandril interrupted, "better not bite off more than they can chew, huh?"

"Oh . . . " Horder considered the problem. "I suppose we can explain that later. The Khalia are more important, aren't they?" He gave a signal to his men to encourage them. "They don't need too many particulars yet, do they?"

"Probably not," said Spandril.

"These Gods will not reveal everything to us," ancient Derir warned Admih. "Gods conceal many things from men. We must be wary so that we will not be misled."

"That is very true," agreed Admih; several of the others showed agreement.

"Look," said Horder, moving a few steps nearer, "we need your help. The Khalia are spreading out, they're getting bolder by the day."

Spandril coughed. "Tell them about Target. Keep it simple, but tell them."

"Yes," seconded Varnig, who had been watching the priests with increasing nervousness for the last several minutes. "Tell them."

"God, I wish we had some place to sit down," complained Horder to his men, and his remarks were duly conveyed to the Highest Caste and priests of Kel by the translating computer they had with them.

"We would be honored if you would accompany us to the Central Temple," said Admih at once.

Horder hesitated and then said, "Sure. That would be fine. You lead the way and we'll follow." He motioned his men to fall in with him. "Keep your eyes open. We don't really know what we're getting into."

"By the look of it, there isn't anything we can't handle," said Ecrilla, apparently to make up for his earlier gaffe.

The gates of Kel were made of precious wood, from the scented arrani tree which grew only in the narrow moderate climate belt. Every time Kel was rebuilt more of the arrani wood had to be brought to the city, a journey that often took most of a year.

"Something stinks," said Ecrilla in an undervoice.

"Stow it, Ecrilla," said Horder.

"Yes, sir."

"God, look at the place," said Spandril as he looked down the narrow streets.

"He said God," the Scribe of Ajna said quietly to Kazei as they moved along the central street of Kel, knowing that though the route was empty, they were being watched by those fortunate enough to live near this Sacred Way.

"Yes; I heard," whispered Kazei.

"How've they managed to survive here?" asked Varnig of nothing in particular.

"They were pretty desperate during the Great Famine, according to the records," said Spandril.

"They'd have to be," said Ecrilla.

"The translator's on," Commander Horder reminded them. "Better think about what you're saying."

"Yes, sir," said Spandril for the men.

Kel had been rebuilt only two generations before and the recent earthquakes had been mild, causing nothing more than minor damage. The paintings on the buildings were still bright; the Artisan Caste was strong in Kel, as in the other cities that must be rebuilt, and they were at pains to keep the city beautiful for the honor of the Gods. In the mining city of Djanrez the Artisan Caste had accomplished more, but nothing as wonderful as the paintings that adorned the Sacred Way of Kel.

"Did you look at those murals?" Spandril asked Horder as they walked along.

"I'm trying not to," answered his Commander.

The Scribe of Ajna made note of this remark and murmured to the priest of Zivi, "He turns away from the exploits of Durga in all Her faces."

"I have noted it," said the priest.

"It is true that the Gods reveal themselves in many ways." The Scribe hesitated at the door to the Central Temple, for he would not enter ahead of those of the Highest Caste, and the priests were above him in honor. In regard to the Visitors, there could be no doubt that they were entitled to enter first.

"What is wisest?" asked Admih of the High Priest of Durga, who was the leader of the Central Temple. "Since the God has not revealed His Godliness?"

"You and I will enter and invite Him and His attendants to enter," said the High Priest. With these words he stepped through the portal and prostrated himself before the enormous altar which dominated the front of the temple.

Admih lowered his head before he crossed the threshold. "The face of the All-Mother is turned to the Celestial River which flows from Janja."

The Highest Caste repeated this reverence as they waited for the Visitors to enter the Central Temple.

Those priests who were entitled to enter the Central Temple arranged themselves in proper order, each beginning to recite their Endless Prayers. The Visitors regarded them in silence which surely revealed again their divinity, for all others would speak their prayers in so holy a place.

"Better go in, Commander," suggested Spandril.

"I guess," he agreed, and moved forward.

The others came after Him, attending Him. The Highest Caste let the proper seven steps separate them from the Visitors before following them within the largest building in the city.

"Where do we sit?" asked Varnig as he looked about the place.

"There are pillows there in the side . . . galleries, I guess they are," said Spandril. "Do you think we could—"

Admih clapped his hands; the priests went for the large pillows and pulled them into the center of the temple so that the Visitors would be able to see the enormous statue of Durga and show Her the courtesy of Gods for one another. "If it is Your wish, it is our honor to obey." He waited while the priest served the Visitors as they were entitled to do.

Gazili came to the side of Admih. "I think I would sacrifice one of my children if I could be permitted to serve a God as they are doing."

"This God has not asked it of you," said Admih, sharing Gazili's zeal. "If I had more than one child, I would wish to do the same."

"Who among us would not?" asked Kazei as he fingered the medallion he wore. "There can be no greater attainment than to serve the Gods."

"Even Vizna, though He is not allied to Durga," sighed Muthali.

"All Gods are allied to Durga," they were reminded by the priest of Yeimei. "She is the All-Mother; all things are Hers, even Janja and Vizna."

The others made gestures of agreement as they watched the Visitors fold onto the pillows.

"We are eager to hear what you will say," said the High Priest of Durga. "Your wisdom will sustain and inspire us."

Commander Horder looked uneasily at the High Priest of Durga and then at his own men. "We want . . . we want to tell you what has happened between us and the Khalia."

Again the name that caught the attention of all the Highest Caste, who moved nearer in order to listen to what the spirit-box told them. Telo, so young and fragile, was the only one who did not press forward, for he needed the support of a pillar to keep from collapsing.

"You spoke of a battle," said the High Priest of Durga, daring to speak out while within his own temple.

"Yes. One of our . . . our bases was destroyed by the Khalia. It was the first major act of aggression on their part." Commander Horder looked at the men of Kel. "You understand that we regarded them as nothing more dangerous than pirates before that happened."

"There was great destruction?" asked the High Priest of Durga.

"Yes," Horder said grimly. "Castleton's . . . slaughter." He looked down, His eyes lowered.

"Ah," said the High Priest of Durga as he nodded toward Her statue. "We must learn more of what these Khalia did."

Horder took a deep breath. "Let's just say that they're crazy in battle. They are as maddened as beasts. They kill for the joy of it, and for the love of battle." It was not easy to keep His voice even. "The loss of life was very high."

"Where was this place, the . . . base you speak of?" asked the High Priest of Durga.

"It was . . . " He stopped and looked at Spandril. "How would you explain it?"

Spandril was willing to attempt a description. "From here you would say it was in the sky, a great distance away, farther than any of you could travel on foot in a dozen lifetimes." He saw Horder signal him to go on. "There were thousands of people there, some of the finest men in the Fleet, and they were wiped out by the Khalia."

"A fine sacrifice," said the High Priest of Durga.

"If losing so many good men can be called fine," said Commander Horder with bitterness.

"'They were honored, these men?" asked the Scribe of Ajna, though it was improper for him to speak in this temple.

Commander Horder looked baffled. "Of course. All of them are heros."

"Indeed," said Derir, his old eyes shining. "The death of heroes."

"It was that," said Commander Horder. "And it's why we're making the effort to locate as many of the old Earth colonies as we can, so that we can protect you, and enlist your aid in fighting the Khalia." He had said these words before, but always to colonies that had remained in some kind of contact with Earth. These isolated colonists were unknown to him, and he did not know how to proceed with them.

"How could such as we fight Khalians?" asked Admih as the Commander stared at him in appeal.

"He's got a point," muttered Varnig.

Commander Horder paid no attention to this. "We need every kind of help. Those Khalia are determined to wreck everything we've tried to build up. They're out to destroy us and all we've accomplished." He looked around the temple. "I can understand why you might doubt what I'm saying. You've been isolated for so long, it's pretty hard to grasp all the changes that have taken place since you were sent out from Earth, but—"

"We came from Janja," the High Priest corrected him politely.

"Yes. From Janja," said Commander Horder impatiently. "Whatever you call it, we all started out there."

"Commander," Spandril said quietly, "it might be better to take a couple of the officials back to the ships and show them the tapes we have. That might make it clearer."

Both Ecrilla and Varnig started to object, but Commander Horder interrupted them. "You've got a point. I don't know what's getting through to them now. And I want to get out of this place. That statue gives me the wobbles."

"He trembles in the presences of Durga," said Derir to Bezin with some satisfaction. "Make note of that."

"This avatar comes from one other than Durga in any of Her faces," Bezin agreed.

Commander Horder looked directly at Admih. "We have . . . records of what happened in the battle. We'll show you. You'll have a chance to see what they do."

"See the battle?" asked Admih, since the High Priest of Durga did not speak. "How can you do this?"

"We have records," muttered Horder.

"Sacred books," said the High Priest of Durga with satisfaction.

"Not quite," Varnig corrected, feeling more uncomfortable than ever in the presence of the Highest Caste. "There are ways . . . we can show you part of what happened."

"Such is your power?" asked the Scribe of Ajna, astonished at his own bravery.

"Something like that," replied Commander Horder as He stood a little straighter. "I think we can accomodate ten of you. If you'll select ten, we'll take you back to the ship and let you see what we've got."

The priests immediately fell to debating among themselves, but the Highest Caste had no such trouble. "Derir is the oldest; he will come with me," announced Admih. "And Kazei and Gazili and the Scribe."

The priests eventually agreed that the High Priest of Durga, the High Priest of Yeimei, the High Priest of Zivi, and the High Priest of Vizna would see these Sacred Books and report to all what they contained.

Once outside the walls of Kel, Commander Horder had Ecrilla and Varnig flank the company of Highest Caste and High Priests. He gave a signal and the doors were opened for Him, and all passed into the great chariot, the celestial ship which had carried Commander Horder to Durga.

Never before had anyone of Durga seen such a thing as the ship that rode the Celestial River. In the Sacred Books there were descriptions of such things, but the chariots of the air were a thing of the distant past, and the ships of the Celestial River were more remote than that. It was with awe that the Highest Caste and the High Priests stepped aboard the ship and saw its wonders.

"There's not much room," Commander Horder explained. "The *Determined* is our base ship, and she's . . . a very long way off." He motioned toward the ceiling. "We're one of nine scouting parties in this sector."

"Yes," said Admih, knowing that the significance of the God's words would be apparent shortly. "Nine scouts. There are nine avatars, then."

"Avata—what?" said Varnig.

"Don't get into that now," Spandril told the others. "It's the translator, probably. You know what it does." He had moved into a bend of the room to give more space to the Highest Caste and High Priests of Durga.

"We'll tell you what's going on, all through the tapes, and we'll answer your questions at the end, if you don't mind," said Commander Horder as He addressed the others. "Most of the tapes are records, but we've had to fill in with a reconstruction here and there."

"That's one way to look at it," said Ecrilla softly to Varnig. "Wholesale propaganda's what it is."

"Shut up, Ecrilla," replied Varnig.

The ship was filled with marvels, and though not ornamented in the way we of Durga expect of a God, none within the ship were disappointed, for there were jewels and sculpture everywhere, and many glowing mysteries that caught the attention of the Scribe of Ajna more than the others. He contended later that most of the jewels were not that, but gauges and instruments, such as are described in the Sacred Maintenance Manuals. He was certain that the faint, whispered voices were from the ship itself and not from the spirits that protected and surrounded it. Only a few in the mining city of Djanrez followed him in this madness, but the Castes there are always extreme in their views.

"There's not much room, but if you can find a place to sit, we'll put the pictures on the library screen there," said Commander Horder, gesturing toward a high, blank wall.

Obediently all the Highest Caste and High Priests did as the God told them.

Lights in the room faded—the God and His attendants were not dismayed, and so the Highest Caste and High Priests of Kel were not dismayed, either—and the wall started to glow softly, and was then replaced with the bright path of the Celestial River.

"You've got to understand that we of the Fleet did not appreciate the danger the Khalia represented at first, since they were acting more like pirates."

On the screen another celestial ship similar to the one they now occupied, though no bigger than a fist, started across the screen, moving among the endless lights that are the beacons of the Celestial River. It was without shape or substance, this ship, and all who saw it knew that it was a vision given by the God.

"The Khalia live to fight. They're ruthless and vicious and completely dedicated to war." Commander Horder spoke in a tone of voice that was flattened by ritual; He had spoken these words before in the same way, and therefore all the Highest Caste and High Priests of Kel strove to remember the words so that they might be able to participate in the ritual later in their own temples.

Two more celestial ships, different from the one already manifested in the vision, darted out of the darkness in pursuit of the first ship. Sparks of light erupted about the celestial ships, showing the potency of the Gods they carried.

"We regarded them as pirates, at first," Commander Horder continued, the ritual observed by His attendants.

In the vision, the first celestial ship was bright with the fires of transformation. For an instant it hung between the other two celestial ships, and then it winked out, entering the Higher Realms.

"The Khalia kept their raids small and fast, selecting small outposts and other isolated ships to attack."

A strange celestial city appeared now in the vision, a great palace with enormous walls and great power that turned in the mind of the God Horder, for it shifted and rotated in the vision, revealing more of its wonders.

"This space station had more than two thousand people on it, and five ships of the line," said Commander Horder with more emotion than he had shown at first. "The Khalia attacked it, coming in forty ships of their own with the greatest firepower we had ever seen from them. The battle lasted for almost five hours, and only eighty-six of our people got away. The space station was a total loss, and four of the ships."

The story unfolded in the vision as the city was surrounded by the strange ships, each of them casting out balls of light that struck at the vast flanks of the celestial city, occasionally breaching them. This time the tiniest attendants of Gods could be seen, not one of them larger than a finger, all working to keep the celestial city from falling to the small celestial ships of those Commander Horder had called the Khalia.

"Where is this place?" asked the Scribe of Ajna, completely fascinated by the vision the God was offering us.

"It's . . . a very long way from here," said Commander Horder after a hesitation. "And this took place many months ago."

"A memory of a battle," said the Scribe of Ajna, and was so much moved that he looked directly at the High Priest of Vizna. "We know of great battles among the Gods that took place long ago. It is in our Sacred Books which crossed the Celestial River from Janja with us. This is the *Beved Hajit*."

All those of the Highest Caste and the High Priests who were in the celestial ship with the God Horder and the Scribe of Ajna were siezed by the same inspiration. The God Horder was recalling the battles of the *Beved Hajit*, so that we would be shown what avatar was with us, and to what purpose. We have often seen that the ways of the Gods are not easily known by men. Now that so much was known to us, we were eager to discover what would be offered to us, the children of those Gods Who continued Their battles.

"The *Beved Hajit*," repeated Commander Horder, His voice changing since He was not repeating His ritual.

"The Holy Book," said the Scribe of Ajna, still held in his inspiration. "The great battles."

"Oh. Yes." He cleared his throat and looked at Spandril.

"I'd go along with it, sir. If they want to be religious about this, let them."

Commander Horder nodded; the vision, which had remained unchanging, now once again moved. "Uh . . . after the space station, we of the Fleet took more precautions. Nothing too extreme. We didn't want to alarm people. We also built up our ships in those quadrants where the Khalia had been strongest."

The vision changed, and in quick succession came larger and more ornamented celestial ships, many of them already revealing their celestial fire as they moved. It was a sight for all to stand in awe of, for these visions were as real as the walls of Kel, or so they appeared. Once Kazei ducked as the celestial ship appeared to hover over him, and everyone made note of it, aware of the importance of his medallion.

"The Khalia grew bolder, more audacious, and they attacked Fleet ships and Fleet space stations with impunity."

The vision continued to change, and the celestial ships were again caught up in battle. Gouts of celestial fire sprung up on many of the ships; at once the ships would wink out as it transcended. Occasionally the fire would not be as pure as was needed and some part of the celestial ship would remain, nothing but a remnant, charred and broken by the touch of the Gods.

"The Fleet has its obligations to protect all our people, those of Earth origin, and those from other planets." World after world were revealed in the God's mind and manifest in the vision. Some were bustling with life, filled with buildings and chariots and celestial ships, some were quiet and simple as a hermit's cave.

"This is Kammille," went on Commander Horder.

There were creatures on the world, the caprice of the Gods, for they were dressed in bright skins like the legendary messengers of Janja, who flew and sang for her long before we set out on the Celestial River. These creatures were seen in large groups, listening to Gods who had descended among them.

"We didn't anticipate trouble on the scale we got it at Kammille. We should have. The Khalia had made their intentions plain enough."

Large numbers of celestial ships, which God Horder identified as being the latest of the celestial ships of the Khalia, swarmed toward the ball named Kammille. This time the battle was long and relentless. Buildings as well as celestial ships fell to the Heavenly Fire.

To see creatures of the Gods siezed by the transcendence that was the Gods' alone! The High Priest of Zakti fell on his face in ecstacy, pleading to be as fortunate as the creatures of Target. Until that day, all of us believed that the Gods would never touch us directly except when our sacrifices were sufficient to bring about a manifestation of Their acceptance, which had not happened in almost a generation. Many had feared that all touch of the Gods had gone, yet here was the assurance, the representation of Their presence more overwhelming than anything in our Sacred Books.

In reverential hush, the High Priest of Durga plucked at his eyes, certain that he would never again witness anything so glorious as the vision of this moment.

"Better ease up a little, Commander," Spandril advised.

"And stop that guy from blinding himself," added Varnig.

The vision froze once more, and the attendants of the God Horder went to the High Priest of Durga and took hold of him.

"Let me, let me," murmured the High Priest of Durga.

"It'll be all right," said the attendant Ecrilla. "Don't do that any more."

"If the God commands it," said the High Priest of Durga, his attention on the suspended vision of the God. "If there is more to see, then I will watch as long as the God wishes it."

"I wish they'd stop calling me a god," Horder said in an undervoice.

"Use it, Commander," Spandril advised him.

"And turn off the translator for a bit." Commander Horder gestured to the spirit-box and at once his words were incomprehensible. In the exalted tongue, Horder and His attendant conversed while the Highest Caste and the High Priests waited, each praying that the God would grant the gift of understanding so that the purpose of the talk would be revealed. To have shown so much and to withhold so much! All knew it was typical of the Gods.

"We will have to make a sacrifice," declared the High Priest of Yeimei. "As great a sacrifice as any we have offered."

"The children," suggested Derir. "We have enough children to offer half of them."

"Or the women," said Admih. "We have not sacrificed women for more than a generation. We could make pyres with the last of the wood from the old forest."

"It is not enough," said the High Priest of Durga. "If we are to achieve what those blessed creatures of Target achieved, we will have to give more than that."

No one could deny the truth of it. Old Derir took his

ancient crossed cords in his hand. "The city of Kel itself. We could emulate what we have seen and give up the city and everyone in it."

"But suppose the Gods wanted more? Even if we burn Kel and ourselves with it, that is only earthly fire. If the Gods will not visit us with Celestial Fire, then the sacrifice will not bring the transcendence we desire." The Scribe of Ajna indicated the God Horder. "Let him continue. He will show us the way. When he has completed his ritual, we will know what we are to do."

All of the High Caste and High Priests of Kel prostrated themselves and began, each of them, to recite their Everlasting Prayers.

The spirit-box spoke again. "Please. Do that later, will you?"

Obediently the High Caste and the High Priests fell silent.

"We've got more to show you," announced the God Horder. "Not too much more of Target. I think you get the picture there."

"Good idea," said Spandril.

"The creatures were consumed with fire," announced Admih, to let the God know he has grasped the significance.

"Yes."

"Better get on with it, Commander," prodded Spandril. "You don't know how much longer you can hold these guys."

"Right." Horder gestured and the vision again sprang into being. "Target was about the worst we've had to face from the Khalia. You can understand why we want to warn everyone about them, put you on the alert."

"We understand," Kazei assured Him.

"Good. Because the trouble is, the Khalia are stepping up their activities. We've been under attack from them ever since Target. It's turning into an all-out war." He indicated the area of his vision. "Now, the Fleet's ready for it. If the Khalia really want to have a fight, we'll give it to them. We aren't about to turn tail and run."

Ecrilla laughed. "We're trying to cover our rear; that's different."

"Ecrilla!" Spandril warned him.

"We have been trying to extend our protection as far as we can. That's why we're looking for lost colonies like you, so that we can be better prepared to—"

Spandril interrupted Commander Horder. "Isolated colonies like this one are likely to be targets, too. The Khalian forces are going to extend their territory of operations, and for that they need planets like this one as a way station. That could mean that you'd be under attack."

"That's putting it pretty bluntly," said Commander Horder. "But it more or less covers the problem."

Admih was so amazed that he found it difficult to speak. "You are telling us that the Khalia might come here, to Durga? That they might wish to engage in battle here?"

"It's possible," Commander Horder said carefully. "We're doing everything we can to prepare for that eventuality." He looked around the walls of his celestial ship. "It might not look like we're ready for them, but—"

"It is the way of the Gods," said the High Priest of Durga. "We do not dispute the way of the Gods."

"Does that mean you'll cooperate?" asked Spandril, looking at Admih. "We'll have to work out terms with you before too long. If you're willing."

Admih did not need to consult his fellow Highest Caste. "It is always the desire of the children of the Gods to be at Their service." He spoke the words as he had every morning since he had entered into adulthood.

"Good," said Horder, relieved. "Because we're worried about places like this. We want you to know that from the beginning. You outlying planets are apt to be more vulnerable than those closer to Fleet headquarters. We're going to have to work out a plan so that you can keep in contact with us."

"But surely—" began the High Priest of Durga. "You are Gods. You have knowledge of all things."

Spandril stepped in. "Even Gods can be distracted. In the chaos of war, Gods do not always have the opportunity to attend to Their children. We have come so that we can decide how best to make sure your prayers are heard and answered."

Admih was puzzled now. "Why has it taken you so long

to do this? For generations we have been in isolation. We have sacrificed and prayed and offered all the treasures of Durga, but have had only silence."

"Yes; we are going to correct that," said Spandril. "Before now, this God did not understand how urgent your need was. Now that the Khalia have made this apparent, He is determined to protect you as you deserve." He looked quickly at Horder before he went on. "You have done well. You and all the others living here on Durga. Had there not been the Khalia, the Gods would have been with you before this time."

"Ah," said the High Priest of Durga. "And the Khalia? What do they know of us?"

"We haven't discovered that yet," said Horder shortly.

The Scribe of Ajna went to the spirit-box and laid his hands on it. "What God lives here? Yaneza had all knowledge. Is this the manifestation of Yaneza?"

"I . . . no, not Yaneza," said Spandril in an abrupt way. "It is a servant of the God Horder."

"Spandril, stop this—" Commander Horder protested.

"We are all servants of the God," went on Spandril as if Horder had said nothing. "We of the Fleet serve many High Gods."

The High Priest of Yeimei nodded in agreement, his fingertips touching and his head bowed over his hands. "It is the war of the High Gods, then."

"Yes. The Khalia are trying to destroy everything we of the Fleet have done. They kill and revel in killing. If they had their way, your entire world would be an empty, burned-out cinder." Spandril faced the High Priest of Durga. "You must try to understand what is at risk here."

"We know," said the High Priest of Durga. "It is in the Sacred Books. There is war among the Gods."

"And if you aid us, we will protect you from the Khalia," said Commander Horder, looking angrily at his second in command. "We of the Fleet are prepared to fight the Khalia to their extinction."

We of Durga had long known that the day would come when there would be confrontation between the Gods, when the fate of Their children would be decided. All of the

High Priests who saw the vision in the celestial ship knew that the time had come when the All-Mother summoned them.

"What of these Khalia?" asked the Scribe of Ajna. "How are they manifest?"

"They are like weasels, like ferrets and stoats," said Commander Horder who had only the vaguest idea of what those animals were.

"What is the nature of these animals?" asked the High Priest of Yeimei.

"They're killers," said Commander Horder. "They're rapacious. The Khalia put the animals to shame."

Once again the vision formed, and there was a creature about half the size of those watching, a fur-covered, sharp-snouted creature wearing a pack on its shoulders, and carrying an Attribute in its hands.

"That's a Khalian." Spandril all but spat the word.

"Are all manifest this way?" asked the High Priest of Durga as he gazed reverently at the vision. "Is this the avatar?"

"They're not quite to scale," admitted Commander Horder. "But that's what they look like. There's some color variation and a few of them have stripes, but that's what you look for."

"A strange avatar," said the Scribe of Ajna.

"It is not for us to question the manifestation of the avatar," the High Priest of Durga rebuked him. "What is that hanging from the pack, God Horder?"

Commander Horder could not conceal His distaste. "Two skulls. Probably trophies."

The High Priest of Yeimei looked at the High Priest of Durga. "Skulls," he said, gesturing acknowledgment. "Thus is the avatar known."

"Yes," said the High Priest of Durga. "We must make sacrifice."

"It wouldn't hurt," said Commander Horder. "Some of those Khalia collect skulls. Be careful that one of them isn't yours." He signaled and another vision appeared. "This is a Khalian scout ship, the sort they might send here. As you can tell, it's smaller than ours—"

Admih laughed on behalf of those with him. Of course it

was smaller, for they saw it in the vision, hardly larger than one of the skulls the Khalians collected. They stared, all of the Highest Caste and High Priests of Kel, at the Khalian scout ship.

"Usually they arrive in threes," Commander Horder went on. "In your case, since you have a few cities here, they might divide up and go to the others as well as this one, but even if all you see is one, you can be sure that there are others around somewhere. It's important to keep that in mind. The Khalia never send out solitary scouts in enemy territory."

The vision faded again, and this time it was replaced by more images of fire and mayhem. Destruction glowed in the vision as walls fell and more of the miniscule people were massacred. It was an act of the utmost homage, and the Highest Caste and High Priests were caught up in the sacred act, each seeing now how woefully inadequate their previous worship had been.

"The All-Mother will forgive us if we correct our error," whispered the High Priest of Durga.

"Even a city is not offering enough," said the Scribe of Ajna.

"The avatar—" began Admih, but was interrupted by Commander Horder.

"We don't want to upset you," He told them. "Isolated like this, you haven't had the chance to see how things have changed. It's unfortunate that it takes a war to—"

The vision faded and the cramped room was once again bright.

"You can count on the Fleet to do everything we can for you," said Spandril, adding, "This war is going to demand a lot from all of us."

"Don't you think that's laying it on a bit thick?" said Ecrilla. "We just found this place. Give 'em some time to get used to us."

"There isn't time," said Spandril.

"You headquarters brats are all alike," Varnig complained.

"And you junior line officers are better?" Spandril asked.

"Stop it," said Commander Horder with fatigue. "We have to settle this before we head for the next city."

"I don't see how you can call a ramshackled place like that a city," Varnig said under his breath, his complaint dutifully translated by the spirit-box.

"I said stop it," Commander Horder repeated more loudly. "We have work to do here."

"Do you think we can do it outside before the stench kills us?" Ecrilla asked sarcastically.

"Good idea," Horder said, and turned once again to Admih. "Let us return to the gates of . . . of Kel."

"Our pleasure and duty are one," replied Admih as he bent double to Commander Horder. "To obey a God is the highest joy."

"All we ask is some help for the Fleet," said Spandril.

Commander Horder turned back to Varnig. "Start preparing a report for Captain Branker."

"Us or the others?" asked Ecrilla.

"Have Fondo do it," said Commander Horder. "I want it on its way before morning."

Ecrilla sighed. "Full report or initial survey?"

"We can't file a full report yet, can we?" Spandril answered for Commander Horder.

Night had taken hold of the land when the Highest Caste and High Priests of Kel left the celestial ship. A high veil of clouds hid the stars so that the vision which had been shown to them was all the more wondrous.

"I'll be glad when I can transfer back to a real ship," said Commander Horder as He looked at the gates of Kel. "These scouting missions are a waste of time."

"Not if it helps us stop the Khalia," Spandril pointed out.

Commander Horder shrugged. "How much chance do you think we have of doing that? Especially here? Lost colonies usually got that way for a good reason." He gave his attention to the Highest Caste and High Priests of Kel. "We will return as soon as possible."

"Will there be a battle? Will the Khalia come?" asked the High Priest of Durga.

"I hope not, for your sake," said Commander Horder.

"We are not yet prepared?" asked Admih.

Horder laughed unhappily. "Nowhere near."

"No one's prepared," said Spandril before Commander Horder could stop him.

"Ah. Then the deciding battle is yet to come. There is time." Admih gestured to the High Priests. "We have much to do."

"We all have much to do," said Commander Horder. "That is why we have to depart now."

The Highest Caste and the High Priests of Kel made gestures of reverence and bowed their farewell. "We will strive to be ready when you return."

"That's good," said Commander Horder. "We ought to be back within the year."

"Unless the Khalia change that," added Spandril.

The spirit-box was silent; the God and His attendants went back to the celestial ship, leaving the Highest Caste and High Priests of Kel huddled against the gates of their city, watching as the celestial ship rose into the air and rushed into the sky.

By morning only two of them—the ancient Derir and the High Priest of Yeimei—were dead and the others were able to stumble back to the Central Temple to prepare to offer the bodies of the newly dead to Durga.

Thus it was that we of Durga came to serve the All-Mother in her aspect of the Destroyer, as She is known when She is Khali, when she strews the ground with corpses and garlands Herself with skulls. We, who feared for so long that our prayers and sacrifices were displeasing to Her, that our devotion was not sufficient to bring her favor to us again.

With the guidance of the High Priests of Kel, our plans were made, and so it was that upon the return of the God Horder, his incarnate flesh and the incarnate flesh of His attendants was offered on Durga's altar in Earthly Fire.

There is no sweeter sacrifice to Khali than flesh, and surely the ruin which has come to Djanrez at the hands of the Khalia shows that we are restored at last to Her favor. It cannot be long before either the Gods of the Fleet or the avatar Khalia claim us with Celestial Fire, and we are at last free of the Turning of Lives, transformed as the creatures of Target were transformed to the higher state where even the Gods are welcome sacrifice to the All-Mother.

INTERLUDE

The assembled admirals sat in various stages of relaxation. One had brought a bottle of Ohio champagne and was passing it around. The Strategy Board was pleased with itself.

The landings on Bethesda had been costly but successful. The Khalia were evacuating Triton and Dibden Purlieu. The Omni was filled with praise for the Fleet, the successful defenders of the Alliance. Outside of Port no member of the Fleet paid for his own drink. Everyone on Port was Fleet, so they bought each other drinks.

Even Smythe was cheerful in his restrained manner. "Let me begin with my congratulations."

Several glasses were raised in response.

"Initial analysis supports our earlier conclusions. The large quantities of materiel captured could not have been manufactured by the Khalia. Nor did they seem capable of more than the most rudimentary of repairs. We have yet to find even one Bethesdan who met a Khalian engineer or scientist."

Several admirals chuckled their approval. If the enemy didn't have any scientists, all the better.

"There was also one disturbing piece of information,"

Smythe sounded concerned now. "Virtually half of the ships we fought at Bethesda were new."

Several glasses froze in midair.

"New?" Meier repeated, the implications of this development just sinking in.

"Dozens, and more were expected," Smythe confirmed.

Meier rose and faced his fellow admirals. "Today we celebrate one victory. But it appears the war will not be over until we can find the source of the Khalian ships and destroy it."

Several *here, heres* agreed.

Smythe spoke again, trying to end on a note of optimism. "We have just freed thousands of Alliance citizens on Bethesda. After a brutal occupation they should be united in their desire to assist us. Perhaps they will have the solution to our mystery."

WHEN THE DEVIL DRIVES
by David Drake

"CAPTAIN MIKLOS KOWACS?"asked whoever was sticking his hand through the canvas curtain to tap Kowacs on the shoulder as he showered with his men. "Could I have a quick minute with you?"

"*Whoo!* I dropped the soap, sweetie," called one of Kowac's Marines in a falsetto. "I'll just bend over and pick it up!"

Kowacs lifted his face to the spray of his shower for an excuse not to look at the guy interrupting. The horseplay of his unit, the 121st Marine Reaction Company—the Headhunters—was as relaxing to him as the steamy hammering of the water. He didn't want to think about anything else just now, and he didn't see any reason why he should.

"If I *was* Nick Kowacs," he said, "I'd have just spent six hours in my hard suit, picking through what used to be the main spaceport on this mudball. Bug off, huh?"

He turned his head slightly. Some of the water recoiling from him spurted through the gap in the canvas to soak the intruder in its rainbow spray.

"Yeah, that's what I wanted to check," the voice continued flatly. "I'm English—I've got the Ninety-Second—and we—"

"Hell and damnation!" Kowacs muttered in embarrassment as he slipped out through the canvas himself. The decontamination showers were floored with plastic sheeting, but the ground outside the facility had been bulldozed bare and turned to mud by overflow and the rain. It squelched greasily between his toes.

"Sorry, Captain," he explained. "I thought you were some rear echelon mother wanting to know why I hadn't inventoried the week's laundry."

"S'okay," English said. "The *Haig*'s about to lift with us, and I needed to check one thing with you about the port."

The Ninety-Second's commander didn't carry Kowacs's weight; but he was a hand's breadth taller, with curly hair and the sort of easy good looks that made him seem gentle to somebody who didn't know English's reputation.

Kowacs knew the reputation. Besides, he'd seen eyes like English's before, pupils that never focused very long on anything because of the things they'd seen already.

Kowacs had eyes like that himself.

Sergeant Bradley, the Headhunters' field first, slipped out of the shower behind his commanding officer. "Anything I can do to help, sir?" he asked.

Stripped, the noncom looked as thin as a flayed weasel. He was missing one toe, a plasma burst a decade before had left half his scalp hairless and pink, and much of the body between those two points bore one or another form of scarring.

"No problem," Kowacs said—and there wasn't, but it was nice to know that there was always going to be somebody to watch his back. It kept you alive in this line of work; and more important, it kept you as sane as you could be. "Captain English heads up the Ninety-Second. This—" shifting his gaze to the taller officer—"is First Sergeant Bradley."

"Toby," said English, shaking with Bradley—both of them with hands wet from the shower. "Not 'captain' yet anyway, though maybe after this last one . . ."

"Hey!" said Bradley with enough enthusiasm to ignore the fact that English was obviously distracted. "You guys did a *hell* of a job on the port! Nothin' left but rubble and cinders. Say, they got you looking for that weasel commando that shot up Post Bessemer two nights ago?"

"Ah," said English. "No, we're about to lift. As a matter of fact—"

Bradley didn't need the glance Kowacs gave him. "Sorry, sir," he said as he ducked back into the shower facility. "*Damn* good to meet you!"

English spent a moment marshaling his thoughts after Bradley had left the two officers alone again—if alone was the right word for men standing beside one of the main roads crisscrossing the huge base.

Base Thomas Forberry—named to commemorate symbolically the hundreds of thousands of civilians whom the Khalia had murdered—had been woodland and farms gone to brush when the Fleet landed to retake Bethesda less than a month before. Now it had a hundred kilometers of perimeter fence with bunkers and guard towers; a nearby spaceport and naval dockyard ten times bigger than the port that had served the planet before the Khalian invasion; buildings to house more people than there were indigenous humans in the portion of the planet now under the Fourth District Military Government installed here at Base Forberry—

And seven thousand five hundred hectares of mud—the inescapable result of any military construction project save those undertaken in deserts, ice caps, or vacuum.

"Ah," said Kowacs—he'd have helped English say what he needed to if he'd had the faintest notion of what it was. "Bradley was right. I don't think—" he paused; but it was true, so he said it, "anybody could've done a better job on the port than you guys did. You'll get your second star for sure."

"Had a lotta help from the indigs," English said, letting his eyes slant away toward the horizon. "They got us through the perimeter, you know?"

"No shit?" said Kowacs. He hadn't heard anything about that.

He was vaguely aware that he was standing stark naked beside the road. Some of the admin types who'd landed when the shooting pretty much stopped might take that badly, but modesty wasn't a useful virtue among troops who spent most of their time either in the field or packed into the strait confines of a landing vessel.

"I guess . . ." said Toby English with a diffidence that must have been as unusual to him as it would have been in the man to whom he was speaking. "That what your sergeant said was the straight goods? Nothing left at the port?"

"Oh, look, man, I'm sorry," said Kowacs who finally thought he knew what was bothering the other officer. "Look, we recovered two of your people. But the third one, the suit transponder still worked but there was half the tail of a destroyer melted across him. Nothing we could do, but we tried."

"Thanks," said English with a smile that was genuine but too brief for that to have been the real problem. "Dead's dead. Don't mean nothin'."

"Yeah," said Kowacs, agreeing with the meaning rather than the words. "We've all sent home eighty kilos of sand with a warning to the family not to open the coffin."

"Ah," English continued, looking away again. "I guess you'd've checked if there was any bunkers under the Terminal Building? I thought there might've been."

"No bunkers," Kowacs said, keeping the frown off his forehead but not quite out of his voice.

"That was downwind of one of the destroyers that cooked off," he continued carefully. "The fission triggers of her torpedo warheads, they burned instead of blowing. But it was hot enough that our suits are still in there—" he pointed toward the plastic dome of the decontamination building, "and they thought we ought to shower off pretty good ourselves."

English smiled falsely. "Yeah," he said. "Look, lift-off was twenty minutes ago, and—"

Kowacs put a hand on the other Marine's arm to stop him. As gently as he could, he said, "There were a lot of bodies inside, but only indigs and weasels. No Marine equipment. What happened out there?"

English shrugged and said, "Don't matter a lot. I told you, the indigs got us through the perimeter. I think most of 'em got out again before things started to pop, but—the

On-the-Spot agent running the unit, Milius . . . She was
keeping the weasels occupied inside the Terminal Building."

He met Kowacs's gaze with clear, pale eyes of his own.
"She had balls, that one."

"Trouble with sticking your neck out . . ." said Kowacs
softly, looking toward a distance much farther in time than
the horizon on which his eyes were fixed. "Is sooner or later,
somebody chops it off."

"Don't I know it," English agreed bitterly. His voice and
expression changed, became milder. "Don't we all. Look, I
gotta run."

He paused, then added, "Hey. If it can't be the Ninety-
Second gets those weasel hold-outs, I hope it's you guys."

"I hope it's us lifts-off tomorrow," Kowacs called to the
taller officer's back; but English was already busy talking to
a truck driver, bumming a ride to the spaceport and a
no-doubt-pissed naval officer.

The Ninety-Second was one of the half-companies shoe-
horned into Fleet combat units instead of being carried in a
purpose-built landing craft the way the Headhunters were.
People whose proper business was starships generally didn't
have much use for the ground-specialty Marines . . . but at
least the destroyer *Haig* hadn't lifted off while the Ninety-
Second's commander did his personal business.

Most of Kowacs's marines were done showering and had
filed back into the changing room. They'd have to don the
same sweaty uniforms they'd worn for six hours under their
hard suits while searching the shattered port, but the shower
had raised their spirits.

Bradley was still waiting behind the canvas. So was
Sienkiewicz, who looked as tough when naked as she did
with her clothes on—and who was just as tough as she
looked.

The twenty nozzles down either side of the canvas
enclosure were still roaring happily, spewing out water that
had been brought twenty kilometers through huge plastic
aqueducts. The drains that were supposed to carry it away
were less satisfactory. At least half the water spilled out of
the enclosure and found its own way slowly toward the
lowest point in Base Forberry.

In an unusual twist of justice, that point was the parade ground surrounded by base headquarters and the offices of the military government, located in a valley where they couldn't be sniped at by the few Khalia still alive on Bethesda.

"Everything copacetic, sir?" Bradley asked with a smile to suggest that he hadn't been listening through the canvas while the officers talked.

"No problem," Kowacs grunted. And there wasn't, not one you could do anything about. Couldn't help the dead, like English had said. "Let's get back to barracks and find fresh uniforms."

"Ah—we were wondering about that, sir," the field first sergeant said. "The trucks are still pretty hot, even after we hosed 'em off."

Kowacs shrugged as he strode toward the changing room. "It's that or walk," he said. "I'll get 'em into a drydock over at the naval base as soon as I can, but Marine ground equipment is pretty low priority over there."

"And this place—" he waved toward the closed chamber in which robot arms were scrubbing the hard suits, "isn't big enough to hold trucks."

Sienkiewicz laughed in a throaty, pleasant—feminine—voice. "What's the matter, sarge?" she asked Bradley. "You expect a little low-level radiation to kill *us?*"

All three of them laughed, but there was no humor in the sound.

The summons set off the bell and red flasher at either end of the barracks: it was a Priority One call. Marines threw down their mid-afternoon tasks and jumped to arms even before they heard the specifics of the message.

There was only one thing on Bethesda now that could justify a Priority One call to the Headhunters. A single Khalian unit, an infiltration commando, hadn't died in heroically useless defense with the hundreds of thousands of other Khalia. The hit-and-run attacks of that surviving handful of weasels had been making things damned hot for the invasion forces.

The problem was beyond the equipment and experience of the Alliance troops that made up the bulk of the ground elements involved in Bethesda's recovery.

But it was made to order for the 121st Marine Reaction Company.

Kowacs slid on his helmet. "Go ahead," he said as his hands fumbled with the shirt he'd hung over the back of the chair he was sitting on. The information would be dumped into the unit's data bank, but he liked to get his orders directly as well. It made him feel that he was involved in a human process, not just an electronic game.

Of course it would be the computer which decided whether they made the strike by truck or loaded onto the *Bonnie Parker* to drop straight onto the weasels, trading longer preparation time for faster transit to the target area. Computers were great for that sort of computation, but humans—

"Captain Kowacs," said the synthesized voice of an artificial intelligence. "You are directed to report to District Governor, Admiral the Honorable Saburo Takami, immediately."

"Huh?"

"A vehicle has been dispatched for you. It will arrive in one-point-five minutes. That is all."

"Aye, aye," Kowacs said dazedly, not that the electronic secretary would have given a damn even if it hadn't broken the connection already. Priority fucking One.

He'd set it up so that all Priority One calls were slaved through the barracks loudspeakers. Everybody was staring at Kowacs as he stomped toward the door, sealing his shirt front while his hands were full of the equipment belt which he hadn't had time to sling on properly yet.

"Daniello," he called to his senior lieutenant, "hold the men in readiness."

Nobody bothered to ask *what* they were to be ready for.

Corporal Sienkiewicz was already waiting outside with bandoliers of ammunition and two unloaded assault rifles. She handed a set to her commanding officer.

Because of the weasel raids, the military government was still treating the Fourth District as a combat zone. Personnel leaving Controlled Areas—bases and defense points—were ordered to carry weapons at all times, though the weapons were to be unloaded except on approved combat operations.

And Sienkiewicz was right: there was no telling what Kowacs was going to hear from Admiral Takami, or how fast the District Governor would expect him to respond.

It was just that Kowacs didn't like to have a gun around when he talked to administrative types. It turned his thoughts in the wrong directions.

The jeep was strack and expensive, running on vectored thrust instead of the air cushion that would have been perfectly satisfactory on the plastic roadways of the base. The vehicle arrived within seconds of the time the AI had given Kowacs; and the driver—an enlisted man—had a voice almost as superciliously toneless as that of the machine when he said, "My orders are to transport one only to District Headquarters."

"Then your orders were wrong," said Kowacs as he and Sienkiewicz got into the jeep. He hadn't intended her to come, and he didn't need a bodyguard at District Headquarters—the sort of guarding that the big corporal *could* do, at any rate.

But neither was some flunky going to tell him he couldn't bring an aide along if he wanted to.

The jeep sagged under the weight of a big man and a very big woman. Cursing under his breath, the driver lowered the surface-effect skirts and pulled back into traffic on the air cushion's greater support.

Base Thomas Forberry was loud with vehicles, construction work, and the frequent roar of starships landing or lifting off from the nearby port. During lulls in the other racket, Kowacs could hear the thumping of plasma cannon from the perimeter. Some officers of the units on guard duty were "clearing their front of areas of potential concealment."

Blasting clumps of trees a kilometer away wouldn't prevent the infiltration attacks the surviving Khalia were making; but it did a little to help the boredom of guard duty in a quiet sector.

The civilian detention facility lay along one side of the road. Scores of wan indigs stared out at the traffic, careful not to come too close to the electrified razor ribbon that encircled the prison camp. The military government had already started rounding up Bethesdans who were reported to have collaborated with the Khalia. They'd be held here until they'd been cleared—or they were handed over to the civilian authorities for trial.

When the Fleet got around to setting up a civilian administration.

"Poor bastards," Kowacs muttered, looking away from the bleak hopelessness of the internees as the jeep crawled past at the speed of the trucks choking the base's main north-south boulevard.

Sienkiewicz shrugged. "They live in the same barracks as us," she said. "They eat the same rations. They sit on their butts all the time without a goddam thing to do, just like we do."

Kowacs met her eyes.

"So tell me where their problem is?" she concluded.

"Same place ours is," Kowacs agreed without much caring whether the driver could hear him also. "And we're going there now."

The parade square in the center of Base Forberry had been covered with plastic sheeting as soon as the three-story Base HQ and the District Government building were finished— and before crews had completed the structures on the other two sides of the square. Tracked machinery had chewed up half the sheeting and covered the remainder with mud of a biliously purple color.

It was the same color as the silt which had seeped into Admiral Takami's office when storm winds flexed the seams of the pre-fab building.

Kowacs saluted as carefully as he could, but he'd never been much of a hand at Mickey Mouse nonsense. The District Governor frowned—then scowled like a thundercloud when he noticed the Marine was eyeing the purple stain along the edge of the outer wall.

The other naval officer in the room, a commander with good looks and only a hint of paunch, smiled at Kowacs indulgently.

"Well, Kowacs," Admiral Takami said, "Sitterson here

tells me we need you in this district. I'm not going to argue with my security chief. What's a government for if not security, eh?"

"Ah?" Kowacs said. He couldn't understand what the governor meant.

He *prayed* that he didn't understand what the governor meant.

"What the governor means," said Commander Sitterson in a voice as smoothly attractive as his physical appearance, "is that the ground contingents are all well and good for large-scale operations, but we need a real strike force. The governor has had the 121st transferred from Naval command to the Fourth District government."

Well, Kowacs had never believed God listened to a marine's prayers.

"Well, I'll leave you men to get on with it," Takami said dismissively. "I have a great deal of work myself."

As Kowacs followed the security chief out of the office, he heard the governor snarling into the microphone embedded in his desk. He was demanding a work crew with mops and scrub brushes.

"I thought you'd rather hear about your reassignment from the governor rather than from me directly," Sitterson said in the anteroom. "Not a bad old bird, Takami. Won't get in the way of our carrying out our job. Did you keep the car?"

"No sir," Kowacs said. He was trying to grasp what had just happened to him and his unit. He couldn't.

"No matter," Sitterson said, though his frown belied his words. "We'll walk. It's just across the square."

He frowned again as he noticed that Sienkiewicz, carrying both rifles, followed them out of the building.

"My clerk," Kowacs said flatly.

"Yes, that reminds me," Sitterson replied. "I'll want one of your men on duty at all times in my outer office. I have living quarters in the building, you know. I can't be too careful."

Kowacs's skin burned as anger drove blood to its surface. "Ah, sir," he said. "We're a Marine *Reaction* Company."

"Well, I *want* men who can react, don't I?" Sitterson retorted.

Kowacs said nothing further.

Security Headquarters was kitty-corner from the government building, a hundred meters away; but Kowacs had never thought Sitterson needed the vehicle for any reason but status. It was a windowless single-story structure, three times as long as it was wide—a module rather than a pre-fab. The door was at one end; Sitterson buzzed for admittance instead of touching the latch himself.

The door opened to reveal an aisle running half the building's length. There were four closed doors to the left and eight barred cells on the right. The individual civilians in five of the cells leaned with their arms against their sides and their foreheads resting against the back wall.

It was an extremely painful position. The petty officer who'd opened the door had a long shock rod with which to prod any of the prisoners who sagged or touched the wall with a hand.

"Interrogation rooms," Sitterson said, gesturing toward the closed doors. He chuckled and added with a nod toward the cells, "I like my visitors to see that we mean business here. This is the only entrance to the building."

"What have they done?" Kowacs asked in a neutral voice.

"That's what we're here to find out, aren't we?" Sitterson replied with a broad grin.

One of the women in the holding cells was sobbing, on the verge of collapse. Kowacs lengthened his stride, drawing the security chief a little more quickly with him to the door at the far end of the aisle.

They weren't quite quick enough into the office beyond. As Sienkiewicz shut the door behind them, Kowacs heard the reptilian giggle of the shock rod loosing its fluctuating current. The woman screamed despairingly.

The senior petty officer behind the huge desk threw Sitterson a sharp salute without getting up. He didn't have room enough to stand because of the data storage modules in the ceiling, feeding the desk's computer.

Sitterson tried to project a sense of his own power—but the quarters assigned his operation were a far cry from even the jerry-built luxury of the District Government Building.

Fleet officers assigned to admin duty on the ground weren't usually the best and the brightest of their ranks.

That was something Kowacs had to remember—though he wasn't sure how it would help him.

"Colonel Hesik has reported, sir," said the petty officer, nodding toward the tall, intense man who had leaped to attention from the narrow couch opposite the desk.

"Wait here, Hesik," Sitterson said as he strode between desk and couch to the room's inner door.

Kowacs eyed—and was eyed by—the tall man as they passed at close quarters.

Hesik's uniform was of unfamiliar cut. It was handmade, with yellow cloth simulating gold braid on the pockets, epaulets, and collar tabs. The slug-throwing pistol he wore in a shoulder holster was a Fleet-issue weapon and well worn.

Hesik's glare was brittle. Kowacs wouldn't have had the man in his own unit in a million years.

Sitterson's personal office had almost as much floorspace as the governor's did, though the ceiling was low and the furnishings were extruded rather than wood.

On the credit side, the floor didn't seep mud.

"Have a seat, Captain," Sitterson said with an expansive gesture toward one of the armchairs. Another door, presumably leading to living quarters as cramped as the reception area, was partly screened by holo projections from the interrogation rooms they had walked past. In the holograms, seated petty officers confronted civilians standing at attention, nude, with their clothes stacked on the floor beside them.

"We'll be working closely together, Captain," the security chief was saying. "I don't mind telling you that I regard this assignment as an opportunity to get some notice. It's a job we can sink our teeth into. If we handle the situation correctly, there'll be promotions all around."

The bearded civilian in the projection nearest Kowacs was babbling in a voice raised by fear and the clipped sound reproduction, "Only eggs, I swear it. And maybe butter, if they asked for butter, maybe butter. But they'd have taken my daughter if I hadn't given them the supplies."

"Ah, Commander," said the Marine, wondering how he would complete the sentence. "I'm not clear why my unit rather than . . ."

Rather than anybody else in the universe.

"Your daughter was involved in this?" asked the hologrammic interrogator. "Where is she now?"

"*She's only eight!* For god's sake—"

Sitterson made a petulant gesture; the AI in his desk cut the sound though not the visuals from the three interrogations.

The security chief leaned over his desk and smiled meaningfully at Kowacs. "I know how to handle collaborators, Captain," he said. "And so do you—I've heard what went on on Target. *That's* why I asked for the 121st."

For a moment, Kowacs couldn't feel the chair beneath him. His body trembled; his mind was full of images of his drop into the Khalian slave pens on Target—and the human trustees there, with their torture equipment and the abattoir with which they aped the dietary preferences of their Khalian masters.

Every trustee in his sight-picture memory wore the features of Commander Sitterson.

Kowacs didn't trust himself to speak—but he *couldn't* remain silent, so he said, "Sir, on Target the prisoners were turning out electronics, stuff the weasels can't make for themselves.".

He lurched out of his chair because he needed to move and by pacing toward the wall he could innocently break eye contact with the security chief. "That stuff, giving the weasels produce so they don't put you on the table instead —that's not collaboration, sir, that's flat-ass survival. It's not the same as—"

But the words brought back the memories, and the memories choked Kowacs and chilled his palms with sweat.

"Well, Captain," Sitterson said as he straightened slightly in his chair. "If I didn't have responsibility for the safety of the hundred and forty thousand Fleet and allied personnel stationed in this district, I might be able to be as generous as you are."

The commander's stern expression melted back into a smile. "Still," he went on, "I think your real problem is that you're afraid you won't see any action working with me. I'll show you how wrong you are.

"Send in Colonel Hesik," he told his desk. The door

opened almost on the final syllable to pass the tall man.

Kowacs started to rise but Sitterson did not, gesturing the newcomer to a chair.

"Hesik here," the commander said, "was head of the resistance forces in the district before our landing. He's been working closely with me, and—" he winked conspiratorially toward the Bethesdan, "I don't mind telling you, Captain, that he's in line for very high office when we come to set up a civilian government."

Hesik grinned in response. The scar on his right cheek was concealed by his neatly groomed beard, but it gave his face a falsely sardonic quirk when he tried to smile.

"Tell Captain Kowacs what happened to your unit three months ago, Hesik," Sitterson ordered.

"Yes sir," said the indig—who had better sense than to try to make something of his shadow 'rank,' which if real would have made him the senior officer in the room. He was willing to act as Sitterson's pet—for the reward he expected when the Fleet pulled out again.

"We were organized by Lieutenant Bundy," Hesik said. He kept his eyes trained on a corner of the room, and there was a rote quality to his delivery.

"Technical specialists were landed six months ago to stiffen local resistance," Sitterson added in explanation. "Bundy was a top man. I knew him personally."

"We were hitting the weasels, hurting them badly," Hesik resumed. His voice had bright quivers which Kowacs recognized, the tremors of a man reliving the past fears which he now cloaked in innocent words. "There were other guerrilla units in the district too—none of them as effective as we were, but good fellows, brave . . . Except for one."

The Bethesdan swallowed. As if the bobbing of his Adam's apple were a switch being thrown, his head jerked down and he glared challengingly at Kowacs. "This *other* unit," he said, "kept in close touch with us—but they never seemed to attack the Khalia. Avoiding reprisals on innocent civilians, they explained."

One of the hologram civilians had collapsed on the floor. Her interrogator stood splay-legged, gesturing with a shock rod which did not quite touch the civilian.

"And perhaps so," Hesik continued. "But we heard very

disquieting reports about members of that unit frequenting the spaceport, where the Khalia had their headquarters. We tried to warn Lieutenant Bundy, but he wouldn't believe humans would act as traitors to their race."

"Kowacs here could tell you about that," Sitterson interjected. "Couldn't you, Captain?"

Kowacs spread his hand to indicate he had heard the security chief. His eyes remained fixed on Hesik.

"They called us to a meeting," the Bethesdan said. "We begged the lieutenant not to go, but he laughed at our fears."

Hesik leaned toward Kowacs. "We walked into an ambush," he said. "The only reason any of us got out alive was that Lieutenant Bundy sacrificed his life to warn the rest of us."

"Doesn't sound like selling butter to the Khalians, does it, Captain?" Sitterson commented in satisfaction.

"Them?" Kowacs asked, thumbing toward the hologram interrogations.

"Not yet," said the security chief.

"But," Hesik said in a voice bright with emotion, "my men have located the traitors, where they're hiding."

"Up for some real action, Captain?" Sitterson asked. "You said you were a reaction company. Let's see how fast you *can* react."

"Download the coordinates," Kowacs said, too focused to care that he was giving a brusque order to his superior. He'd taken off his helmet when he entered the building. Now he slipped it on again and added, "How about transport?"

Sitterson was muttering directions to his AI. "You have trucks assigned already, don't you?" he said, looking up in surprise.

"You bet," Kowacs agreed flatly. "Priority One," he said to his helmet. "This is a scramble, Headhunters."

His helmet projected onto the air in front of him the target's location, then the route their computer had chosen for them. That decision was based on topographical data, ground cover, and traffic flows along the paved portion of the route.

"How many bandits?" Kowacs demanded, pointing a blunt finger at Hesik to make his subject clear.

"Sir," said Daniello's voice in the helmet, "we still don't have the hard suits back from decontamination."

"Twenty perhaps," said Hesik with a shrug. "Perhaps not so many."

"Fuck the hard suits," Kowacs said to his First Platoon leader. "We got twenty human holdouts only. Pick me and Sienkiewicz up in front of the security building when you come through the parade ground."

"On the way," said Daniello.

"We're going too," said Commander Sitterson, jumping up from behind his desk as he saw to his amazement that the Marine was already headed for the door.

"Please yourself," Kowacs said in genuine disinterest.

It occurred to him that the weasel commando in the area might have human support. And a group of turncoats like these could tell him something about that—if they were asked in the right way.

Satellite imagery reported seventeen huts in the target zone, which made Kowacs think Hesik had underestimated the opposition. By the time the four trucks were in position, each in the woods half a kilometer out from the village and at the cardinal points around it, Kowacs had better data from long-term scanning for ion emissions and in the infrared band.

The Bethesdan was right. There couldn't be as many humans at the site as there were dwellings.

For the last five kilometers to their individual drop sites, the trucks overflew the woods at treetop level on vectored thrust. It was fast; and it was risky only if the target unit had more outposts than seemed probable, given their low numbers.

"Probable" could get you dead if one guy happened to be waiting in a tree with an air-defense cluster, but that was the chance you took.

"Hang on," warned the driver—Bickleman from Third Platoon. Kowacs didn't trust somebody assigned from the motor pool to know what he was doing—or be willing to do it in the face of enemy fire, when people's lives depended on their transport bulling in anyway.

The truck bellied down through the canopy with a hell of

a racket, branches springing back to slap the men facing outward on the benches paralleling both sides. A limb with a mace of cones at its tip walloped Kowacs, but his face shield was down and the scrape across his chest was nothing new. He held the seat rail with one hand and his rifle with the other, jumping with the rest of his unit as soon as they felt the spongy sensation of the vehicle's underside settling into loam.

The bustle of Third Platoon taking cover briefly, then fanning out in the direction of the village, was only background to Kowacs for the moment. He had the whole company to control.

Bradley and Sienkiewicz covered their commander while he focused on the reports from the other three platoons—"Position Green," the drop completed without incident—and the hologram display a meter in front of him which was more important than the trees he could see beyond the patterns of light.

"Advance to Amber," Kowacs said. A blue bead glowed briefly in the hologrammic heads-up display projected by his helmet and all the others in the unit, indicating that the order had been on the command channel.

They moved fast through the forest. The Headhunters were used to woods—as well as jungles, deserts, or any other goddam terrain weasels might pick to stage a raid—and here speed was more important than the threat of running into an ambush.

Kowacs couldn't see much more of Third Platoon than he could of the rest of the company. The undergrowth wasn't exceptionally heavy, but there were at least two meters between each marine and those to either side in the line abreast.

"Gamma, Amber," reported the Third Platoon leader, somewhere off to the left. Kowacs knelt with the rest of the unit around him, rifle advanced, waiting for the remaining platoons to reach the jump-off point.

"Beta Amber"/"Alpha Amber," reported Second and First Platoons in near simultaneity. There was a further wait before Delta called in, but they were the Heavy Weapons Platoon and had to manhandle tripod-mounted plasma guns through the undergrowth.

Anyway, Delta had reported within a minute of the others, not half a lifetime later the way it seemed to Kowacs as his fingers squeezed the stock of his rifle and his eyes watched green beads crawl across the ghostly hologram of a relief map.

The only difference between Position Amber and any other block of woodland was that it put each platoon within a hundred meters of the village. The huts were still out of sight, though Second and Heavy Weapons would have clear fields of fire when they wriggled a few meters closer.

"Alpha, charge set," reported Daniello whose platoon had the job of driving a small bursting charge a meter down into the soil.

"Beta, sensors ready," answered his Second Platoon counterpart who had set the echo-sounding probes on the other side of the village.

"Fire the charge," Kowacs said.

As he spoke, there was a barely audible thump off to the right and somebody shook his arm to get attention.

"What's going—" demanded Commander Sitterson, whose helmet received all the unit calls—but who didn't have the background to understand them.

He didn't have sense enough to keep out of the way, either. Kowacs was very glad that because of the angle, he hadn't swung quickly enough to blow Sitterson away before understanding took over from reflex.

"Not *now,* sir!" he snapped, turning slightly so that Sitterson's head didn't block the pattern of lines dancing across his display as the unit's computer mapped the bunkers and tunnels beneath the village in the echoing shock waves.

There weren't any bunkers or tunnels. The target was as open as a whore's mouth.

"Was that a shot?" the security chief insisted. Hesik lay just back of Sitterson, his face upturned and the big pistol lifted in his right hand.

"Assault elements, *go!*" Kowacs ordered as he rose to his feet himself, so pumped that he wondered but didn't worry whether the wild-eyed Bethesdan colonel was going to shoot him in the back by accident.

First and Third platoons swept into the village clearing

from two adjacent sides, forming an L that paced forward
with the sudden lethality of a shark closing its jaws.

"Everyone stay where you are!" Kowacs boomed through
the loudspeaker built into the top of his helmet. The speaker
was damped and had a strong directional focus, but it still
rattled his teeth to use the damned thing. Still, *he* was in
charge, and the holdouts in the village had to know that.

Even if it meant that he'd catch the first round if the fools
tried to resist.

The civilians in plain sight seemed scarcely able to stand
up.

Two women—neither of them young, though one was
twenty years younger than Kowacs thought at first glance—
were scraping coarse roots on a table in the center of the
straggle of huts. Beside them on a straw pallet lay a figure
who might have been of either sex; might have been a
bundle of rags, save for the flicker of lids across the
glittering eyes, the only motion visible as the line of rifles
approached.

"Don't move, dammit!" Kowacs bawled as a man directly
across from him ducked into the hut.

There was a pop and a minute arc of smoke from
Bradley's left hand—the hand that didn't hold the leveled
shotgun. The smoke trail whickered through the doorway as
suddenly as the civilian had—then burst in white radiance,
a flare and not a grenade as Kowacs had half-expected.

Bawling in terror, the man flung himself back outside and
danced madly as he stripped away the flaming rags of his
clothing while the hut burned behind him. A marine
knocked him down with his rifle butt, then kicked dirt over
the man's blazing hair.

Both platoons were among the huts in seconds. "Empty!"
a voice called, and, "Empty!", then, "Out! Out! Out!"

Three of them tried to get out the back way as somebody
was bound to do. That was fine, always let 'em *think* they
had a way to run. The dazzling whipcrack of a plasma bolt
streaking skyward, all the way to the orbit of the nearer
moon, caught the trio in plain sight.

They didn't flatten on the ground or raise their hands,
just froze in place and awaited the cross fire which would
vaporize them if it came. Marines from Second Platoon

threw them down and trussed them scornfully.

"He can't move, he's wounded!" a woman was screaming desperately from the hut beside Kowacs. That didn't sound like an immediate problem, so he glanced around for an eyeball assessment of the situation.

Everything had gone perfectly. The one hut was afire. Several Marines held an extra weapon while their buddies grasped the civilian who'd been carrying it. The woman didn't have to tell anybody that the fellow two of his men were dragging was wounded. Kowacs could smell the gangrene devouring the prisoner's leg.

The only shot fired was the warning round from the plasma weapons placed in ambush. Very slick. So slick that it probably looked easy to Sitterson and Hesik, pounding up from the treeline where they'd been left flat-footed by the Marines' advance.

The elder of the women who'd been preparing food cried shrilly at Kowacs, "Why are you here with guns? We need help, not—"

Then she saw Hesik. Kowacs caught her by one arm and Sienkiewicz grabbed the other when they saw what was about to happen, but it didn't keep the old woman from spitting in Hesik's face.

The Bethesdan colonel slapped her across the forehead with the barrel of his pistol.

The younger of the pair of women broke away from a marine who was more interested in the drama than in the prisoner he was holding. She jumped into the dark entrance of a hut. The three marines nearest lighted the opening with the muzzle flashes of their automatic rifles.

The prisoner flopped down with only her torso inside the hut. Her legs thrashed while one of the Marines, more nervous or less experienced than the others, wasted the rest of his magazine by hosing down her death throes.

The air stank with the oiliness of propellant residues. Hesik looked dazed. He was making dabbing motions with his right hand, apparently trying to put his weapon back in its holster. He wasn't even close.

"Right," said Kowacs, angry that his ears rang and that a screwup had marred a textbook operation. "Get the trucks up here and load the prisoners on while we search—"

"Not yet," ordered Sitterson. Everybody paused.

"Hold him," Sitterson added to the marine gripping the man—boy, he was about seventeen—with his hair singed off. "You too—" pointing at Sienkiewicz. "Make sure he doesn't get loose."

The big corporal obeyed with an expression as flat as those of Kowacs and Bradley while they watched the proceedings. She gripped the boy's left elbow with her own left hand and angled her rifle across her chest. Its muzzle was socketed in the prisoner's ear.

Sitterson took something from his pocket—a miniature shock rod—and said to the boy in a caressing voice, "Now, which of this lot is Milius?"

"Go to—," the boy began.

Sitterson flicked him across the navel with his shock rod. It gave a viper's hiss and painted the midline hairs with blue sparks. The boy screamed and kicked. Sienkiewicz interposed her booted leg, and the security chief punched the prisoner in the groin with the rod.

"Sir!" Kowacs shouted as he grabbed Sitterson by the shoulder and jerked him back. "Sir! People are watching!" He tapped his rifle on the side of his helmet where a chip recorder filed every aspect of the operation for rear echelon review.

Sitterson was panting more heavily than his physical exertion justified. For a moment, Kowacs thought the commander was going to punch him—which wasn't going to hurt nearly as much as would the effort of not blowing the bastard away for doing it.

Instead, the security chief relaxed with a shudder. "Nothing to worry about," he muttered. "Not a problem at all. What's your unit designator?"

"Huh?" Kowacs replied.

Sienkiewicz was spraying analgesic on the prisoner while the other marine stood between the boy and any possible resumption of Sitterson's attack. Maybe they were worried about what their recorders would be saying at a court-martial.

Maybe they didn't like Sitterson any better than their CO did.

Sitterson stepped behind Kowacs, holding the marine officer steady when he started to turn to keep the security chief in sight. Kowacs froze, waiting for whatever was going to come, but there was no contact beyond Sitterson's finger tracing the serial number imprinted in the back of the helmet rim.

"There," he said as he let Kowacs face around again. "I'll take care of it when we get back. I'll have the file numbers of all the recorders in this company transferred to units in storage on Earth."

Kowacs looked blank.

"That's the way to do it," Sitterson explained with an exasperated grimace. "Don't try to wipe the data, just misfile it so nobody will *ever* be able to call it up."

"Where're those *trucks?*" Bradley demanded to break the sequence of words and events. The vehicles were arriving with their intakes unshrouded for efficiency, howling like demons and easy to hear even for ears deadened by rifle blasts.

Two Marines came out of the hut where the woman sprawled. One of them carried a submachinegun he'd found inside. The other held, of all things, an infant whose wails had been lost in the noise and confusion of the raid.

"Check it for bullet splinters," Kowacs ordered with a black scowl, knowing that if the baby had taken a round squarely it would have bled out by now.

"It just needs changing, sir," said Sienkiewicz unexpectedly.

"Then *change* it!" Kowacs snapped.

"All right," said Sitterson. "I think you're right. We'll take them back to headquarters for interrogation."

Marines faced outward toward the treeline with their weapons ready—just in case. The trucks bellowed in, brushing the upper limbs with thrust and their belly plates.

Switching to the general unit push because he couldn't trust his unaided voice to be heard as a truck settled in the clearing before him, Kowacs asked, "Bradley, how many we got all told?"

"Thirteen with the kid," the sergeant replied, flashing Kowacs a double hand plus three fingers to reiterate his radio message. "That fits, right?"

Bradley frowned, then added, "Fourteen with the mother."

"Yeah, they'll need that too for identification," Kowacs said with no more emotion than the static hiss of his radio. "But we'll sling it to a cargo rail, all right?"

The draft from the truck exhausts stirred the burning hut into a mushroom of flame, then collapsed it in a gush of sparks spiraling into several of the huts downwind.

"Beta, Delta," Kowacs ordered on the command channel. "Pack up and let's split before it turns out there's an explosives cache here the sensors missed but the fire doesn't."

"Come on, come *on!*" Bradley was demanding on the general frequency. "Three prisoners to a truck. And *secure* them to tie-downs, will you? They're going to tell us things."

Commander Sitterson had begun to sneeze. The vehicle exhausts were kicking up dust, smoke, and the smell of the corpse being dragged past him.

Kowacs really wanted to be away from this place, though he didn't have any objective reason for the way it made him feel. The only problem was, when they got back to Base Forberry, the interrogations were going to resume.

And if the "Milius" the security chief was looking for was the same woman Toby English had been talking about, Kowacs didn't think he was going to like *that* much either.

As the trucks hovered at the base perimeter, waiting to be keyed through the automatic defenses by the officer of the guard, Commander Sitterson said, "Well, Kowacs. Now that you're under my command, I want you to be comfortable. What can I do for you? Are your barracks satisfactory?"

"Huh?" said Kowacs. He'd been watching the prisoners lashed to the forward bulkhead, the burned kid in the center with an old woman on either side of him. "Barracks? Nothing wrong with them. They leak a bit."

So does the governor's office.

"But you know, there is something you could maybe do . . ."

"Name it," Sitterson said, beaming.

The column got its go-ahead and vectored out of hover mode with a lurch. One of the women called the boy "Andy" when she asked if he were all right.

Andy told her to shut her mouth and keep it shut.

"Well, these trucks," Kowacs explained. "We couldn't decontaminate them properly after we searched the spaceport this morning, just hosed 'em off. If you've got any pull with the yard facilities, maybe you could get us time in a drydock to—"

"Trucks?" gasped the security chief. He half-rose from his bench seat before he realized how far out over the road that left him poised. *This* truck hasn't been decontaminated?"

"Sir," Sergeant Bradley interrupted with a flat lie, delivered in as certain a tone as that of the Pope announcing Christ is risen. "They've undergone full field procedures and are perfectly safe. But *we* may have to spend twelve hours a day for the next month aboard them, so we'd like to be twice safe."

"Yes, well," Sitterson said, easing back down on the bench with a doubtful expression. "I understand that. Of course I'll take care of it."

Sitterson wanted the prisoners at his headquarters, not the internment facility. The trucks and their heavily armed cargo wallowed through traffic to the parade square, drawing looks of interest or disgust—depending on personality —from the rear echelon types they passed.

The Headhunters were in dual-use vehicles with enough power to keep a full load airborne without using ground effect. They could have flown above the traffic—except that above ground flight was prohibited by base regulation, and Base Thomas Forberry came under Naval control instead of that of the district government. The Shore Police would have been more than happy to cite Commander Sitterson, along with Kowacs and all four of his drivers.

When the trucks grounded in front of the Security Headquarters, dimpling the plastic matting, Kowacs's men began unfastening the prisoners and Sitterson called into his helmet microphone, "Gliere, open the holding cells. We'll keep all the prisoners here for now."

Kowacs couldn't hear the response, but as the building opened, Sitterson added, "Oh—there's a body also. Have someone from forensics work it up for identification and then take care of it, will you?"

"This isn't right!" shouted the boy, Andy, as the marines to either side of him manhandled him along faster than his burn-stiffened legs wanted to move. "You should be helping us! You should be *helping* us!"

"Come on ahead," Sitterson ordered Kowacs. "I want you with me during the interrogation. They know you mean business."

"Right," Kowacs said on his command channel. "Daniello, you're in charge till I get back. Keep everybody in the barracks, but we're not on alert status till I tell you different."

He strode along beside Sitterson and Hesik. The Bethesdan colonel seemed to be recovering somewhat, but he hadn't spoken since the prisoner made her ill-advised leap for a weapon.

Or for the baby. Well, a bad idea either way.

Sienkiewicz was a half-step behind him. Kowacs looked over his shoulder—looked up—and said, "Did I tell you to come along, Corporal?"

"Yessir," Sienkiewicz said. With her extra bandoliers of ammunition and grenades, and the heavy, meter-long plasma weapon slung behind her hips against need, she looked like a supply train on legs.

Hell, he did want her around.

The cells were open and empty. The guard and the trio of petty-officer interrogators saluted the security chief as he stepped past them, then roughly took the prisoners from the marines and pushed them into the cells—the men alone, the women in pairs. One of the women held the infant. The doors clanged shut when the cells were filled.

In the outer office, Sitterson said, "You can wait here." Not as brusque as "Wait here," but the same meaning. His entourage—Kowacs a big man, Sienkiewicz huge, and Hesik looking thin and trapped—glanced at one another and at the petty officer behind the desk. There wasn't enough room for any of them to sit on the couch.

"Gliere," the security chief said as an afterthought on his way to his private quarters. "Get the number from Kowacs's helmet and see to it that the recordings go to File

Thirteen. The whole company. You know the drill."

"Yes *sir,"* Gliere replied. "Just a minute while I take care of the cells."

The non-com was watching miniature holos of the holding area. He touched a switch on his desk. Another of the cells closed with a ringing impact.

Sitterson was back within five minutes. He was wearing a fresh uniform; the skin of his face and hands was pink with the enthusiasm with which he had scrubbed himself.

Kowacs hoped the security chief never learned how hot the trucks really were. He'd order a court-martial, beyond any question. It was easy to forget just how nervous rear echelon types got about their health and safety.

"All right," the security chief said brightly. "Let's get down to it, shall we? Gliere, we'll take the man in the end cell."

Andy.

"He thinks he's tough." Sitterson added with a laugh which Hesik echoed.

Kowacs said nothing. He tossed his automatic rifle to Sienkiewicz and gestured her to stay where she was. The corporal's grimace could have meant anything.

Andy tried to walk when they moved him across the aisle into an interrogation room, but he was barely able to stand. He had no clothes to strip off. The sealant/analgesic Sienkiewicz had sprayed on from her first aid kit had dried to mauve blotches like the camouflage of a jungle animal.

When the door shut behind them, the boy wavered and caught himself on the room's small table.

"Attention, damn you!" Sitterson ordered, pulling out his shock rod.

"Why are you doing this to me?" the boy cried. Delirium, drugs, and the decay toxins loosed by his injuries turned his voice into a wail of frustration.

"Why didn't you turn yourselves in?" Sitterson shouted. "Why were you hiding out with your guns?"

"We *did* call in!" Andy said. "And your toady Hesik said wait, he'd send vehicles for us."

"Liar!" Hesik said as he swung the butt of his pistol at the boy's mottled forehead.

You don't learn a damned thing from dead prisoners, and

the blow would have killed had it landed.

It didn't land because Kowacs caught the Bethesdan colonel's wrist in one hand and twisted the weapon away with the other as easily as if Hesik were a child.

"Sir," Kowacs said to the security chief. "I think this'll go better if you and I do it alone for a bit, you know?"

"He'll lie!" Hesik said. The marine wasn't looking at him, but his grip was as tight as it needed to be.

Kowacs shrugged toward Sitterson. "He'll talk," he said simply. "Dead, he won't talk."

Sitterson's expression was unreadable. At last he said, "Yes, all right. You and I. Hesik, wait outside. Don't worry."

"He'll *lie!*" the Bethesdan repeated, but the tension went out of his muscles and Kowacs let him go.

Kowacs handed back the pistol. His eyes were on Hesik, and they stayed on him until the door closed again behind the Bethesdan.

"We can have him back anytime," Kowacs said without emotion to the prisoner. "We can leave the two of you alone, or we can help him with you. If you don't want that, start talking now."

"You think I care?" the boy muttered.

But he did care. He was naked and hurt, badly hurt. Kowacs was huge in his helmet and equipment belt, still black with the grime of the raid; and the marine was a certain reminder of how thorough and ruthless that raid had been.

"Tell us about Lieutenant Milius," Sitterson said. He started to wave his shock rod before he realized that the threat of Kowacs's presence was greater than that of temporary pain. "Where is she?"

"Dead, for God's sake!" the boy blurted. "She was in the terminal building when everything started to go. Ask the marines we took in there. *They'll* tell you!"

Sitterson slapped him with a bare hand. "You're lying! You're covering for a traitor who murdered a fellow officer!"

It wasn't a powerful blow, but it knocked Andy back against the wall. He would have slumped to the floor if Kowacs hadn't caught him and jerked him upright.

"Hesik told you that?" the boy said. His lip was bleeding.

"All right, sure—she shot that bastard Bundy. They came to us, told us to back off—we were stirring up the weasels too badly."

Kowacs released the boy when he felt him gather himself and straighten.

"Milius told 'em go fuck 'emselves," Andy continued with real venom. "And your precious Bundy, *he* says, if she won't stop for him, maybe the weasels will take care of the problem. *That's* why she blew the bastard away. I just wish we'd taken out Hesik and the rest of the mothers in that cell then when we had the chance."

"Lying little swine!" Sitterson cried. He grabbed the boy by the hair with one hand, throwing him against the wall while he poked the shock rod toward the prisoner's eye.

The singed hair crumbled. Sitterson's hand slipped in a gooey pad of sealant and serum from the burned skin beneath.

"Sir," said Kowacs as he slid between the collapsing boy and the security chief who stared at his hand with an expression of horrified disgust. "We made a mistake. If these guys are the ones got the Ninety-Second into the port, then they're straight. Even if they did shoot your o.t.s. agent."

"If!" the security chief repeated. "He's a dirty little liar, and he's covering for a traitor who didn't come *near* the port during the assault."

"No sir," Kowacs said. He was standing so close to Sitterson that he had to tilt his head down to meet the eyes of the senior officer. "Milius did lead them in. And she did buy it during the attack."

Sitterson flung himself backward, breathing hard. "Who the hell says?" he demanded. His left hand was clenching and uncurling, but his right held the shock rod motionless so that it did not appear to threaten the marine.

"Toby English," Kowacs said. "Lieutenant English, CO of the Ninety-Second."

Sitterson looked at the Marine. "You're . . ." he began, but his voice trailed off instead of breaking. He swallowed. "Oh, Christ," he said very quietly. "Oh Christ help me if that's true."

"Sure, you can ask Toby," Kowacs said. "The *Haig* lifted

off this morning, but you can send a message torp after her
for something this important."

"He's off-planet?" the security chief asked. His face
regained the color it had lost a moment before.

"Yeah, but—"

"That's all right," Sitterson interrupted, fully himself
again. He opened the door. "We'll adjourn for now, Captain."

Gesturing toward the petty officers waiting for direction,
he added, "Two of you, get this one,"—Andy was on the
floor, unconscious from shock or the medication—"into
his cell and hold him. Just hold them all until I get back to
you."

"Sir, I—" Kowacs began.

"Return to your unit and await orders, Captain,"
Sitterson said crisply. "This operation has been a success
thus far, and I don't intend to spoil it."

Kowacs didn't like to think about the implications of that
while he and Sienkiewicz hitched a ride back to the barracks
on a fuel truck going in the right direction. He didn't like to
think about Colonel Hesik's smile, either.

But he couldn't forget either thing.

Kowacs was typing his report, hating the job and hating
worse what he was having to say, when Bradley and
Sienkiewicz pushed aside the sound-absorbent curtains of
his "office."

"Bugger off," Kowacs said, glaring at the green letters
which shone demurely against the white background of the
screen. "I've got today's report to do."

"Figured you'd get Hoofer to do that," Bradley said.
"Like usual."

Kowacs leaned back in the chair that was integral with
the portable console and rubbed his eyes. Hoofer, a junior
sergeant in First Platoon, was good with words. Usually
he'd have gotten this duty, but . . .

"Naw," Kowacs said wearily. "It's knowing how to say it
so that nobody back on Tau Ceti or wherever gets the wrong
idea. And, you know, burns somebody a new one for
shooting a woman in the back."

"She shouldn't have run," Sienkiewicz said.

"Right," said Kowacs. "A lot of things shouldn't happen. Trouble is, they do."

He looked expectantly at the two non-coms. He was waiting to hear why they'd interrupted when they, of all people, knew he didn't like company at times like this.

Bradley eased forward so that the curtain surrounding the small enclosure hung shut. "We went for a drink tonight at a petty officers' club with Gliere, the Tech 8 in Sitterson's office. The Mil Gov bars have plenty of booze, even though you can't find enough to get a buzz anywhere else. He got us in."

"Great," said Kowacs without expression. "If you'd brought me a bottle, I'd be glad to see you. Since you didn't—"

"Thing is," the field first continued as if he hadn't heard his commander speak, "Gliere's boss called him back after the office was supposed to be closed."

Kowacs raised an eyebrow.

"Pissed Gliere no end," Bradley said. "Seems Sitterson wants him to clear the data bank of all records relating to the bunch we brought in today. Wants it just like that lot never existed—and the file overwritten so there aren't any gaps."

Nick Kowacs got up from the console. The chair back stuck; he pushed a little harder and the frame bent thirty degrees, out of his way and nothing else mattered.

He began swearing, his voice low and nothing special about the words, nothing colorful—just the litany of hate and anger that boils from the mouth of a man whose mind is a lake of white fury.

"What does he think we are?" Sienkiewicz asked plaintively. "They were on *our* side."

"Right," said Kowacs, calm again.

He looked at his console for a moment and cut its power, dumping the laboriously created file into electron heaven.

"That's why it's Sitterson's ass if word gets out about what he did." Kowacs continued. He shrugged. "What we all did, if it comes to that."

"They're still in the holding cells," Bradley said. "The

prisoners. I sorta figure Sitterson's going to ask us to get rid of that part of the evidence. 'Cause we're conscienceless killers, you know."

"Except the bastard won't ask," Sienkiewicz said bitterly. "He gives orders."

"Right," said Kowacs. "Right. Well, we're going to solve Sitterson's problem for him."

He sat down at the console again, ignoring the way the damaged seat prodded him in the back.

"Sergeant," he said, "book us to use the drydock late tonight to wash the trucks—between midnight and four, something like that."

"Ah, sir?" Bradley said. "The main aqueduct broke this afternoon. I'm not sure if the naval base has water either."

Kowacs shrugged. "Sitterson said he'd get us a priority," he said. "We'll operate on the assumption that he did."

"Yessir," said Bradley.

"Who do you have on guard duty at Sitterson's office tonight?" Kowacs went on.

"I haven't finalized the list," Bradley said unemotionally. "It might depend on what his duties would be."

"The doors to the holding cells are controlled by the desk in Gliere's office," Kowacs said.

"Yessir," Bradley repeated. Sienkiewicz was starting to smile. "I got a lot of paperwork to catch up with. I'm going to take the midnight to four duty myself."

"So get your butt in gear," Kowacs ordered. He powered up his console again.

"Sitterson ain't going to like this," Sienkiewicz said with a smile that looked as broad as her shoulders.

Kowacs paused, glancing up at two of the marines he trusted with his life—now and a hundred times before. "Yeah," he agreed. "But you know—one of these days Toby English and me are going to be having a drink together . . . And when we do, I don't want to look him in the eye and tell him a story I wouldn't want to hear myself."

As his men slipped out to alert the rest of the company, Nick Kowacs started to type the operational order that would be downloaded into the helmets of all his troops. Green letters hung in the hologram field, but instead of them he saw images of what would be happening later in the night.

He was smiling, too.

A jeep, its skirts painted with the red and white stripes of the Shore Police, drove past the District Government Building. Neither of the patrolmen spared more than a glance at the trucks hovering at idle along the four sides of the otherwise empty square.

Kowacs let out the breath he had been holding.

"Hawker Six," Bradley's voice whispered through the helmet phones. "They don't want to come."

"*Get* them out!" Kowacs snarled without bothering about proper radio discipline.

There were more vehicles moving along the main northsouth boulevard of Base Thomas Forberry. Every moment the Headhunters waited was another chance for somebody to wonder why a truck was parked in front of Security Headquarters at this hour.

Eventually, somebody was going to come up with the obvious right answer.

"On the way, Hawker Six," Bradley replied.

They'd raised the sidings on each vehicle, so that you couldn't tell at a glance that the trucks held the entire 121st Marine Reaction Company, combat-equipped.

You also couldn't tell if Kowacs's own truck carried thirteen internees—who would revert to being Bethesdan civilians as soon as the trucks drove through the Base Forberry perimeter on their way to the naval dockyard three kilometers away.

If everything worked out.

"Alpha Six to Hawker Six," reported Daniello, whose platoon waited tensely in its vehicle on the south side of the square. "A staff car approaching with a utility van."

"Roger, Alpha Six," Kowacs replied.

Officers headed back to quarters after partying at their club. Maybe cheerful—and maybe mean—drunks looking for an excuse to ream somebody out. Like whoever was responsible for trucks parking in the parade square.

"Hawker Five—" Kowacs muttered, about to tell Bradley to hold off on the prisoners for a moment.

He was too late. The first of the Bethesdans was coming out between the arms of two Marines, just like he'd been carried in. Andy, a boy trying to look ready to die; and with his injuries and fatigue, looking instead as if he already had.

"What—," Andy demanded.

Sienkiewicz stepped close, ready to club the boy before his shouts could give the alarm. Kowacs shook his head abruptly and laid a finger across his own lips.

The car and van *whooshed* by, their headlights cutting bright swathes through the ambience of Bethesda's two pale moons. The van's axis and direction of movement were slightly askew, suggesting that the driver as well as the passengers had been partying.

"Listen, kid," Kowacs said, bending so that his face was within centimeters of Andy's. "We're going to get you out of the perimeter. What you do then's your own look-out. I don't think Sitterson's going to stir things up by coming looking for you, but Hesik and your own people—that's *your* business. Understood?"

"Whah?" Andy said. The rest of the prisoners were being hustled or carried out. Andy stepped aside so that they could be handed into the back of the truck. "Why are you doing this?"

"Because I'm fucking stupid!" Kowacs snapped.

There was an orange flash to the south. Kowacs's boots felt the shock a moment before the air transmitted the explosion to his ears. It must have been a hell of a bang to people who weren't a couple kilometers away like Kowacs was.

"Motor pool," Sienkiewicz said, making an intelligent guess. "Late night and somebody got sloppy, drove into a fuel tank." Shrugging, she added, "Maybe it'll draw everybody's attention there."

"I'd sooner all the guards were asleep, like usual," Kowacs replied with a grimace.

"Hawker Six," Bradley called. "Some of these aren't in the best of shape. It'll hurt 'em to be moved."

"They'll hurt a lot worse if we leave 'em for Sitterson, Hawker Five," Kowacs replied. "Get 'em out."

"Alpha Six to Hawker Six," said Daniello. "Two vans headed north. They're highballing."

"Roger, Alpha Six," Kowacs said. "No problem."

What *could* be a problem was the way lights were going on in the three-story officers' quarters lining the boulevard in either direction from the square. The blast had awakened a lot of people. The officers gawking out their windows couldn't see a damn thing of the motor pool, now painting the southern horizon with a glow as red as sunrise—

But they could see Kowacs's trucks and wonder about them.

Two marines stepped out of the building with an old man who hung as a dead weight. Bradley followed, kicking the door closed behind him. The sergeant held his shotgun in one hand and in his left arm cradled a six-year-old who was too weak with fever for his wails to be dangerous to the operation.

"Here's the last of 'em, sir," Bradley reported, lifting the child to one of the marines in the vehicle.

Andy looked at the sergeant, looked at Kowacs, and scrambled into the truck himself.

"Watch it!" warned Daniello's voice without time for a call sign.

Air huffed across the parade square as the two vans speeding north braked to a halt instead of continuing on. One of the vehicles turned in the center of the square so that its cab faced the District Government Building.

"What the hell?" muttered Kowacs as he flipped his face shield down and switched on the hologram projection from his helmet sensors. His men were clumps of green dots, hanging in the air before him.

The van began to accelerate toward the government building. The driver bailed out, to Kowacs's eyes a dark smudge on the plastic ground sheathing—

And a red dot on his helmet display.

"Weasels!" Kowacs shouted as he triggered a long burst at the driver. His tracers gouged the ground short of the rolling target, one of them spiking off at right angles in a freak ricochet.

Most of his men were within the closed trucks. Bradley's

shotgun boomed, but its airfoil loads spread to clear a room at one meter, not kill a weasel at a hundred times that range. Where the *hell* was—

The weasel stood in a crouch. The bullet that had waited for Kowacs to take up the last, least increment of trigger pressure cracked out, intersected the target, and crumpled it back on the ground.

—Sienkiewicz?

The square hissed with a moment of dazzling brilliance, false lightning from the plasma gun Corporal Sienkiewicz had unlimbered instead of using the automatic rifle in her hands when the trouble started. Her bolt bloomed across the surface of the van, still accelerating with a jammed throttle and twenty meters from the front door of the District Government Building.

The explosives packed onto the bed of the van went off, riddling the building's facade with shrapnel from the cab and shattering every window within a kilometer.

Kowacs had been steadying himself against the tailgate of his truck. It knocked him down as the blast shoved the vehicle sideways, spilling Headhunters who were jumping out to get their own piece of the action.

But the explosion also threw off the weasels in the second van who were spraying bright blue tracers in the direction from which the marines' fire had come.

Klaxons and sirens from at least a dozen locations were doing their best to stupefy anyone who might otherwise be able to respond rationally.

Kowacs lay flat and aimed at the weasels. There was a red flash from their vehicle. Something flew past like a covey of banshees, trailing smoke in multiple tracks that fanned wider as they passed. Twenty or thirty rooms exploded as the sheaf of miniature light-seeking missiles homed on the folks who were rubbernecking from their barracks windows.

It was the perfect weapon for a Khalian commando to use to spread panic and destruction as they sped away in the night in a Fleet-standard van—presumably hijacked at the motor pool, where the previous explosion didn't look like an accident after all.

The missile cluster wasn't a goddam bit of good against

the Headhunters, blacked out and loaded for bear.

Only a handful of marines from each platoon was clear of the hampering trucks, but their fire converged on the Khalian vehicle from four directions. Tracers and sparks from bullet impacts flecked the target like a festival display—

Until Sienkiewicz's second plasma bolt turned it into a fluorescent bubble collapsing in on itself.

One of the weasels was still alive. Maybe it'd been in the cab and shielded when the bolt struck the back of the van. Whatever the cause, the weasel was still able to charge toward Security Headquarters, firing wild bursts from its machine pistol.

You expected the little bastards to be tough, but this one was something special. Kowacs himself put four rounds into the Khalian's chest, but it had to be shot to doll rags by the concentrated fire of a dozen rifles before what was left finally collapsed.

Kowacs rolled to his feet. His whole left side was bruised, but he couldn't remember how that had happened. He flipped up his face shield and called, "Cease fire!" on the command frequency.

Sienkiewicz's second target was still burning. Fuel, plastics, and weasel flesh fed the orange flames. There was only a crater where the first van had blown up, but burning fragments of it seemed to have started their own little fires at a dozen places around the parade square.

Kowacs switched to the general Base Forberry push and crashed across the chatter with a Priority One designator. "All Fleet personnel. The Headhunters are in control of the vicinity of the Mil Gov complex. Don't fire. Keep your heads down until we've secured the area."

Kowacs turned around.

"Bastards got in through the aqueduct," Bradley snarled beside him. "Sure as shit."

Light from the open door to Security Headquarters blinded Kowacs.

"Kowacs!" shouted Commander Sitterson, a shadow behind his handheld floodlamp with the dimmer shadow of Colonel Hesik behind him. "What are you doing? And where are the—"

Andy stuck his burned face from the back of the truck beside Kowacs.

"You *traitor!*" Sitterson screamed at the marine captain. "I'll have you shot for this if it's the last thing I—" and his voice choked off when he saw that Kowacs had lifted his rifle to his shoulder because that was what you were trained to do, never hip-shoot even though the target's scarcely a barrel's length away.

And Kowacs couldn't pull the trigger.

Not to save his ass. Not in cold blood.

Not even Sitterson.

When Kowacs heard the first shot, he thought one of his men had done what he couldn't. As Sitterson staggered forward, dropping his light, Colonel Hesik fired his pistol twice more into the commander's back and shouted, "I'm on your side! Don't hurt me! I won't—"

The muzzle blast of Bradley's shotgun cut off Hesik's words as completely as the airfoil charge shredded the Bethesdan's chest.

"I was wrong about how the weasels got in," Bradley said in the echoing silence. "Hesik was a traitor who led 'em here before he greased his boss."

Liesl, CO of the Third Platoon, had gotten sorted out from his men and was standing beside Kowacs. "Gamma Six," Kowacs said, nodding as he slapped a fresh magazine into his rifle, "get aboard and get this truck over to the dock for washing, just like we planned."

"Aye aye, sir," Liesl said. Bickleman was driving again. He boosted engine thrust as soon as he heard the order. The vehicle and its cargo began to move with marines still lifting themselves in over the tailgate.

"Alpha Six," Kowacs said on his command frequency, "secure the boulevard to the south. Maybe there's not another load of bandits, but I don't like surprises. Beta Six, spread your men out and search the trucks we nailed. And *watch* it."

There was a long burst of automatic fire, but it came from a barracks and wasn't aimed anywhere in particular. Somebody whose room had taken a Khalian rocket had survived to add to other people's confusion.

"Headhunter Command to all Fleet personnel!" Kowacs

said. "Stop that wild shooting or we'll stop it for you."

All the real problems were over for now. Kowacs didn't think he'd ever be able to tell the true story. Maybe to Toby English over a beer.

That didn't matter.

All that mattered was that he didn't have to admit, even to himself in the gray hours just before dawn, that he'd murdered thirteen civilians to cover an administrative error.

BESTSELLING
Science Fiction
and
Fantasy